T0295535

Marketing and Sustainability

Contradiction or the Path to Profitable Businesses and Sustainable Societies

Pia A. Albinsson
Hugo Guyader
Mikael Ottosson
Anders Parment

WILEY

This edition first published 2025

© 2025 John Wiley & Sons Ltd

All rights reserved, including rights for text and data mining and training of artificial technologies or similar technologies. No part of this publication may be reproduced, stored in a retrieval system, or transmitted, in any form or by any means, electronic, mechanical, photocopying, recording or otherwise, except as permitted by law. Advice on how to obtain permission to reuse material from this title is available at http://www.wiley.com/go/permissions.

The right of Pia Albinsson, Hugo Guyader, Mikael Ottosson, and Anders Parment to be identified as the authors of this work has been asserted in accordance with law.

Registered Office(s)
John Wiley & Sons, Inc., 111 River Street, Hoboken, NJ 07030, USA
John Wiley & Sons Ltd, The Atrium, Southern Gate, Chichester, West Sussex, PO19 8SQ, UK

For details of our global editorial offices, customer services, and more information about Wiley products visit us at www.wiley.com.

Wiley also publishes its books in a variety of electronic formats and by print-on-demand. Some content that appears in standard print versions of this book may not be available in other formats.

Trademarks: Wiley and the Wiley logo are trademarks or registered trademarks of John Wiley & Sons, Inc. and/or its affiliates in the United States and other countries and may not be used without written permission. All other trademarks are the property of their respective owners. John Wiley & Sons, Inc. is not associated with any product or vendor mentioned in this book.

Limit of Liability/Disclaimer of Warranty
While the publisher and authors have used their best efforts in preparing this work, they make no representations or warranties with respect to the accuracy or completeness of the contents of this work and specifically disclaim all warranties, including without limitation any implied warranties of merchantability or fitness for a particular purpose. No warranty may be created or extended by sales representatives, written sales materials or promotional statements for this work. This work is sold with the understanding that the publisher is not engaged in rendering professional services. The advice and strategies contained herein may not be suitable for your situation. You should consult with a specialist where appropriate. The fact that an organization, website, or product is referred to in this work as a citation and/or potential source of further information does not mean that the publisher and authors endorse the information or services the organization, website, or product may provide or recommendations it may make. Further, readers should be aware that websites listed in this work may have changed or disappeared between when this work was written and when it is read. Neither the publisher nor authors shall be liable for any loss of profit or any other commercial damages, including but not limited to special, incidental, consequential, or other damages.

Library of Congress Cataloging-in-Publication Data is Available:

ISBN 9781394273768 (Cloth)
ISBN 9781394273775 (ePDF)
ISBN 9781394273782 (ePub)

Cover Design: Wiley
Cover Images: © Westend61/Getty Images, © MAD.vertise/Shutterstock, © Black Salmon/Shutterstock, © PPR109103/Shutterstock, © fran_kie/Shutterstock, © LightField Studios/Shutterstock

Set in 11.5/14pt and BemboStd by Straive, Chennai, India

SKY10085587_092024

To Emmelie, Evelynne, and David.
– Pia

To my loving friends and family.
– Hugo

To Henry, Lykke, and Susanne.
– Mikael

To Greta, Knut, and Karin.
– Anders

Contents

Foreword

We are at a very crucial time in how sustainability impacts our future. Over the last 100 years our society has become more dependent on resources that challenge the natural environment and interface with economic and social development. As sustainability relates to minimizing damage to the environment over time, marketing and most business activities play an important role in minimizing negative outcomes and protecting all stakeholders. Sustainability overlaps with social responsibility in attempting to address stakeholder concerns and respond to issues with appropriate strategies, policies, and operations. Sustainability is also linked to ethical decision-making and the ability to address ethical issues or dilemmas. We are in the midst of a profound historical shift, and it's urgent to address sustainability. This book provides a foundation for addressing opportunities to contribute to our society's welfare.

The four authors of this textbook are highly qualified experts in the field of marketing and sustainability. The authors have extensive research experience, and they have collected case studies over time that they use as illustrative examples of how sustainability can be connected to business practices. In addition, their involvement in business transformation as consultants, i.e. practical experiences from the implementation of sustainability in marketing for real, is very useful in creating cases that appeal to students.

The case for sustainability is made for the field of marketing but relates to all aspects of business planning, strategy, and implementation. Since a central focus of the book is marketing, it is appropriate that the content presents various factors affecting consumption patterns that support more sustainable marketing practices.

The question of a sustainable consumer discusses changing consumer behavior, something that is crucial in driving the transition toward more sustainable consumption. Examples are provided related to new product development where firms are changing their operations and processes to be more sustainable.

Business model innovation may contribute to sustainability, especially in supply chain management, marketing channels, logistics, purchasing, and operations. These areas are targeted for opportunities to become more sustainable. Reducing the cycle time and resources in reaching the consumer are goals while maintaining profitability and hence mirroring the necessity of financial sustainability to make environmental and social sustainability happen.

This contribution is important because many stakeholders are calling for the long-term well-being of the natural environment, including all biological entities. Sustainability includes assessment and improvement of marketing strategies, work practices, lifestyles, and consumption practices. A dilemma is facing business about whether the cost of sustainability practices will be passed on to consumers or absorbed by firms. The balancing act will be for firms to remain competitive, control costs, and target responsible consumers who understand the value of sustainability to society. That, in turn, will make the firm more attractive for various stakeholders.

Sustainability can have different definitions particularly in different cultures. As a global issue it has been addressed by the United Nations, which introduced Brundtland Commission on Economic and Development views of sustainable development in terms of environmental, economic, and social well-being for both current and future generations. The authors provide directions for reaching these goals from a marketing perspective.

There is an integration of sustainable principles throughout the book, and the authors provide examples globally. Business examples are provided that encourage eco-innovation and a sustainable focus in their operations to balance, cost, resources, and outcomes to serve all stakeholders. While most of the book is concerned with consumer markets, there are implications for business-to-business markets. Topics such as circular business models, sustainability ecosystems, and the sharing economy are thoroughly discussed and illustrated with models and figures.

The importance of this book goes beyond a narrow definition of sustainability to focus on the natural environment. Sustainability is linked to social responsibility and a firm's obligation to maximize its positive impact on stakeholders and minimize its negative impact. As sustainable development is linked to environmental, economic, and social well-being for both current and future generations, a comprehensive view of sustainability considers an agenda to gain favorable stakeholder responses.

From a marketing perspective, it is pointed out that sustainable marketing practices can create a competitive advantage. Firms can use sustainable products to not only create social value but communicate quality and create brand loyalty. Examples are provided of firms that have used their sustainable and socially responsible decisions to differentiate and promote their products. An example of a company is Patagonia that uses organic cotton in its apparel. A sustainable firm can use certified green labels by environmental organizations identifying their organization as green marketers. For example, in Europe, companies can voluntarily apply for the EU eco-label to indicate products that are less harmful to the environment than competing products.

Firms are taking steps to become more sustainable and gain competitive advantage because consumers want to contribute to a more sustainable world. To reach consumers and other stakeholders, this book makes a unique contribution by covering endeavors to communicate the role and importance of sustainability. Companies with sustainability activities need to communicate their involvement and reach consumers that appreciate these efforts. This communication can be through advertising, labeling, or any other form of communication related to the firm or product. Since most consumers are expecting firms to be more sustainable, the promotion can have a positive effect on sales. Avoiding greenwashing requires managers to be honest, to be transparent, and to present the firm's actions as authentic.

The authors make a significant contribution and provide a holistic overview of the opportunities to address sustainability in marketing and business. All aspects of marketing strategy are covered in sufficient detail to provide a road map for an organization to use in improving sustainability efforts. There is adequate coverage of why sustainability is important from a historical perspective and the necessity to include sustainability in current and future marketing practices. The focus on consumers and their sustainability choices is at the center of encouraging more sustainable consumption practices. It also takes a view of what consumers can do to contribute to sustainability.

This book is valuable for business practitioners and makes an excellent textbook for marketing and sustainability courses. The content suggests that marketing and consumers can play a key role in making the world more sustainable. It makes a strong argument that building both student and business community into sustainability leaders can make a difference. The authors are optimistic that we can use knowledge on this topic and can contribute to the economic, social, and environmental advancement of society.

O.C. Ferrell, PhD
James T. Pursell, Sr. Eminent Scholar in Ethics
Director, Center for Ethical Organizational Cultures
Harbert College of Business
Auburn University

Preface

Increased demands for sustainability are affecting all parts of the business world such as prices and inflation, resource constraints, resource depletion, logistic and supply chain bottlenecks and delays, and consumer demands. Many of the forthcoming challenges are due to climate change, resource depletion, and increased costs related to escalated volatility in weather patterns. This book provides frameworks, models, and concepts needed as current and future business leaders must be aware of sustainable business practices to stay competitive and be responsible market actors. Marketing is a core business function, and knowing how it relates to sustainability is key for current students and practitioners who will become future responsible business leaders.

Marketing and Sustainability: Contradiction or the Path to Profitable Businesses and Sustainable Societies will provide students at the undergraduate and graduate levels as well as business professionals with an overview of marketing and how it relates to sustainability practices.

This book results from each of the four authors' long-term interests and efforts at incorporating sustainability initiatives in research, business practice, and marketing classes. While based in both the United States and Sweden, the international author team has experience from working in many countries, universities, and various industries. For example, Anders Parment and Mikael Ottosson, two of the authors of this book, wrote the first version of *Sustainable Marketing: how social, environmental and economic considerations can contribute to sustainable businesses and markets* for the Swedish market in 2012. Hugo Guyader was then invited to update the book in 2020, still focusing on the Scandinavian higher education market.

Pia Albinsson was invited to co-author the latest version you hold in your hands: the global edition.

The combined expertise of the European and U.S. markets and business practices adds to the breadth of the knowledge presented. The book invites marketing students and teachers from these regions to reflect upon the models provided therein to illustrate with examples they're most familiar with and to draw local parallels. Nevertheless, the authors have aimed to bring up global brand examples and research findings from scholars around the world that have impacted sustainability research and business practices.

This book integrates sustainable development principles and marketing. From consumer behavior to sustainable pricing, we provide examples from across the globe, e.g. how businesses use design thinking for the environment, eco-innovation, biomimicry, and a general sustainable focus in their operations to face increasing costs, limited resources, and increased global competition among other contemporary challenges. *Marketing and Sustainability* covers both business-to-business markets and consumer markets, considering marketing practices as part of business administration. Up-to-date and topical areas of research such as circular business models, sustainability ecosystems, and the sharing economy are thoroughly discussed and illustrated with models and figures.

We have extensive research experience and exemplify these with cases that are used as illustrative examples of how sustainability can be connected to various business practices – we package some of these cases with a longer description as "vignettes" in each chapter. In addition, we have been involved in business transformation as consultants and analysts and hence have experience integrating sustainability in marketing practices.

It is our conviction that our textbook will provide the target market with a profound contribution. The book provides invaluable contributions to undergraduate, graduate, and post-graduate students as well as managers in companies, the public sector, and civil society – all under increasing pressure to deal with marketing and sustainability for strategic purposes as well as in everyday practices. Our book integrates sustainable development principles throughout – sustainability is a cornerstone – and we integrate and relate it to marketing frameworks, models, and concepts. This involves the relationships between sustainability and the marketing mix (product, place, price, promotion), consumer behavior, service, business models, marketing channels, branding, and operations. We believe that this comprehensive approach will equip readers with the knowledge and tools necessary to navigate and excel in an ever-evolving market landscape. Ultimately, our textbook aims to foster a deeper understanding of the crucial interplay between marketing and sustainability, empowering professionals and students alike to make impactful decisions.

The book addresses marketing and sustainability from various perspectives.

Chapter 1, Marketing and Sustainability: An Overview

This chapter introduces the way the field of marketing relates to the broad phenomenon of sustainability. It also introduces the term *sustainability*, its role today, and the historical significance of sustainability in marketing and business. Three dimensions of sustainability will be presented from several perspectives. In addition, the chapter discusses the necessity to include sustainability in current and future marketing practices.

Chapter 2, Factors Influencing Consumers and Their Sustainability Choices

Numerous factors impact consumption, spanning from broader environmental and contextual circumstances to aspects of individual personality and psychological processes. This chapter covers general factors at first that can pose challenges to encouraging more sustainable consumption practices among consumers and to which marketers can bring solutions, before focusing on how pro-environmental attitudes shape consumer behavior such as shopping for organic groceries, commuting by sustainable transportation alternatives, choosing to recycle, etc.

Chapter 3, Is There Such a Thing as Sustainable Consumers?

This chapter builds on Chapter 2 as we continue to discuss consumer behavior and sustainable consumption. Using a global view, the content presents various factors affecting consumption patterns and enabling sustainable consumption. We also discuss how a group of consumer researchers have shifted from the unbalanced view of acquisition and consumption by also considering the social impact of their work. This shift to focus on consumer well-being and social impact had its beginnings in the leadership of the Association for Consumer Research and has been named Transformative Consumer Research. The chapter also introduces the attitude-behavior gap, also referred to the *green gap*, that exists in the marketplace. Different ways of exerting influence over consumption and what the individual consumer can do to contribute to sustainability is also discussed.

Chapter 4, Sustainable Marketing Practices

This chapter initiates an exploration into research concerning the sustainable operations of companies, which many perceive as not only beneficial but also obligatory.

Historically, companies have often been viewed as unsustainable entities, but a notable shift has occurred due to the growing emphasis on sustainability. For example, sustainability oriented companies may use biomimicry, design for the environment, or cradle-to-cradle design concepts when developing new products. Within this chapter, we highlight examples of companies embracing sustainability. We examine the potential benefits these sustainable companies can gain in the market and delve into various reasons why certain companies may resist transitioning toward a more sustainable approach.

Chapter 5, Sustainability by Service Provision

Much of the early work regarding companies and sustainability focused on manufacturing firms and their emissions to air, water, and soil. In this chapter we introduce services research, which increasingly has started to analyze how service provision could become more sustainable. We uncover innovative ways to reduce environmental impacts within the service sector, which plays a crucial role in modern economies. Additionally, a deeper understanding of sustainability in service provision can drive the development of new practices that support long-term ecological balance and social well-being.

Chapter 6, How to Communicate Sustainability Initiatives

In Chapter 6, we discuss marketing communications and sustainability, two areas that strongly influence each other: companies with sustainability claims must carry out marketing communications differently, and marketing communications will be different when sustainability is part of the communication. Meanwhile, consumers and other stakeholders are increasingly expecting companies to be sustainable, whereas many companies actually engage in greenwashing. Sustainability requires honesty, transparency, and a societal orientation, and these characteristics must be reflected in messages that are being communicated.

Chapter 7, Sustainability and Branding

For many decades, companies have worked intensively with their brands to enjoy a range of advantages that come with strong brands. Branding practices have become widespread, and organizations in civil society and the public sectors alike have put a lot of effort into strengthening their brands. Brands communicate promises and result in expectations that are linked to how companies and others communicate. For organizations attempting to have sustainable practices, it is very important to be able to play along in the so-called branded society to enjoy the advantages that come with the establishment of strong brands.

Chapter 8, Sustainable and Circular Business Models

Business models represent the starting points and end results of all business activities. They start with a thorough understanding of how consumers think, act, and behave while taking market characteristics into consideration, and if successful, they will provide consumers, employees, and other stakeholders with great value. Regarding sustainability and circularity, the things that evolve around business models look different. This chapter discusses what sustainable and circular business models are and how they differ from traditional business models without sustainability concerns.

Chapter 9, Sustainable Value Chains and Marketing Channels

For a very long time, a century or so, marketing channels have had the key function of physically distributing goods from manufacturers to buyers via intermediaries such as retailers. An increasing service share in the economy, more competition, and stronger consumer rights have put a lot of demands on marketing channels to evolve. Moreover, the advent of sustainability concerns is a key factor that is fundamentally reshaping marketing channels. In this chapter, we discuss sustainable marketing channels and the challenges that they bring.

Chapter 10, Prices of Sustainable Products and Pricing Strategies

Sustainable business practices often lead to higher costs that may be passed on to consumers or assumed by companies. In this chapter we discuss prices of sustainable products and pricing strategies. Many studies show that there is an estimated green premium that consumers are willing to pay for sustainable food products. However, because of the attitude-behavior gap, consumers' stated willingness to pay is far from always materialized in all purchase decisions. Companies may need to re-think their pricing strategies to balance the difficulty of being competitive in the marketplace, selling more sustainable products, and reaching profitability.

Each chapter provides vignettes – short cases, illustrations, or essay-like reflections – that provide readers with additional perspectives and examples on the themes of each chapter.

Resources for Teaching Needs

Each chapter contains the following:

- Learning objectives
- Vignettes
- References

In addition, the index cross-references topics presented across the book.

Finally, the book contains the following instructor materials for Chapters 1–10 (downloadable from the book's companion website at www.wiley.com/go/albinsson/marketingandsustainability):

- PowerPoint presentations
- Test banks
- Short 3–5 minute videos

Chapter 1

Marketing and Sustainability: An Overview

This chapter introduces the way the field of marketing relates to the broad phenomenon of sustainability. It also introduces the term *sustainability*, its role today, and the historical significance of sustainability in marketing and business. Three dimensions of sustainability will be presented from several perspectives. In addition, the chapter discusses the necessity to include sustainability in current and future marketing practices.

Learning Objectives

- Understand the historical shift from traditional marketing to sustainability marketing and the conceptual development toward the triple bottom line, e.g. ecological and social (equity), in addition to economic aspects of marketing activities
- Define and understand the difference between sustainability and sustainable development and the three pillars of sustainability: long-term economic viability, societal and ethical concerns, and the protection of the environment and future generations
- Understand that different countries follow different sustainability reporting regulations
- Understand the importance of the Brundtland Commission, the Sustainable Development Goals (SDGs), and Fit for 55
- Be able to apply hard and soft applications of sustainability

Introduction

It is no exaggeration to claim that the issue of sustainability has become increasingly important over the last few decades – one might even argue that it is now the foremost important topic in society. Regardless of whether we talk about climate change, declining biological diversity (i.e. reduced number of plant and animal species), child labor, or corruption, sustainability issues are of such key importance today that they concern all companies, consumers, organizations in the public sector, and organizations in civil society. Today, politicians and chief executive officers (CEOs) make important pronouncements about shifting from *traditional business as usual perspective* to more sustainable-oriented business practices on a daily basis. As discussed in the Harvard Business Review, companies committing to environmental, social, and governance (ESG) principles are taking strategic approaches toward influencing the sustainability of their supply chains, business models, and broader business ecosystems (Kaplan and McMillan 2021; Polman and Winston 2022). Sustainability is thus a concept against which all questions facing companies and organizations can be set, that is, choice of suppliers, strategies for recruiting and retaining employees, product development, choice of marketing channels, marketing campaigns, and communication strategies.

Changing societal demands, climate change, and ecological transition put pressure on companies to modify their business practices to integrate social and environmental concerns (Allal-Chérif et al. 2023). In line with these demands, the need for operational transparency is ever increasing (Buell 2019), which means that demand expectations on companies and organizations sustainability efforts are growing. The demand by regulators and other stakeholders for more sustainable business practices also puts pressure on companies and public organizations to report what they perform when it comes to sustainability. The regulation for sustainability reporting has been heavily increased during the last decade and will continue to be tightened and expanded significantly in the coming years.

Meanwhile, the transition toward more sustainable businesses, and society, can't be taken for granted. Populism and lack of trust in societal institutions and systems, geopolitical challenges and wars, increasing societal polarization especially in the labor market, and increasing financial inequalities, and political fragmentation are significant driving forces that may counteract sustainability efforts. The necessity of a transition toward a more sustainable society is beyond any doubt, and the solution is to do good, spread the word, and make sure that substantial progress is being made. *Greenwashing*, the opposite of well-conceived sustainability strategies, gives those who are against the transition good arguments, while good practices create a guiding star for others to follow. To create good practices, we'll need support from governments, companies, consumers, employees, and other stakeholders. Young consumers are particularly sensitive to greenwashing, something that should be seen as a driver in the sustainability transition.

Sustainability Reporting – Increased Demands on Large Companies

Regardless of the size of the company, it is becoming increasingly obvious that all companies must relate their business to sustainability today. It is a necessity for companies in today's markets to take responsibility for all aspects of their operations and create trust. Many stakeholders, for example business-to-business (B2B) buyers, place higher sustainability demands on their suppliers.

In the United States

In 2024 there is still no mandatory sustainability reporting. However, the United States Securities and Exchange Commission (SEC) has some reporting requirements related to information material to investors such as related to ESG risks (Silk and Lu 2024). Instead, much of the ESG reporting is left as voluntary, but this is a rapidly changing area, and the United States is likely to see stricter guidelines soon.

In the European Union

In contrast, the Non-Financial Reporting Directive (NFRD) in the European Union contains requirements for certain companies to produce a sustainability report. Those affected are companies of general interest that have more than 500 employees. The report must contain such sustainability information as is needed to understand a company's results, position, development, and the consequences of its operations. The directive specifies environmental, social, and personnel issues; respect for human rights; and the fight against corruption and bribery.

The EU directive on corporate sustainability reporting (Corporate Sustainability Reporting Directive, CSRD) means that current rules are revised and tightened. The requirements are extended to include all large companies and all listed companies within the European Union. In addition, more detailed reporting requirements and requirements to report according to mandatory EU standards are introduced. The standards are developed by the European Financial Reporting Advisory Group (EFRAG). For example, US companies doing business in the European Union need to adhere to EU guidelines and need to get their readiness efforts underway to comply with a range of sustainability topics that they may not have had to disclose information about, e.g. circularity (Tomlinson 2023).

(Continued)

(Continued)

The guidelines from the Global Reporting Initiative (GRI) are used by an increasing number of companies since they provide support for potentially relevant sustainability aspects and performance indicators. In connection with the European Union's work with the renewed directives, new standards will also be introduced.

Even if a company is not one of the large companies covered by the legal requirement for sustainability reporting, there can be great value in having a sustainability report in one form or another, for example to be able to take part in public procurement or meet the high demands of customers or suppliers.

Source: Finansinspektionen (2024); Silk and Lu (2024).

Sustainability Integrated in Everyday Practices

The majority of medium- and large-sized companies, as well as major civil society organizations and actors in public administration, have one or more members of staff working solely with sustainability and reporting. In 2011, only 16% of S&P 500 companies had a chief sustainability officer (CSO). In 2023, this number had grown to 81%. This means a concern for sustainability is integrated into most companies' operations, underlining the fact that sustainability issues are not some short-term trends but more likely an extremely palpable and real issue for today's organizations. Interestingly, companies with a CSO often score higher on their ESG performance (Urso 2022).

Despite these developments, sustainability issues continue to play a subordinate role in basic textbooks used in marketing courses. At best, these issues are discussed in a chapter (Kotler and Armstrong 2023), but they are usually mentioned as a current trend together with, for instance, e-marketing or mobile marketing in the form of a paragraph, a case, or some discussion points (Fahy and Jobber 2022), a recent exception being Peterson's book (2021).

It has been half a decade since the first books on marketing and the ecological crisis (Fisk 1974) and ecological marketing (Henion and Kinnear 1976) were published. However, marketing textbooks still have a great responsibility when it comes to capturing an increasingly important part of the practices addressed by the subject of marketing since millions of business and marketing students are introduced to the subject area of marketing each year.

Some authors have taken a different approach, not writing a textbook for students but rather a how-to guide for entrepreneurs, such as the books by Carvill et al. (2021), by Grant (2020), and by Dahlstrom and Crosno (2024). There is a lot of room for improvement, though, and we are far from a situation where sustainability is a natural and integrated part of teaching at business schools. Not even in Sweden, which is often considered a leading country when it comes to sustainability, with a solid and leading education system, has it really taken off. Sweden has been portrayed as ". . . by far the most sustainable country within the world. The country has the highest renewable energy usage, lowest carbon emissions, as well as . . . some of the best education programs" (Berry 2021). Sweden is frequently used as the example of sustainable production and consumption in Europe (Jansson et al. 2017; Alfredsson and Malmaeus 2019).

To sum up, the need for sustainability in marketing is beyond any doubt. Various stakeholders are adapting a more sustainable approach, but there are counteracting forces and some criticism that may slow down the transition. In addition, business schools should have a stronger emphasis on sustainability. Our hope is that this book will meet the need for a marketing textbook and contribute toward an increased awareness of sustainability issues among business students, professionals, and other key stakeholders in the transition toward a more sustainable society.

Henion and Kinnear, the Forerunners

In North America, Karl E. Henion (lecturer in marketing at the University of Texas) and Thomas C. Kinnear (assistant professor at the University of Western Ontario) were among the first academics to consider the growth of the environmental movement (e.g. the first Earth Day was celebrated in 1970; Greenpeace was founded in 1971) and the legislative progress toward environmental protection (e.g. the Clean Air Act and Clean Water Act in 1970 and 1972, respectively). They took an interest in researching the segment of consumers who care for the environmental impact of their consumption and published a series of scientific papers on the topic (Henion 1972; Kinnear et al. 1974).

In 1975, they organized the American Marketing Association's (AMA's) First National Workshop on Ecological Marketing (see Henion 1981), which led to the publication of the seminal book *Ecological Marketing* (Henion and Kinnear 1976). They wrote: "In relation to the marketing component, ecological marketing is concerned with all marketing activities: (i) that have served to help cause environmental problems and (ii) that may serve to provide a remedy for environmental problems. [. . .] Thus, ecological marketing is the study of the positive and negative aspects of marketing activities on pollution, energy depletion and nonenergy resource depletion." (p. 1) This led to the contemporary marketing concept (cf. Kotler and Zaltman 1971), later called societal marketing concept, to propose an improvement of environmental quality and resource conservation proactively in the business sector, rather reactively through public regulations.

How Does Sustainability Relate to Marketing?

Sustainability and marketing are two concepts that can create ambiguous associations. Is "sustainability marketing" an oxymoron? On the one hand, traditional marketing encourages growth, promotes an endless quest for satisfying needs and wants, and seems to look upon resources as forever abundant. On the other hand, a sustainability focus suggests that utilized resources can be renewed by mimicking the circular flows of resources in nature, and it respects the fact that the capacity of both resources and the environment are limited (e.g. White et al. 2019).

So, how can marketing, which in the minds of the general public is usually seen as only concerned with increasing sales of products (i.e. goods, services, and solutions), contribute toward sustainability? To answer this critical question, we first have to define what marketing is as an academic discipline, a professional activity, and a subject (with multiple subdisciplines) of scientific research. This will help us to understand that marketing and sustainability are inextricably intertwined. In relation to this, the American Marketing Association (AMA) – the most influential authority in our discipline, whose website (ama.org) is full of useful resources for students, academics, and professionals – selected the following definition for the discipline (2017):

> Marketing is the activity, set of institutions, and processes for creating, communicating, delivering, and exchanging offerings that have value for customers, clients, partners, and society at large.

The latter point is what distinguishes sustainable marketing from marketing as it has traditionally been conceived. AMA is very prominent in the marketing field and publishes five journals: *Journal of Marketing*, *Journal of Marketing Research*, *Journal of Public Policy & Marketing*, *Journal of International Marketing*, and *Journal of Interactive Marketing*. Other subdisciplines are macro marketing, services marketing, retailing, distribution/marketing channels, advertising, value creation, consumer behavior, marketing analytics, etc., many of which also have specific journal publications associated with them.

In other words, marketing scholarship is no longer concerned only with selling more and more products. If we for a moment return to the AMA definition, the actual value process between the company, its market, and the wider society is of key importance in the definition. Already in the early days of the discipline, there was a concern for such sustainability. For instance, not only is Robert Bartels considered one of the fathers of the marketing discipline, but he was also among the first scholars to contest the evolution of marketing concepts – which at the time proclaimed providing to customers what they want – and their implementation in businesses (Bartels 1968):

Society, not the business entrepreneur, is the basic undertaker of all activity. Marketing is that activity undertaken by society at large to meet its consumption needs – the producing, distributing, and consuming of products needed for human existence.

In other words, Bartels criticized the contemporary assumption that "the bottomless marketing cornucopia would provide rich harvests to society forever" (Iyer 1994, p.127), and he argued that aligning societal, environmental, and business values would be essential for the long-term welfare of society (Bartels 1968).

Nowadays, there is a well-established environmental and societal imperative for marketers to recognize the sustainability issues related to globalization and cultural differences, the role of the Internet and social media, the proliferation of brands, the increased retail concentration, and the 2023 economic recession for example. Moreover, many influential scholars argue that marketing is no longer only about selling but also about interactions within complex and dynamic multi-actor systems aimed at co-creation of value (Vargo et al. 2023).

Today, most marketing theorists assume that buyers and sellers co-create value, a fundamental shift in marketing focus (Ranjan and Read 2016; Perera et al. 2017; Saha et al. 2022). Such a perspective is particularly important when it comes to marketing and sustainability – a shared effort by customers, companies, and other stakeholders as well.

A key factor in building up long-term customer relations relates to the analyzes of customer needs, followed by focusing value-creation in such a way that products and offerings correspond to needs and desires. In this context, it is relevant to think about which customer to focus on and whether their short-term needs should always be met. An approach that questions what products should be provided combines satisfying short-term consumer wants with a societal orientation that aligns with sustainability concerns and hence provides an application of the so-called societal marketing concept, a cornerstone in contemporary marketing practices. There are many examples of companies choosing to desist from attempting to meet certain customer requirements. Tobacco, pornography, and alcohol are examples of products that may be problematic from a societal perspective. Accordingly, many countries have implemented strict rules about how such products can be marketed and consumed. Companies must ask themselves whether they should merely focus on short-term exchanges with today's customers – or also attempt to create long-term relations with the customers of the future. Depending on which strategy a company chooses in this regard, its sustainability decisions will be affected.

Green Marketing, Sustainability Marketing – Same, Same, But Different?

In the AMA dictionary, the term *sustainability marketing* is unfortunately not mentioned. The AMA prefers the older term *green marketing*, which is rather defined from a manufacturing and retailing approach, with an environmental twist.

(Continued)

(Continued)

Green marketing refers to the development and marketing of products that are presumed to be environmentally safe (i.e. designed to minimize negative effects on the physical environment or to improve its quality). This term may also be used to describe efforts to produce, promote, package, and reclaim products in a manner that is sensitive or responsive to ecological concerns. (marketing-dictionary.org).

This definition is very much in line with Polonsky (1994), who conceptualized green marketing activities as the generation and facilitation of marketplace exchanges with a minimal detrimental impact on the natural environment. It also recognizes the contribution of Peattie (2001) by emphasizing marketing activities that attempt to reduce the negative impact of existing products and manufacturing processes and to promote more environmentally sound products and services.

While focusing on "green" manufacturing (i.e. improving the systems of production) is in line with long-term environmental and economic perspectives, it lacks the complete sustainability approach that includes social and societal improvements at all stages of the production and consumption processes aiming to improve individual, environmental, and societal well-being (Ostrom et al. 2015; Guyader et al. 2019). Accordingly, green marketing is inconsistent with the view of consumers as co-creators of value for a variety of stakeholders.

Eventually, one may note that it has almost been four decades since the Brundtland Report (WCED 1987) and "the 'euphoric' discovery of the environment by marketing practitioners and academics" (i.e. Peattie and Crane 2005, p. 357). As such, the nomenclature and terminology around green marketing have evolved. Thus, we can denote three phases:

- "Ecological" green marketing in the late 1970s and early 1980s, with a rapid increase in green consumerism due to a concern from businesses to help solve environmental problems (e.g. pollution and waste issues)
- "Environmental" green marketing in the late 1980s when the focus shifted to clean technology, new green product design, and the widespread implementation of International Organization for Standardization (ISO) standards and third-party certifications
- "Sustainability" (green) marketing since the 1990s and early 2000s, which is the most common term relating marketing activities to all three pillars of the SDGs established by the UN (For an evolution of terminology used (see Figure 1.1)

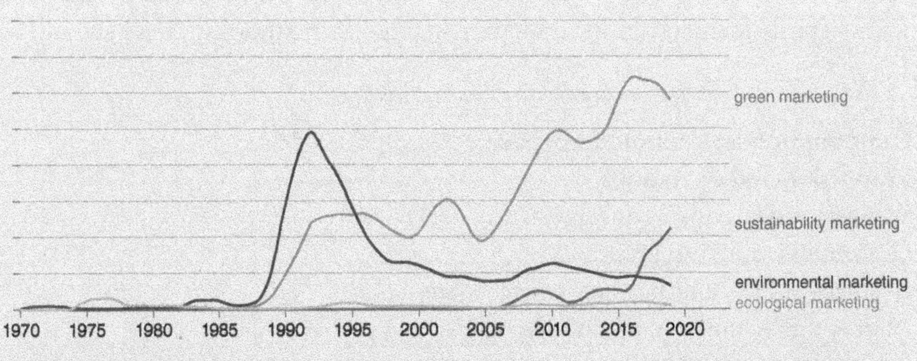

Figure 1.1 Evolution of the terms related to green marketing. While ecological (1980s), environmental (1990s), and sustainability (2000s) marketing have followed each other over time as definitions have been revised, *green marketing* has been the preferred term in books.
Source: Created in Google Books Ngram Viewer (2024).

While AMA does not currently use the term *sustainability marketing* in their online dictionary, available on their website, in 2023 the first special interest group (SIG) focusing on sustainability and innovation was officially announced. The description of the group is as follows (e.g. AMA Special Interest Groups n.d.):

> *The Sustainable Marketing & Innovation SIG is an emerging community of scholars who believe that the business of business is more than business. To this end, we strive to understand how environmental, social, and/or governance initiatives undertaken by companies influence pivotal business and societal outcomes. The specific research interests of our SIG members span numerous topics, including: demonstrating the business case for sustainability, driving innovation in a circular economy, empowering entrepreneurs at the base of the pyramid with marketing knowledge, understanding drivers of consumer decision making, linking marketing to the United Nations Sustainable Development Goals, and clarifying when and how sustainability can serve as a basis for competitive advantage. Given the strong push to also incorporate sustainability into the curriculum, we also facilitate collaborative exchange of research ideas and teaching resources.*

Relating the Field of Marketing to Sustainability in this Textbook

The aim of this book is to highlight, discuss, and problematize subareas where it is particularly important to relate the field of marketing to sustainability. These subareas deal with key parts of marketing where the link to sustainability issues is seldom problematized in introductory marketing textbooks. These subareas are as follows:

- Consumption and consumer behavior
- Production and operations
- Services and sharing economy
- Communication and branding
- Business models and product service systems
- Marketing channels and value chains
- Pricing strategies and prices

There are, of course, many other areas that may be just as interesting. This book is not comprehensive – textbooks seldom are – and we could have added more material regarding, for instance, the interconnected development of digitization and sustainability, or sustainable entrepreneurship and innovations. Our hope, nevertheless, is that we emphasize the parts that are crucial by following established ways of relating to marketing activities (i.e. consuming, producing, service, communicating, and distributing). The format of this book limits our ability to discuss every conceivable aspect, and our hope is that the discussions conducted in this book will contribute toward greater knowledge and more reflection on sustainability issues within businesses in general and the practice of marketing in particular. Hence, an attentive reader will be able to identify and digest many examples beyond what we deal with in this book.

In each respective chapter, we include insights from contemporary research and present theoretical concepts with examples from around the world. For the previously mentioned subareas, there are clear links between marketing and sustainability. In a nutshell, the concepts of marketing and sustainability might be seen as polar opposites, but in our book, it means focusing on how companies and other organizations work in an integrated way with the social, environmental, and economic aspects of marketing activities at various levels from strategic planning to practical implementation. Our ambition in writing this book is thus to get past the superficial examples that used to be common in some of the literature on corporate social responsibility (CSR) – such as companies that donate funds to schools in under-developed countries but that otherwise conduct their business in an unsustainable way. Our conviction is that sustainability cannot be achieved if these issues are not given strategic significance and permeate core activities. A basically unsustainable business can thus never be laundered using statements about sustainability and expensive advertising campaigns – a rather common practice called *greenwashing*, a concept that we will come back to in later chapters.

The three aspects of sustainability – social, environmental, and economic – are well-established and allow not only for catching the richness of sustainability but also the difficult trade-offs between the three dimensions. The Cambridge dictionary definition of sustainability is

> "the ability to continue at a particular level for a period of time" and "causing little or no damage to the environment and therefore able to continue for a long time."

Sustainable things can either be material or immaterial. It is often difficult to assess in advance what will last (Bonnedahl et al. 2022). For instance, the time horizon is critical. If we apply a sufficiently long-term perspective, then hardly anything will be sustainable. Another key question concerns what is worth preserving over time – maybe some products should be abandoned for the better, like substituting combustion engine vehicles with electric ones, a transition that is moving forward but will take several decades. Moreover, many of the resources we are naturally consuming today did not even exist a couple of decades ago. A moment's reflection enables us to quickly realize that interpretations of what sustainability entails are far from unambiguous. We return to this discussion later in the book.

By adding the term *development* to sustainability, another dimension is introduced (Bonnedahl et al. 2022). The Cambridge dictionary definition of development is "the process *in which someone or something grows or changes and becomes more advanced.*" Development is normally a term with positive associations, often equated with progress. The term *sustainable development* owes its breakthrough to the prominent 1987 Brundtland Report, "Our Common Future," compiled by the UN World Commission on Environment and Development under the leadership of the then prime minister of Norway, Gro Harlem Brundtland (WCED 1987). This report became significant as it paved the way for a new and less confrontational view on the link between economics and sustainability. The concept of sustainable development was developed by the American environmental scientist Lester R. Brown, founder of the Earth Policy Institute. Following acceptance of this as a principle, large parts of the environmental movement, the world's politicians, and trade and industry would all start working together from the 1990s and onward. Instead of emphasizing that sustainability and economic growth are incompatible, which has been a dominant perception, the Brundtland Commission argued that economic growth was possible while being based on sustainable considerations.

Lester Brown: A Key Figure in the Transition Toward Sustainable Business

Lester Brown started his career as a farmer, growing tomatoes in southern New Jersey with his younger brother during high school and college. Shortly after earning a degree in agricultural science from Rutgers University in 1955, he spent six months living in rural India where he became intimately familiar with the food/population issue. In 1959 Brown joined the US Department of

(Continued)

(Continued)

Agriculture's Foreign Agricultural Service as an international analyst. Brown also studied agricultural economics at the University of Maryland and public administration at Harvard University.

Few people have done more for the sustainability transition than Lester Brown, and since the 1980s, it has been clear that Lester Brown has already strongly affected thinking about problems of world population and resources. The *Washington Post* has called him "one of the world's most influential thinkers."

He has founded many initiatives that drive the transition, too. In 1969, he left the government to help establish the Overseas Development Council. In 1974, with support of the Rockefeller Brothers Fund, he founded the Worldwatch Institute, the first research institute devoted to the analysis of global environmental issues. In 2001, he founded the Earth Policy Institute.

He is one of the world's most widely published authors on the topic of sustainability. At the Worldwatch Institute, Lester Brown launched the Worldwatch Papers series, the World Watch magazine, and the annual State of the World reports among numerous other publications. He has also written more than 50 books, translated into more than 40 languages. Books such as *Building a Sustainable Society* and *Who Will Feed China?* have challenged established ways of thinking. While at the Earth Policy Institute, he published *Eco-Economy: Building an Economy for the Earth* as well as *Full Planet, Empty Plates* – the titles describe well what sustainability-related themes the books deal with.

He is the recipient of many prizes and awards, including 25 honorary degrees, a MacArthur Fellowship, the 1987 UN Environment Prize, the 1989 WorldWide Fund for Nature Gold Medal, and the 1994 Blue Planet Prize for his "exceptional contributions to solving global environmental problems." In 2012, he was inducted into the Earth Hall of Fame Kyoto. Lester Brown's mission has been clear: to chart a course toward a sustainable future for our planet. With deep insights and challenging thinking on climate change, deforestation, and dwindling resources, he has pursued his goal of doing what he can to contribute toward a sustainable future for existing and future generations.

The Brundtland Report was highly inspired by the work of Lester Brown. The report of the commission, published in 1987 by the UN, has been highly influential with its definition of what "sustainable development" means for the world, and it became the basis for the Earth Summit and, ultimately, the adoption of the "Agenda 21" by 178 governments (in 1992 in Rio, Brazil). The report of the commission, published in 1987 by the UN, has been highly influential with its definition of what "sustainable development" means for the world, and it became the basis for the Earth Summit and, ultimately, the adoption of the "Agenda 21" by 178 governments (in 1992 in Rio, Brazil).

In a sustainable society, begging to make a living is avoided. The Brundtland Commission's original definition of the term *sustainable development* reads as follows (WCED 1987, Chapter 2, p. 2):

> Sustainable development is development that meets the needs of the present without compromising the ability of future generations to meet their own needs.

It contains within it two key concepts:

- The concept of "needs" in particular the essential needs of the world's poor, to which overriding priority should be given
- The idea of limitations imposed by the state of technology and social organization on the environment's ability to meet present and future needs

As marketing is concerned with satisfying the needs and wants of consumers – and building profitable relationships with them, something that may imply selling more than the customer needs – the principles of sustainable development are highly relevant here. In particular, the UN 12th SDG is actually about "responsible consumption and production," something that businesses, nonprofit organizations, and governmental bodies should strive for in our global marketplace (see Figure 1.2). In other words,

Figure 1.2 The report "Our Common Future" published in 1987 by the UN has become one of the most influential reports related to sustainable development.
Source: Halytskyi Olexandr/Adobe Stock.

organizations can satisfy the desires of consumers today in a way that is responsible (i.e. sustainable) and not jeopardize the lives of future consumers. Although marketers began emphasizing sustainability as early as the 1970s, awareness of its importance and complexity increased significantly with the Brundtland Commission in the 1980s. As a result, it has become urgent for marketers to understand what sustainable development means and to integrate sustainability concerns into their practices.

The Triple Bottom Line

Nowadays, we emphasize three responsibilities in sustainable development, referred to as the triple Es, the triple Ps, or the triple bottom line (see Figure 1.3):

- Economic prosperity, i.e. economic capital
- Environmental integrity, i.e. natural capital
- Social equity, i.e. human capital

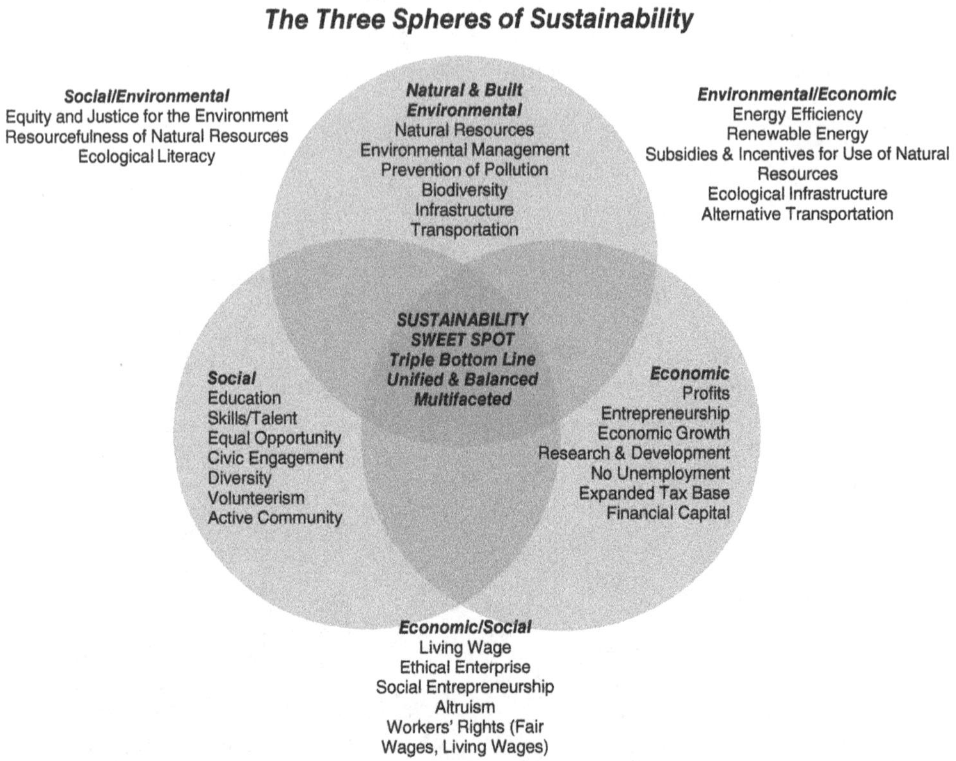

Figure 1.3 The three spheres of sustainability.
Source: Adapted by the authors from A Framework for Sustainability Indicators at EPA (2012a).

In detail, economic sustainability – realized by companies that show steady profits over time – comprises factors concerning how we can create sound economic growth without, for example, bribes and corruption. Environmental (sometimes called ecological, environment, or planet) sustainability emphasizes that economic growth should not occur at the expense of our nature, environment, and ecology. Social (sometimes called societal, often referred to as equity, or people) sustainability, finally, is about building a long-term sustainable society in which people's basic needs are met. This includes working conditions and income equality. It is often difficult to keep the three different parts of the sustainability concept apart, as economic, environmental, and social sustainability frequently touch upon and even overlap with each other (see Figure 1.4). Introducing new energy-efficient ventilation systems into industrial manufacturing can, for instance, reduce energy consumption and costs, improve the working environment of the staff, and create economic growth in the environmental technology industry. In other instances, there is a clear conflict between the sustainability dimensions, i.e. in building a new railway that will force families out of their homes – expropriation legislation is necessary to make society prepare for the future. Air travel obviously could contribute toward social sustainability – understanding others and gaining perspectives on one's own life make the world a more decent and peaceful place. At the same time, air travel creates dangerous pollution. All in all, it is often difficult for organizations to balance the three pillars of sustainable development.

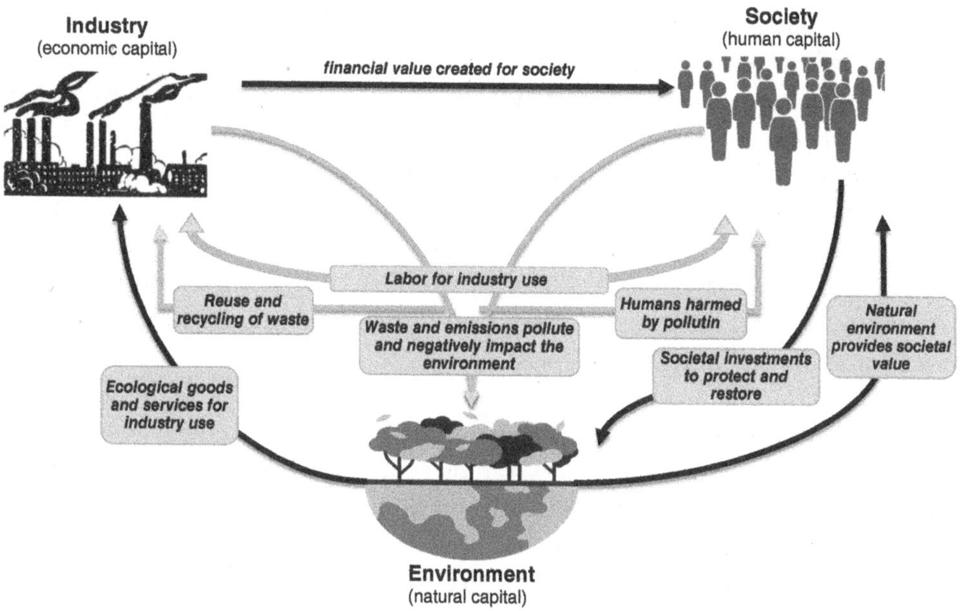

Figure 1.4 Sustainable development is concerned with economic, environmental, and social factors.
Source: Adapted by the authors from EPA (2012b).

Fit for 55 – Tricky Balancing in Many Dimensions

Fit for 55 is a recent European Union initiative to revise legislation to reduce emissions by at least 55% by 2030, compared to 1990 levels a legal requirement. This may sound like an ambitious goal, but already EU emissions trading system (ETS), a carbon market, which has been in place since 2005, has reduced the union's emission by 41% (European Council 2024; European Union 2024).

The package includes a wide range of measures across various sectors, including energy, transport, industry, and agriculture. Key components of Fit for 55 include the following:

- *Revised ETS*: Expanding the scope of the ETS to include new sectors like shipping and aviation, tightening the cap on emissions, and introducing a carbon border adjustment mechanism (CBAM) to prevent carbon leakage
- *Effort Sharing Regulation (ESR)*: Setting binding national targets for emissions reductions in sectors not covered by the ETS, such as buildings, agriculture, and waste
- *Renewable Energy Directive (RED II)*: Increasing the European Union's renewable energy target to 40% by 2030 and implementing measures to support the deployment of renewable energy sources
- *Energy Efficiency Directive (EED)*: Strengthening energy efficiency measures in buildings, industry, and transport to reduce energy consumption and promote energy-saving practices
- *Fuel Quality Directive (FQD)*: Introducing stricter requirements for the carbon intensity of fuels used in transportation, encouraging the use of low-carbon alternatives such as biofuels and renewable electricity
- *Alternative Fuels Infrastructure Directive (AFID)*: Enhancing the infrastructure for alternative fuels such as electric vehicle charging stations and hydrogen refueling stations to support the transition to cleaner transportation
- *Land Use, Land Use Change, and Forestry (LULUCF) Regulation*: Setting rules for managing carbon sinks, such as forests and agricultural land, to ensure they contribute to climate mitigation efforts

Fit for 55 represents a significant overhaul of EU climate and energy policies, aiming to accelerate the transition to a low-carbon economy while promoting innovation, investment, and job creation. However, its implementation will require cooperation and coordination among the European Union's member states, as well as ongoing monitoring and adjustment to ensure its effectiveness in achieving climate targets.

The principles may be implemented differently in the EU member states. For instance, the Swedish government intends to apply the three dimensions of sustainable development – economic, environmental, and social – in a way that concordantly and mutually support each other. Sweden's goal is to be a leading nation when it comes to reaching the Agenda 2030 goals (Government Offices of Sweden 2022). Sweden also has high goals related to climate change and greenhouse gas reduction, according to the Swedish Environmental Protection Agency (2017):

"By 2045 at the latest, Sweden must have no net emissions of greenhouse gasses into the atmosphere, in order to subsequently achieve negative emissions. The goal means that the emissions of greenhouse gases from Swedish territory must be at least 85% lower by the year 2045 than the emissions in 1990."

This objective can be achieved only by sending clear signals to the market already today (i.e. an economic factor). For example, considering that a private car has a life span of around 20 years, vehicles powered by a combustion engine (fueled by gasoline or diesel) either must use renewable fuels or should not be sold anymore. For the transition to start as soon as possible, marketing efforts (i.e. product design, pricing, communication, incentives for behavioral change, etc.) are necessary – for example communicating the lower usage costs of electric vehicles to balance the higher up-front costs that consumers usually consider when purchasing a new car. Similarly, industrial projects like fossil-free steel and sustainable fertilizer production must move from idea to implementation for Sweden to reach its high sustainability and climate goals.

The UN SDGs

The 2030 Agenda for Sustainable Development, adopted by all UN member states in 2015, provides a shared blueprint for people and the planet, now and into the future. At its heart are the 17 SDGs, which represent an urgent call for action by all countries (i.e. developed and developing) in a global partnership. They recognize that ending poverty and other forms of deprivation must go hand in hand with strategies that improve health and education, reduce inequality, and spur economic growth – simultaneously as they tackle climate change and work to preserve our oceans and forests.

Source: United Nations.

The term *sustainability* is clearly ambiguous – like the term CSR. For instance, Dahlsrud (2008) found 37 different definitions of the term CSR in a review of its use. The advantage of the term *sustainability* vis-à-vis CSR, however, is that it has a clearer (but far from unambiguous) definition – thanks to the Brundtland Commission – which is applied internationally. At the UN summit on sustainable development in Johannesburg in 2002, the concept of sustainable development was recognized as a superordinate principle for all UN work, underscoring the widespread application of initiatives for sustainability in society and the prevalence of the term nowadays.

A Soft and Hard Interpretation of Sustainability

It is commonplace to differentiate between a soft and hard interpretation of sustainability. A *soft* interpretation of the term – "weak sustainability" – refers to the substitution of certain resources with others (Bonnedahl et al. 2022). To build homes and reduce homelessness, we have to produce, for example, timber, concrete, bricks, and windows. This kind of production will utilize and consume finite resources and generate emissions. A supporter of the soft interpretation of sustainability would accept a certain amount of environmental impact to increase social sustainability (i.e. providing more people with a roof over their heads). The most important aspect, according to this perspective, would thus be balancing the various parts of the sustainability concept while not reducing the ability for future generations to generate prosperity.

On the other hand, a *hard* interpretation of the term – "strong sustainability" – would reject this line of reasoning that allows different parts of sustainability to be traded off against one another (Bonnedahl et al. 2022). No compromises can be made for supporters of the hard interpretation. Of course, such a line of reasoning, according to the critics, presupposes that all the various resources can actually be fully substituted. Natural resources that are depleted and animal species that become extinct due to their loss of habitat can never be re-created; thus, it is impossible to regard these as a necessary evil price to pay for a new road, a new mine, or a tourism facility for example. Consequently, critical natural resources must be protected and cannot be regarded as substitutable.

Bonnedahl et al. (2022) argues that the too soft interpretation of sustainability as formulated and popularized by the Brundtland report and manifested in the UN's 2030 Agenda for Sustainable Development is problematic since it has yet not solved any major sustainability problems. Such a view on sustainable development is ultimately strictly anthropocentric – it is based on and revolves around humankind and its current and future needs (Bonnedahl et al. 2022). According to critics of the weak sustainability view, the failure of the present sustainable development policy is due to ". . . its rootedness in assumptions and values of weak sustainability" (Bonnedahl et al. 2022, p. 156). Rather than letting anthropocentric views on sustainability determine future policies, ecological balance should, according to supporters of the hard interpretation of sustainability, be the foundation of sustainable development.

At the same time, the specific focus on needs does not mean what consumers associate with wanting things like "an iPhone," or "enter any product or service brand experience here . . ." but a few suggestions are fashion, aesthetics, design, technical innovations, and premium products. In the Brundtland Commission's discussion, the term *need* refers to people's basic needs: like physical needs (food, water, shelter, etc.), social needs (e.g. belonging, affection), and individual needs (e.g. knowledge, self-expression) – these needs are not created by marketers but part of human nature. The Brundtland Commission states: "the concept of 'needs,' in particular the essential needs of the world's poor, to which overriding priority should be given" (WCED 1987, p. 54). It carries on saying:

> "Living standards that go beyond the basic minimum are sustainable only if consumption standards everywhere have regard for long-term sustainability."

In this respect, the Brundtland Commission makes it clear that distribution-related injustices between different regions and countries of the world, resulting in different types of consumption, are not sustainable. Not until the basic needs of all people have been met is some other type of consumption legitimate, provided that it occurs within what can be regarded as environmentally sustainable. At the same time, the Brundtland Commission emphasized that people's needs are largely socially and culturally influenced, once again resulting in a vagueness in the applicability of the concept. For instance, in terms of need for food, Frenchmen might prefer to eat bread and cheese, Swedes would prefer meatballs and potatoes, Americans may prefer fried chicken and fries, while Chinese may prefer fish and rice due to cultural differences. Another problematization with sustainable consumption is the increase in natural disasters due to changes in wind (forest and wildfires, hurricanes, tornados), water (flooding), and temperature (heatwaves, freezing temperatures) in more areas that changes consumers' priorities in their consumption needs.

To conclude this introductory chapter, we have to accept that the term *sustainability* incorporates a certain amount of vagueness. However, according to Solow (2000), the term provides comprehensive guidance with regard to showing consideration to coming generations, but this has to be broken down and operationalized by organizations to be used more concretely. This opening chapter discussion shows that we have to systematically problematize the contribution of marketing to a sustainable society – and this book is our contribution to moving discussions forward.

References

Alfredsson, E. C., & Malmaeus, J. M. (2019). Real capital investments and sustainability - the case of Sweden, *Ecological Economics,* 161, 216–224.

Allal-Chérif, O., Climent, J. C., & Berenguer, K. J. U. (2023). Born to be sustainable: how to combine strategic disruption, open innovation, and process digitization to create a sustainable business, *Journal of Business Research*, 154, 113379.

AMA (2017). American Marketing Association. What is Marketing? https://www.ama.org/the-definition-of-marketing-what-is-marketing (accessed 16 January 2024).

AMA Special Interest Groups (n.d.). Sustainable Marketing and Innovation. https://www.ama.org/pop-up-sig-sustainable-marketing (accessed 14 March 2024).

Bartels, R. (1968). The general theory of marketing. *Journal of Marketing*, 32, 29–33.

Berry, I. (2021). Top 10 Greenest Countries. *Sustainability Magazine.* https://sustainabilitymag.com/top10/top-10-greenest-countries-2 (accessed 1 April 2024).

Bonnedahl, K.J., Heikkurinen, P., & Paavola, J. (2022). Strongly sustainable development goals: overcoming distances constraining responsible action, *Environmental Science & Policy*, 129, 150–158.

Buell, R.W. (2019). Operational transparency. *Harvard Business Review*, 97, 102–113.

Carvill, M., Butler, G., & Evans., G. (2021). *Sustainable Marketing: How to Drive Profits with Purpose.* Bloomsbury Business.

Dahlsrud, A. (2008). How corporate social responsibility is defined: an analysis of 37 definitions. *Corporate Social Responsibility and Environmental Management*, 15, 1–13.

Dahlstrom, R., & Crosno, J. (2024). *Sustainable Marketing* (Kindle ed.). Sage

EPA (2012a). Three Spheres of Sustainability. https://comdev.osu.edu/sites/comdev/files/imce/Comprehensive%20Planning%20based%20on%20Sustainability%20-%20Final.pdf (accessed 2 April 2024).

EPA (2012b). Sustainability Indicators. https://www.epa.gov/sustainability/report-framework-sustainability-indicators-epa (accessed 2 April 2024).

European Council (2024). Fit for 55. https://www.consilium.europa.eu/en/policies/green-deal/fit-for-55-the-eu-plan-for-a-green-transition/#what (accessed 15 February 2024).

European Union (2024). Fit for 55, https://commission.europa.eu/strategy-and-policy/priorities-2019-2024/european-green-deal/delivering-european-green-deal/fit-55-delivering-proposals_en (accessed 9 April 2024).

Fahy, J., & Jobber, D. (2022). *Foundations of Marketing* (7th ed.). London: McGraw-Hill Education.

Finansinspektionen (2024). Hållbarhetsrapportering. https://fi.se/sv/hallbarhet/regler/hallbarhetrapportering (accessed 5 May 2024).

Fisk, G. (1974). *Marketing and the Ecological Crisis.* New York: Harper and Row.

Government Offices of Sweden (2022). Agenda 2023 för Hållbar Utveckling. https://www.regeringen.se/regeringens-politik/globala-malen-och-agenda-2030 (accessed 13 February 2024).

Grant, J. (2020). *Greener Marketing.* Wiley

Guyader, H., Ottosson, M., Frankelius, P., & Witell, L. (2019). Identifying the resource integration processes of green service. *Journal of Service Management*, 31(4), 839–859.

Henion, K.E. (1972). The effect of ecologically relevant information on detergent sales. *Journal of Marketing Research*, 9, 10–14.

Henion, K.E. (1981). Energy usage and the conserver society: review of the 1979 AMA conference on ecological marketing. *Journal of Consumer Research,* 8(3), 339–342.

Henion, K.E., & Kinnear, T.C. (1976). *Ecological Marketing.* American Marketing Association.

Iyer, E. (1994). Book review. *Journal of Marketing*, 58(2), 127–129.

Jansson, J. Nordlund, A., & Westin, K. (2017). Examining drivers of sustainable consumption: the influence of norms and opinion leadership on electric vehicle adoption in Sweden, *Journal of Cleaner Production*, 154, 176–187.

Kaplan, R.S., & McMillan, D. (2021). Reimagining the balanced scorecard for the ESG era. *Harvard Business Review* https://hbr.org/2021/02/reimagining-the-balanced-scorecard-for-the-esg-era?ab=hero-main-text (accessed 3 February 2021).

Kinnear, T.C., Taylor, J.R. and Ahmed, S.A. (1974). Ecologically concerned consumers: who are they? Ecologically concerned consumers can be identified. *Journal of Marketing*, 38(2), 20–24.

Kotler, P., & Armstrong, G. (2023). *Principles of Marketing* (Global Edition). Pearson.

Kotler, P., & Zaltman, G. (1971). Social marketing: an approach to planned social change. *Journal of Marketing*, 35, 3–12.

Ostrom, A.L., Parasuraman, A., Bowen, D.E., Patrício, L., & Voss, C.A. (2015). Service research priorities in a rapidly changing context. *Journal of Service Research,* 18, 127–159.

Peattie, K. (2001). Golden goose or wild goose? The hunt for the green consumer. *Business Strategy and the Environment,* 10, 187–199.

Peattie, K., & Crane, A. (2005). Green marketing: legend, myth, farce or prophesy? *Qualitative Market Research: an International Journal*, 8(4), 357–370.

Perera, B. Y., Albinsson, P. A., & Shows, G. D. (2017). Value co-creation in consumer-intensive service encounters: a dyadic perspective. *Journal of Creating Value*, 3, 19–32.

Peterson, M. (2021) Sustainable Marketing: A Holistic Approach. Sage.

Polman, P., & Winston, A. (2022). *Net Positive: How Courageous Companies Thrive by Giving More Than They Take*, Harvard Business Review Press

Polonsky, M.J. (1994). An introduction to green marketing. *Electronic Green Journal*, 1, 2–3.

Ranjan, K. R., & Read, S. (2016). Value co-creation: concept and measurement. *Journal of the Academy of Marketing Science*, 44, 290–315.

Saha, V., Goyal, P., & Jebarajakirthy, C. (2022). Value co-creation: a review of literature and future research agenda. *Journal of Business & Industrial Marketing*, 37, 612–628.

Silk, D.M., & Lu, C.X.W. (2024). Environmental, Social & Governance Law 2024. The International Comparative Legal Guide 17-01-2024. http://iclg.com/practice-areas/environmental-social-and governance-law (accessed 19 January 2024).

Solow, R.M. (2000). Sustainability: an economist's perspective. In R. N. Stavins (ed.). *Economics of the Environment,* Chapter 26 (5th ed.). New York: W. W. Norton & Co.

Swedish Environmental Protection Agency (2017). Sveriges klimatmål och klimatpolitiska ramverk. https://www.naturvardsverket.se/amnesomraden/klimatomstallningen/sveriges-klimatarbete/sveriges-klimatmal-och-klimatpolitiska-ramverk (accessed 13 February 2024).

Tomlinson, B. (2023). Corporate Sustainability Reporting Directive: the rush to get ready. Ernst & Young. https://www.ey.com/en_us/assurance/csrd--the-rush-to-get-ready (accessed 15 February 2024).

Urso, F. (2022). Number of company sustainability officers triples in 2021 - study, Reuters, May 4, 2022. https://www.reuters.com/business/sustainable-business/number-company-sustainability-officers-triples-2021-study-2022-05-04 (accessed 10 January 2024).

Vargo, S.L., Peters, L., Kjellberg, H., Koskela-Huotari K., Nenonen, S., Polese, F., Sarno D., & Vaughan, C. (2023). Emergence in marketing: an institutional and ecosystem framework. *Journal of the Academy of Marketing Science,* 51, 2–22. 10.1007/s11747-022-00849-8

WCED (1987). *Our Common Future.* World Commission on Environment and Development. Oxford University Press.

White, K., Habib, R. and Hardisty, D.J. (2019). How to SHIFT consumer behaviors to be more sustainable: a literature review and guiding framework. *Journal of Marketing*, 83, 22–49.

Chapter 2

Factors Influencing Consumers and Their Sustainability Choices

Numerous factors impact consumption, spanning from broader environmental and contextual circumstances to aspects of individual personality and psychological processes. This chapter first covers general factors that can pose challenges to encouraging more sustainable consumption practices among consumers and to which marketers can bring solutions, before focusing on how pro-environmental attitudes shape consumer behavior such as shopping for organic groceries, commuting by sustainable transportation alternatives, choosing to recycle, etc.

Learning Objectives

- Understand the key factors generally influencing consumer behavior
- Describe the consumption process and distinguish its different stages
- Recognize different ways to influence consumers to embrace sustainability practices

- Be able to differentiate the various principles of influence
- Understand the SHIFT framework
- Recognize nudging practices

Introduction

Consumption poses economic, social, and environmental challenges, with a historical trend of consumers acquiring more goods and services. Despite the promotion of sustainable consumption, there's a noticeable inclination for increased consumption, even when companies integrate sustainability into their models. This underscores the necessity to evaluate consumption patterns and their impacts locally, regionally, and globally. Consumer demand significantly influences the adoption of sustainable development principles. Ultimately, the supply of responsibly produced products and consumers' willingness and capacity to engage in sustainable consumption are intertwined. Therefore, both companies and consumers bear responsibility in advancing societal sustainability.

General Factors Influencing Consumption

There are key factors influencing consumer behavior, such as cultural factors, social factors, personal factors, psychological factors, and contextual factors (Belz and Peattie 2012; Kotler and Armstrong 2023). Let's look at each of these:

Cultural Factors

Cultural factors include culture (e.g. American or Swedish), subculture (e.g. hip-hop, hippies), and social group membership. A social group is a group of individuals with similar values, interests, and lifestyles. Group membership, however, is not a given – individuals can, for instance, identify with the working class while objectively being high-earners (e.g. hipsters) or with the young generation of consumers while being objectively old. By and large, shifts have occurred in these categories as new subcultures have emerged, as consumers have become more interested in sustainability issues, and as social behavioral patterns have changed.

Social Factors

Among social factors influencing an individual's purchasing behavior, reference groups play a noticeable role – bloggers, musicians, politicians, business leaders, or other famous individuals acting as shapers of public opinion and setting different types of trends. Other factors include family members and the role and status of the individual. Roles (e.g. professional roles like professors or doctors, or familial roles like parents or siblings) confer a given status that reflects the general perception ascribed by society to that role. Roles and status also influence purchase decisions, since a certain type of product will be socially accepted to varying degrees in relation to the individual's different roles. Consumer behavior can thus be explained through the symbolic meanings that certain goods/services represent to people (e.g. a wedding dress is not just any dress) – which can also include the image of a particular brand.

The Influence of Descriptive Social Norm Information to Ditch the Car

Let's consider the following problem: people's commuting habits are "locked in," and difficult to change. Could social norms help them "walk the talk" for more sustainable transportation? In Canada, Kormos et al. (2015) tested the following hypothesis: *people in a high social norm condition (i.e. who were told that many others had reduced their private vehicle use) exhibit a greater reduction in private vehicle use than people in a low social norm condition (i.e. who were told that relatively few others had reduced their private vehicle use).* There were three experimental conditions with different information provided to the participants:

- *Low local norm*: "Since 1993, only 4% of commuters at our university have switched to more sustainable modes of transport to campus" (i.e. under-reporting others' successful efforts at their university to switch to sustainable transportation)
- *High local norm*: "Since 1993, 26% of commuters at our university have switched to more sustainable modes of transport to campus" (i.e. over-reporting others' successful efforts at their university to switch to sustainable transportation)
- *Control group*: No manipulation

The experiment results supported the hypothesis that when people are given information about how others use sustainable transportation (basically, making sustainable transportation the more normal behavior to adopt), they start using such alternative commuting options instead of private cars (see also Figure 2.1).

(Continued)

(Continued)

Figure 2.1 Sustainable commuting is about using transportation methods that are environmentally friendly, energy-efficient, and socially responsible by choosing alternatives to traveling by single-occupancy vehicles, such as public transportation (buses, trains, subways, etc.), cycling, walking, carpooling, or vanpooling with employees, or using micro-mobility options (e.g. e-scooters, e-bikes, and other small, battery-powered vehicles) instead of taxi rides. Sustainable commuting minimizes the negative impacts from traveling on the environment, it reduces carbon emissions, and it also promotes overall well-being.
Source: Photostock 2287899005.

Personal Factors

Personal factors play a key role in our purchase decisions. Naturally, our age and our economic circumstances affect what and how much we consume. During our lifetime, we will consume different things on the basis of our needs and our economic circumstances. Other factors affecting our consumption include lifestyle and profession, as well as personality and self-image. Holiday trips and choice of car/residential area can indicate, for example, our value to those around us (e.g. conservatism or innovative thinking).

There is also a clear generational component in terms of explaining purchasing behavior (e.g. Kotler and Armstrong 2023); in marketing, it has proved to be effective to appeal to the individual's feelings linked to events during their *coming-of-age years* (i.e. age 17–23).

Psychological Factors

Psychological factors also affect an individual's purchasing behavior. One such factor is the nature and strength of individual motives. *Motivation* concerns a need that is sufficiently palpable that an individual will attempt to satisfy it. There can be different types of needs, ranging from the most elementary physiological needs (water, food, shelter) to more complex needs linked to human self-realization (finding meaning in performing arts and other needs for personal growth). People can rank these needs in different order of importance: for some it is more important to find free Wi-Fi before coffee.

Perception is also a key psychological factor. This is the process by which individuals choose, organize, and interpret the information forming a meaningful picture of the world they inhabit. This means consumers can weigh the functional benefits and relative affordability of a product/service differently. The perceived benefits and costs make up the perceived net benefit – the value associated with a purchase – thus, for sustainability marketers, there is a need to increase the perceived net benefits of sustainable solutions compared to conventional offerings. Moreover, perception is generally about how we humans are affected by all the stimuli we constantly encounter. For example, the number of stimuli varies considerably between different geographical locations – in Sao Paolo, Brazil, (which in 2007 banned all advertising in public space), the number of stimuli is considerably lower than in Tokyo, Hong Kong, or New York.

Recent consumer research by Sokolova et al. (2023) investigated why when holding the amount of plastic in product packaging fixed, adding more paper to it leads to higher perceived environmental friendliness (PEF), even though it's not. In general, a bias is a tendency to favor one thing, person, or group over another, often in an unfair way. Perception bias is a type of cognitive bias that occurs when our expectations, experiences, and beliefs influence how we perceive and interpret information and events. A bias can occur consciously or unconsciously and can affect our judgment and decision-making. Therefore, the PEF bias means that consumers tend to perceive overpackaged products, wrapped in **plastic plus paper** (as the pictured fruit salad in Figure 2.2 in a plastic container with an additional strip of cardboard paper around), as having more environmentally friendly packaging than their *plastic-only*-wrapped counterparts (e.g. the fruit salad in a plastic container without anything else). The PEF bias is driven by consumers' beliefs "paper = good, plastic = bad" and by proportional reasoning, wherein packaging with a greater paper-to-plastic proportion is judged as more environmentally friendly. Good news! This bias can be mitigated by a "minimal packaging sticker" intervention, which increases the environmental friendliness perceptions of plastic-only packaging, rendering plastic-packaged products to be preferable to their plastic-plus-paper-packaged counterparts.

(Continued)

(Continued)

Figure 2.2 The fruit salad is packaged in plastic and further wrapped with paper.
Source: Shutterstock 1891942888.

Among the psychological factors affecting the consumer's purchase process, we also note *learning* (i.e. the experience consumers draw on as a consequence of previous encounters). Positive associations linked to a specific brand or product increase the probability of the consumer choosing the same brand again and vice versa.

Convictions and attitudes held by consumers also influence their willingness to act more sustainably (e.g. "What do I think is important?" "What do I believe about sustainability?" "What does it mean for me?" "Do I share some responsibility?" "Can I make a difference?" "How do I look upon myself?"). A *conviction* is a conception held by a consumer regarding a product, and this conviction can be based both on real knowledge and on opinions or ideologies. A consumer who is a vegan for ideological and moral reasons chooses not to eat meat. Eventually, there is also a spectrum of different attitudes. *An attitude* describes an individual's relatively consistent feelings, evaluation, and experience of something – like a positive (or negative) attitude toward environmental conservation.

Contextual Factors

Finally, we can consider several contextual factors, as discussed by Belz and Peattie (2012):

- *Geographic context*: Consumption (food, clothing, energy, etc.) is influenced by where we live in the world

- *Purchases as context*: The level of compromise (e.g. performance, further travel) and the level of confidence (in addressing a genuine sustainability issue) of a purchase for consumers will influence their behavior. Moreover, the value of the purchase (car versus newspaper), frequency (food versus house), social visibility (e.g. fair-trade coffee), complexity (milk versus computer), for self or others (e.g. gift), necessity or indulgence (need versus luxuries) are also important contextual factors
- *Circumstance as context*: Situational influences during the purchase phase (e.g. time pressure, being alone or not, the purchase environment) and structural influences during the postuse phase (e.g. recycling facilities, availability of secondhand stores) are part of circumstances of consumption
- *Macro context*: The citizen consumer (ethical/political consumption) is motivated by and linked to social solidarity rather than simply being an ethically inspired act of individualism. Such important external influences include the institutional context, business practices, the existence of a community, the government's approach, and the broad cultural context

The following Table 2.1 summarizes the general factors affecting consumer behavior discussed thus far.

Table 2.1 General factors influencing consumer behavior.

Factors	Examples
Cultural	Culture
	Subculture
	Social group
Social	Reference groups
	Family
	Roles and status
Personal	Age and generational affinity
	Profession
	Economic situation
	Lifestyle
	Personality and self-image
Psychological	Motivation
	Perception
	Learning
	Convictions (belief) and attitudes
Contextual	Geographic
	Purchases as context
	Situational circumstances
	Macro context

The case of e-scooter rental is used to illustrate how these factors play a role in consumer adoption (see Figure 2.3).

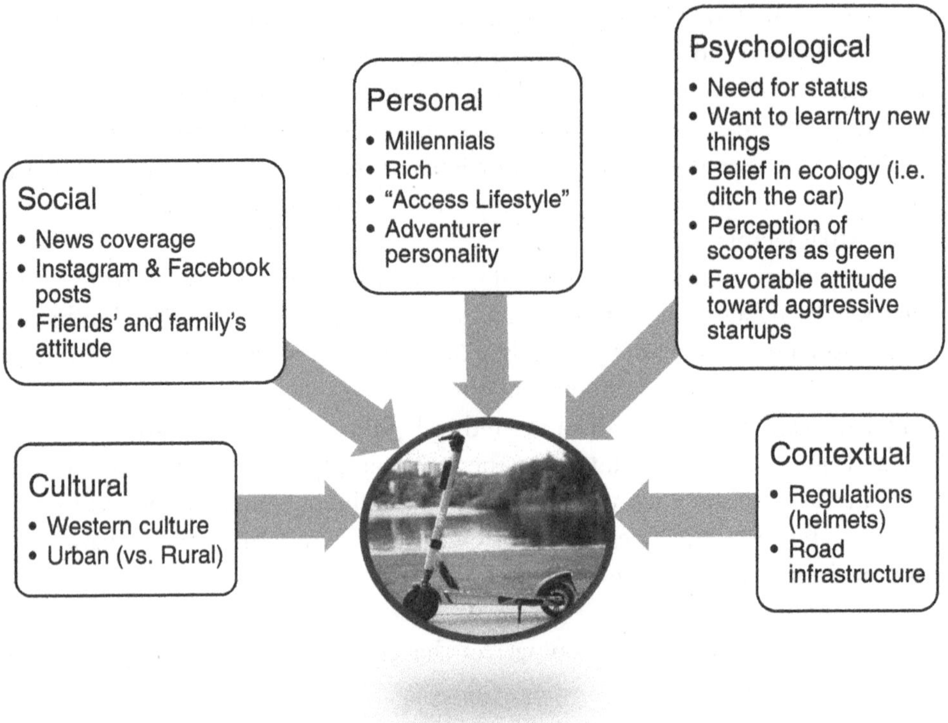

Figure 2.3 Example of factors affecting consumer adoption of electric scooters.
Source: Authors' own.

The Purchase Decision Process

The purchase decision process – often called the *buying process* – is key for understanding consumption decisions. Traditionally, the term *consumer* refers to the ultimate user of goods, ideas, and services. However, the person buying a product does not need to be the same person who uses it after purchase. A parent can, for instance, buy clothes for their child, who then wears these clothes, while a manager can buy a business phone for an employee.

There are three stages or phases during the buying process:

- *The prepurchase phase*: Various purchasing criteria arise, and the consumer seeks information and is influenced by word-of-mouth, personal selling, advertising, etc.
- *The purchase phase*: The purchase-triggering decision is made, making it important for companies to reach the consumer by using different types of marketing

communication and activating associations contributing to the purchase decision being made

- *The postpurchase phase*: Postpurchase feelings are activated, and, here too, companies can use advertising to provide customers who have already made purchase decisions with confirmation that they have made the right choice

However, the *consumption process* reaches far beyond the purchase transaction itself, when the exchange between the buyer and the seller takes place in the market. As such, marketing scholars commonly divide the consumption process into five phases (Kotler and Armstrong 2023):

1. Need recognition
2. Information search
3. Evaluation of alternatives
4. Purchase decision process
5. Postpurchase behaviors: use and postuse

This is based on the same logic as the three phases above (i.e. that there is a prepurchase process, a purchase process, and a postpurchase process); here, however, the different stages are more refined. For instance, for routine low-involvement purchases, such as everyday commodities like milk or orange juice, many consumers go straight from need recognition to purchase decision. These are relatively uncomplicated; consumers seldom put a great amount of energy into evaluating

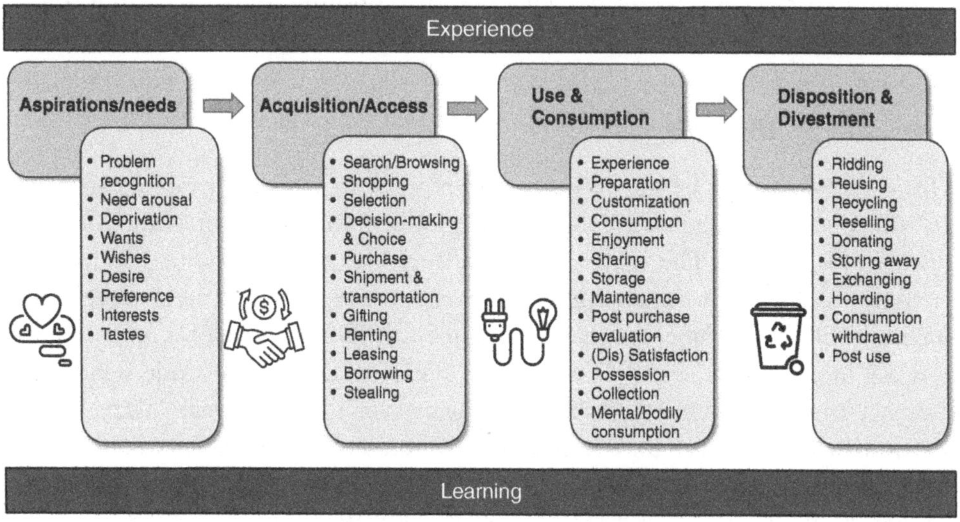

Figure 2.4 The stages of the consumption and disposition process.
Source: Adapted from Pham (2013); Albinsson and Perera (2009).

their purchase and choose their usual breakfast items for example. In contrast, high-involvement purchases, such as buying an electric mountain bike, require significantly more time, especially in the prepurchase phase. Some people enjoy this part of the process where they create a comparative table with different criteria (e.g. brand, price, bike weight, battery capacity, color) to help them choose the best alternative for them. (See also Figure 2.4 for another representation of the consumption process with many diverse activities)

Need Recognition

This is the first stage of the consumption process, in which consumers recognize a problem or need. During need recognition, the consumer realizes, via internal or external stimuli, that there is a need to solve a problem or satisfy a need. Internal stimuli can include hunger or thirst, while external stimuli can include an ad or word of mouth (e.g. hearing about a new flavor of chocolate). If the consumer has a strong driving force, such as thirst, they will then find a way to satisfy their thirst such as buy a bottle of water immediately without gathering any more information.

Information Search

This is the second stage of the consumption process, in which consumers are motivated to search for more information. It is normal to have a period of information search via, for example, personal sources (family and friends), commercial sources (ads, personal selling), public sources (mass media, blogs, consumer organizations), or previous experiences. The relative effect on the consumer of these various sources varies from person to person and with the type of purchase.

Evaluation of Alternatives

This is the third stage of the consumption process, in which consumers use information to evaluate alternative brands or products in the set of choices (see for example Figure 2.5). The same consumer, during a certain type of purchase, can carefully work out, for instance, interest charges when buying a car; however, when making another purchase, she may instead trust in friends' assertions or pure intuition. All in all, consumers' behavior is complex and difficult to understand when it comes to decision-making – that is why talk of the proverbial "black box" of decision-making continues. For instance, consumers cannot always explain why they make certain purchases. At a basic level, it can be said that consumer decision-making models involve two steps (Shao et al. 2008; Wästlund et al. 2015): screening (i.e. the decision-makers eliminate alternatives) and choice (i.e. the actual consideration of alternatives resulting in a purchase decision), which is the next stage in the consumption process.

Figure 2.5 When choosing an eco-friendly detergent or fabric softener, there are many options with different features. This makes the information search and evaluation stages crucial. Marketers should offer a unique value proposition that stands out from the competition and clearly communicate this with trusted labels and third-party certifications (Guyader et al. 2017). *Source:* Shutterstock 2121827021.

Purchase Decision

This is the fourth stage of the consumption process, in which consumers decide which brand or product to buy. The actual purchase decision can be further influenced by, for example, personal selling or unexpected situational factors, such as when consumers feeling that the level of service is inferior voting with their feet and going to another shop where the envisaged product might not be in stock but a similar one would be. As mentioned, decision-making is not always rational (Kahneman 2011). Emotional values are very important for the consumer in the purchase decision process (e.g. joy or sadness). Moreover, consumers can make purchase decisions on the basis of their self-image and the image they want to project socially (Dunning 2007). It is not until afterward (i.e. postpurchase) that they rationalize their behavior in terms of defense strategies to make them seem more rational than is actually the case (Cialdini 1984, 2016).

Postpurchase Behaviors

This is the last stage of the consumption process, in which consumers take further action after purchase, influenced by the outcome of consumption (evaluated as satisfying or dissatisfying). In the case of high-involvement purchases, the postpurchase behavior constitutes a critical part of the consumption process. Whether or not the consumer is satisfied during this phase is normally based on whether the product lived up to expectations – this also means that sales staff, ads, etc. should avoid promising things that the product cannot deliver. Many purchases result in cognitive dissonance (i.e. the buyer is considering whether the right purchase decision has been made). Many consumers feel that it is painful to be confronted by the disadvantages the chosen alternative entails, while simultaneously missing the advantages that the non-purchased products might have entailed – something similar to "fear of missing out" (FOMO) feelings (Chan et al. 2022). Managing the postpurchase phase is thus crucial for creating customer satisfaction. In particular, there are two specific behaviors consumers engage in after buying products: using them and disposing of them.

In the *use* phase, convenience is key. This is determined by the attributes of the product. Convenience, such as how easy it is to use something, influences consumer behavior in all the key markets (e.g. grocery shopping, transportation). An interesting development seeking to counterbalance the consumption of fast food (which is successful for being cheap but also very convenient) is the "slow food movement," an eco-efficient form of consumption or consumer movement where the desire for speed in consumption and production that traditionally leads the pace of innovation in the marketplace is considered unsustainable (e.g. Chaudhury and Albinsson 2015).

The *postuse* (i.e. product disposal) phase relates to concerns for the environment and the growing shortage of landfill space. As such, there are increasing efforts to reuse, remanufacture, and recycle used products and packaging. Changing product disposal behavior requires no compromise from the consumer in terms of their level of consumption or the nature of the products. That is to say that it suits consumers unwilling to change their lifestyles – in other words, the use phase. Moreover, it is possible for companies to reclaim used products from consumers and make them available for manufacturing or recycling through reverse engineering channels. It requires manufacturers to access used products that have become dispersed among households, which will return to the supply chain in varying conditions and at a convenient time for the customer. The key challenge concerns figuring out how to make returning end-of-life or used products to the value creation system as convenient and easy for consumers as simply throwing them away, as well as more attractive – which is what the circular economy principles are all about.

Note that a former editor of the *Journal of Consumer Psychology* wrote that the first of the seven sins of his discipline is the narrow scope of consumer behaviors (Pham 2013). Basically, researchers are too focused on the acquisition stage of the consumption process and there is a direct lack of research on the other stages. Moreover, "businesses are not interested only in purchasing behavior (the acquisition stage), they are also interested in what consumers need and want (the desire stage) and how products and services are actually used and consumed in the marketplace (the use and consumption stage)" (Pham 2013, p. 413). Nowadays, there is still much left to understand about disposal and divestment practices that take place postuse (e.g. recycling, reselling, donating), and these are essential responsibilities for marketing professionals and researchers (see Albinsson and Perera 2009).

How to Influence Consumers to Behave More Sustainably

We previously covered the difference between low-involvement and high-involvement products, which has an impact on consumers' decision-making. For instance, a banana (low-involvement) is chosen differently than a car (high-involvement). There are other influences on consumer behavior, such as culture, social relationships, or psychological factors. Actually, psychology and consumer behavior research in marketing are intrinsically linked. Another important influence is the nature, the amount, and the means of giving information to consumers (or the lack of knowledge altogether).

Next, we review how information (among other things) is processed by consumers.

The Six Principles of Influence

The book *Influence: The Psychology of Persuasion* (Cialdini 1984) has sold more than three million copies in more than 40 languages. It was written by Robert Cialdini, a trained psychologist who spent two-and-a-half years studying salespeople and how they get their clients to say yes. Cialdini argues that we live in a complex world and that we are (cognitively) lazy or do not have time to consider all the information available when making a decision, which is why we use mental shortcuts (i.e. heuristics, cues). One example is that something expensive means it is of good quality. This works well most of the time.

Cialdini (1984) narrowed down all these influential ways to six "universal principles" – a range of persuasive techniques to influence behavior that marketers may use:

- *The principle of reciprocity*: We want to repay, in kindness, what another person has provided us. Those who give are likely to get others to agree with them. For instance, the Hare Krishna Society used this principle in the 1970s to raise funds, offering passersby a gift (the magazine *Back to Godhead* or a flower) and then requesting a monetary donation – which was more likely to be given than without any gift. Supermarkets offering free stuff is another example of the principle put to use so that consumers reciprocate by buying more
- *The principle of likability* (or *similarity*): We say yes to people we like. People who are physically attractive or who give us compliments have an impact on us. Moreover, we also like people who are similar to us (e.g. same clothes, same background, same interests). This principle is very evident in salespeople
- *The principle of social proof* (or *consensus*): To determine what is correct, we find out what other people think is correct. Consider the fake laughs in TV shows such as *Friends* or *The Big Bang Theory*. We know the laughs are part of the soundtrack,

yet we also tend to laugh (at least smile) when we hear them compared to when we do not. Online reviews (positive and negative) also have a great impact on our behavior – if 13 people said this pizzeria was great, it must be true, right? Similarly, "three persons booked this place in the last two hours" is shown to visitors of Hotels.com or Booking.com to influence people to book a hotel stay. This principle works especially well when we do not know what constitutes appropriate behavior, when we are uncertain, or when we are in an unknown situation (e.g. in a new town looking for a dinner place)

- *The principle of authority*: We have a deep-seated sense of duty to authorities. We learn early on as a child to trust authority figures such as parents and teachers because they are wiser than we are but also because they control rewards and punishments. As we get older, we shift these authorities to, for example, employers, judges, and political powers. That is why there are often diplomas on the walls of doctors – these tell us that they have the necessary expertise. Similarly, health-related products (e.g. toothpaste) are often advertised on TV by actors wearing white blouses or lab coats, since this type of uniform conveys a sense of authority – although we have to be aware that authority and expertise are two different things
- *The principle of consistency* (or *commitment*): This is the desire to be (and appear) consistent with what has already been done. Once a choice is made, there is personal and interpersonal pressure to behave consistently with that commitment. For instance, people committing to quit smoking to their Facebook friends are more likely to do it – they want to appear consistent with the claim they have made
- *The principle of scarcity*: Limitation enhances desirability. People want more of what is in limited supply, such as products in "limited edition" (e.g. for Christmas) or "only three left" often seen in online stores. We assume that things in short supply have more value – especially when they have recently become restricted (i.e. more than if those things were restricted all along)

Motivating Hotel Guests to Reuse Their Towels

Goldstein et al. (2008) applied the principle of social proof (consensus) in two experiments to test the effectiveness of different formulations and presentations of the now common message we can find in hotel rooms, supporting environmental protection – and whether this message could motivate hotel guests to engage in sustainable behavior: reusing towels as part of an energy conservation program (see Figure 2.6).

The first experiment was designed as follows: when staying in a hotel room, guests were getting information about descriptive norms, which "motivate

Figure 2.6 Motivating guests to reuse hotel towels.
Source: Shutterstock 1450857164.

both private and public actions by informing individuals of what is likely to be effective or adaptive behavior in a situation" – basically how most people behave. The message was:

> "JOIN YOUR FELLOW GUESTS IN HELPING TO SAVE THE ENVIRONMENT. Almost **75% of guests** who are asked to participate in our new resource savings program do help by using their towels more than once. You can join your fellow guests in this program to help save the environment by reusing your towels during your stay."

Experiment 1 shows a 26% increase in reuse rates with this group behavior message ("majority reuse towels").

The second experiment was designed as the following: This time, when staying in a hotel room, guests were getting information about provincial norms, which refer to hotel guests' immediate surroundings – in contrast with the norm of guests' less immediate surroundings, the global norm. The message on the towel hanger was:

> "JOIN YOUR FELLOW GUESTS IN HELPING TO SAVE THE ENVIRONMENT. In a study conducted in Fall 2003, 75% of the guests **who stayed in this room** participated in our new resource savings program by using their towels more than once. You can join your fellow guests in this program to help save the environment by reusing your towels during your stay."

(Continued)

(Continued)

Experiment 2 showed that provincial norms (immediate surroundings: "in this room") provoked 33% behavior change. This confirmed that individuals are, in fact, more likely to be influenced by descriptive norms when the setting, (i.e. the room) in which those norms are formed is comparable to the setting those individuals are currently occupying.

These two experiments demonstrate the power of social norms in influencing people's behavior. As mentioned, social norms are powerful because they tap into fundamental human needs for social acceptance, guidance, and conformity, making them a key driver of consumer behavior. They influence individuals both consciously and subconsciously, shaping their preferences and purchase decisions in significant ways. Social norms can be harvested to promote more sustainable behavior (e.g. reusing hotel towels) Goldstein et al. (2008).

Most recently, Cialdini (2016) has argued that there is a seventh principle: unity. That is, there is a certain type of identity that best characterizes a "we relationship," which can lead to more acceptance, cooperation, liking, help, trust, and assent. In other words, *unity* is the principle of "we": being together (kinship, place) or acting together.

In light of this influential work – without a play on words – and with sustainability as a backdrop, marketers should be interested in shifting consumers to behave more sustainably, not only because firms should by now be aware that the consumption mindset encouraged by conventional (economic-focused) marketing is a key driver of unsustainable consumption and its negative impacts on the environment but mostly because firms that are actually capable of adapting to the demands of our changing world are the ones most likely to thrive in the long term and enjoy strategic benefits (White et al. 2019). For instance, car manufacturers such as Volvo or BMW who traditionally focused on selling ownership such have been considering new business models, such as car rental through Volvo On Demand and SHARE NOW (respectively) in the "sharing economy" paradigm. Accessing a car on demand is much more environmentally friendly than owning a car. We will discuss this more in Chapter 8.

The SHIFT Framework

The attitude-behavior gap or so-called green gap is the most important challenge, not only for businesses and marketing managers but also for public policymakers or nonprofit organizations. We will discuss this in more depth in the next chapter. A review of 280 articles provides a framework for shifting consumers toward sustainable consumer behaviors based on the following psychological factors (White et al. 2019):

- Social influence
- Habit formation
- Individual self
- Feelings and cognition
- Tangibility

Social influence is about social norms, social identities, and social desirability, the psychological factors that can influence sustainable consumer behavior (White et al. 2019).

Social norms are unwritten rules in society indicating what is appropriate and what is not. Such social norms informing us what other people usually do in a similar situation are called *descriptive norms*. They can be very efficient in helping consumers behave according to their beliefs – as social norms are a necessary condition for attitudes and intentions to translate into actual behaviors. For example, there has been a significant shift in consumer behavior toward using reusable shopping bags instead of single-use plastic bags. In many communities, using reusable bags has become a visible and common practice – we regularly see shoppers bringing their own bags. This visibility acts as social proof, reinforcing the idea that using reusable bags is the standard behavior and thus, when consumers observe that a majority of people are using reusable bags, they are more likely to adopt this behavior themselves, perceiving it as the socially approved and environmentally responsible choice.

Eventually, "injunctive norms" indicate which behaviors other people approve and disprove of – compared to what is actually done by others informed by descriptive norms. As such, injunctive norms are particularly relevant for people's personal networks and community, such as influencing people within a group to behave according to what the other group members think is okay or not (White et al. 2019).

A sense of *social identity* can also come from group memberships. When people see themselves as part of a group, as insiders, they are more likely to engage in sustainable behaviors if other "ingroup members" do the same. Moreover, social identities also lead to people not wanting their group to be mixed with or even outperformed by other groups (White et al. 2019).

Social desirability means that people act according to what makes a good impression on other people. In particular, signaling theory suggests that people might engage in costly prosocial behaviors such as environmental conservation particularly when they are motivated to attain a certain socially desirable status. Since the purchase of eco-friendly products enables people to signal that they are both willing and able to buy a product that benefits others at the cost of their own wallet, activating a motive for status might lead them to engage in sustainable consumption behavior.

Habit formation relates to the fact that sustainable consumption can involve a one-shot decision, such as switching to a renewable electricity provider, but many behaviors involve repeated actions over time, which means people need to change their habits, giving up old routines for new ones. For instance, reducing water consumption at home requires creating new habits such as taking shorter showers or not using running water while washing dishes. As such, habit change and formation are a critical component of shifting consumers toward sustainable behaviors (White et al. 2019). In particular, there are two main strategies for doing so: a negative one that breaks bad habits and a positive one that reinforces good habits.

Negative behavior change strategy: Forms of interventions that break repetitions and disrupts bad habits:

- *Discontinuity*: A disruption in the stable context that makes it difficult to carry on with the usual habits that would otherwise automatically occur
- *Penalties or punishments*: A tax, fine, or tariff that decreases the tendency to engage in an undesirable behavior – however, penalties are complicated to enforce

Positive behavior change strategy: Forms of interventions that reinforce repetitions and strengthen good habits:

- *Increased convenience*: This is about making it easier to start and keep up with sustainable behaviors (e.g. placing recycling bins closer to where people need them). Behavioral economists would argue that nudges can also be very useful when designing the set of choices offered to consumers (e.g. making renewable energy the default option for electricity when it is offered to new clients (Pichert and Katsikopoulos 2008)
- *Prompts*: Messages delivered just before a behavior, such as information about driving slower to reduce pollution provided on the handles of fuel dispensers in gas stations
- *Incentives*: Monetary incentives such as rebates, tiered pricing, and cashbacks, as well as free gifts, rewards, and other extrinsic incentives. Note that overly small monetary rewards are often less motivating than free gifts, a lottery entry, or even social praise. Moreover, the induced behavioral change can just disappear with the incentive
- *Feedback*: Informing consumers about specific aspects of their environmental performance compared to their own previous performance (e.g. month-to-month water and energy use) or, compared to others, encourages sustainable habit formation. This is particularly effective when the feedback is provided live (i.e. in real time), over an extended period of time, and in a clear and easily understandable manner (White et al. 2019)

Individual self is about how people think of themselves, and other personal factors have a strong impact on consumer behaviors, in particular the self-concept, self-interests, consistency, self-efficacy, and individual differences (White et al. 2019).

The *self-concept* refers to how a consumer perceives herself, which attributes constitute her personality. A positive self-concept and the desire to maintain it emphasizes the negative environmental impacts of certain behaviors for the self, but it might also make some behavioral change more difficult due to the self-sacrifice (e.g. boycotting air travel [*flygskam*] is not particularly common outside of Sweden). Thus, positively associating the self-concept with sustainable consumption through self-affirmation or the endorsement of important self-values reduces the perception of self-sacrifice.

Self-interests can be leveraged to promote sustainable consumption. Marketers can highlight the self-benefits associated with a given sustainable product, service, or behavior – when it may counteract the common barriers evoked earlier (e.g. reduced performance, high up-front costs). For instance, emphasizing the better taste or personal health benefits from consuming organic food products (rather than environmental benefits such as reducing water pollution) has become common.

As argued by Cialdini (1984), *consistency* is highly valued in society, and a lack of consistency is socially undesirable. In other words, people want to see themselves as being consistent. As such, people who reaffirm an attribute of their self-concept (e.g. being concerned with the environment) or engaging in a sustainable behavior at one point in time often lead to consistent sustainable behaviors in the future (White et al. 2019). For instance, making a pledge on Facebook that one will commute by bike to work this entire month instead of driving motivates people to stick to their initial commitment once they start.

Self-efficacy refers to the belief that a particular behavior (e.g. shopping for Fairtrade products) will make a difference and that it will have positive consequences (e.g. improving farmers' living conditions). This is also referred to as *perceived consumer effectiveness* (PCE) (Kinnear et al. 1974; Webster 1975; Ellen et al. 1991). If consumers believe that engaging in a behavior is inefficient from an environmental sustainability perspective, they will not even try. For instance, one research team tested the influence of such PCE on recycling behavior (and two types of messages: those highlighting the positive consequences of recycling and those presenting the problems of failing to recycle). PCE was expected to increase consumers' willingness to move beyond the psychological discomfort arising from negative messages, such as fear appeals. The results showed that people with a high PCE turn out to be more receptive to negatively framed messages than those with low PCE (Lord and Putrevu 1998).

There are individual differences shown to influence consumer behavior toward sustainability. For instance, people expressing personality traits such as mindfulness, extraversion, agreeableness, conscientiousness, and, of course, environmental concern or the feeling of being connected to nature are driving pro-environmental behaviors (White et al. 2019). That is also why demographics are often used for segmentation purposes (e.g. consumers engaging in sustainable consumption are often younger, more liberal, and highly educated).

Feelings and cognition refer to the influence these psychological factors have. Indeed, when making decisions, people either use their gut feelings and emotions or carefully and attentively analyze the different alternatives before choosing. Psychologists talk about System 1 and System 2 (Evans 2008; Kahneman 2011). Whereas System 1 (based on feelings) is fast and intuitive, System 2 (based on cognition) is slow, effortful, and rational (see a more detailed comparison in Table 2.2). Regarding System 1, both negative and positive emotions can impact pro-environmental behaviors. Regarding System 2, it is important to consider issues of information and learning, eco-labeling, and framing. We will come back to System 1 and 2 later in this chapter.

Negative emotions come into play when consumers evaluate the consequences of performing or not performing certain sustainable consumption behaviors. In particular, fear can be used in combination with information concerning efficacy (explained earlier) and which actions to take to overcome this fear. Guilt is also used to create a sense of responsibility for unsustainable outcomes, even if it is only "anticipated" or "collective guilt." Sadness is another negative emotion, although once it dissipated, differences in sustainable actions were eliminated (White et al. 2019).

Positive emotions such as joy, pride, and hope result in "warm-glow feelings" that increase overall satisfaction with the consumption experience. It makes sense that people are more likely to consume sustainably when they enjoy it, when it is pleasurable. For instance, price increases the feelings of effectiveness (White et al. 2019).

Information, learning, and knowledge. As mentioned, a lack of information and lack of understanding (i.e. confusion) are important drivers for unsustainable consumption. Hence, presenting information to consumers that is relevant to the desired (and undesired) consumer behaviors and their environmental consequences increases the likelihood that they engage in and perform these behaviors, for instance

Table 2.2 System 1 and System 2.

System 1 (feelings-based)	System 2 (cognition-based)
Automatic	Controlled
Experiential	Rational
Heuristic	Systematic
Implicit/tacit	Explicit
Heuristic	Analytic
Associative	Rule-based
Intuitive	Analytic
Holistic	Analytic
Adaptive unconscious	Conscious
Reflexive	Reflective
Stimulus bound	Higher order
Impulsive	Reflective

helping consumers find products in a store with visual aids such as green-colored price tags for eco-friendly products, or signaling products from the local region or information on what fair-trade production entails (Guyader et al. 2017). White et al. (2019) argue that knowledge is actually essential to the entire SHIFT framework: "consumers must have knowledge of the social norm, must be aware of and understand the prompt or feedback, and must comprehend information related to self-values, self-benefits, self-efficacy, etc." (p. 31).

Eco-labeling is another means of informing consumers about the sustainable attributes of a product. Certifications from third parties are considered more transparent and unbiased than when brands create their own. Moreover, "labels that are attention-grabbing, easily understandable, and consistent across categories can enable consumers to make better informed eco-friendly decisions" (White et al. 2019, p. 31). For example, Max Havelaar Foundation, Rainforest Alliance, and Fairtrade International are three organizations that deliver certifications for distinguishing fair-trade products from conventional ones based on a set of specific social, environmental, and economic standards designed to promote sustainable and equitable trade (we further discuss fair-trade eco-labeling in Chapter 3 and fair-trade pricing in Chapter 10, see also Figure 2.7). The UK and France are adopting a color-coded system to indicate the nutrition of manufactured food

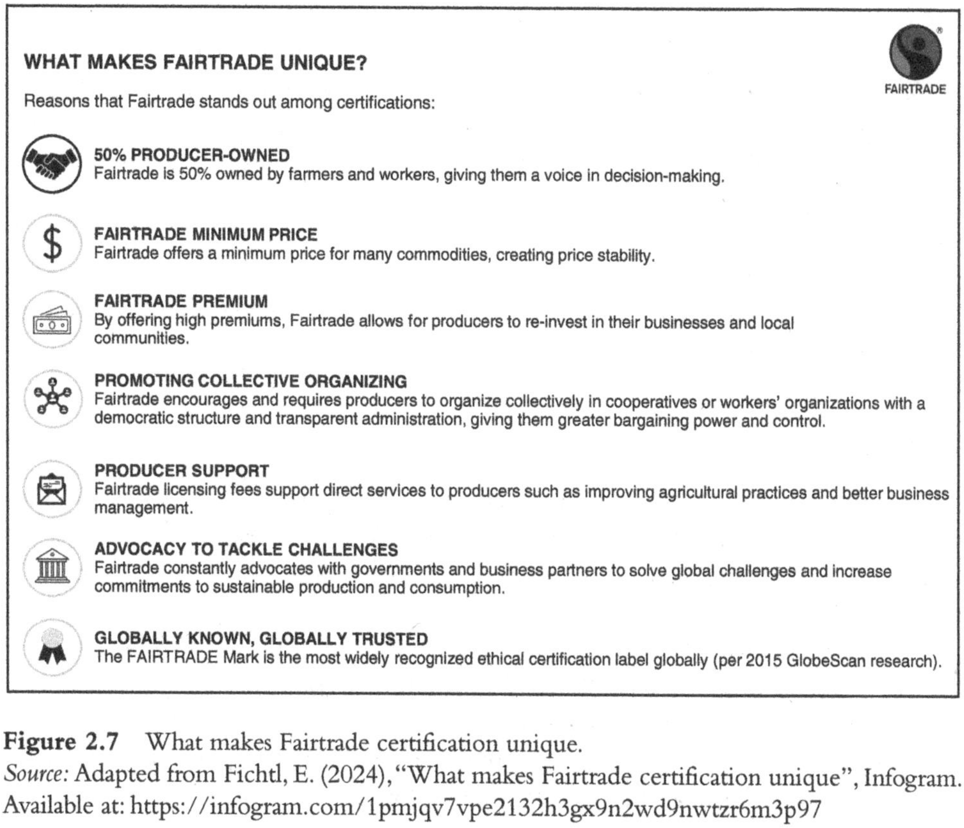

Figure 2.7 What makes Fairtrade certification unique.
Source: Adapted from Fichtl, E. (2024), "What makes Fairtrade certification unique", Infogram. Available at: https://infogram.com/1pmjqv7vpe2132h3gx9n2wd9nwtzr6m3p97

(the "Nutri-score"), following a traffic-light scheme going from a green A (the best nutrients) to a red E (the worst nutrients). The Swiss multinational Nestlé has adopted the Nutri-score for all its products (e.g. KitKat, Cheerios, Nestea, Smarties, etc.) in Europe (Nestlé 2019).

Framing certain information in a strategic way may encourage sustainable consumption (White et al. 2019). For instance, the European Union's energy labels on household appliances (e.g. TVs, fridges, washing machines) indicate their energy efficiency, also from a green A to red D. This way of emphasizing energy efficiency rather than cost-savings frame information regarding environmental product attributes that become clear during consumers' decision-making.

Tangibility, or the lack of, refers to that sustainable consumer behaviors and their outcomes are by definition long-term-oriented (e.g. some people will not even experience the results of their sustainable consumption – only future generations), and they often seem abstract, vague, and distant to the consumer. According to White et al. (2019), this problem of tangibility can be altered by:

- *Matching temporal focus*: Engaging consumers to think about the future benefits of their actions
- *Communicating local and proximal impacts*: Immediate consequences of the consumers' actions so that they are more relevant
- *Concrete communication*: Communicating the immediate impacts of environmental problems, such as the influence of climate change at the city level
- *Encouraging the desire for intangibles*: The servitization and the dematerialization of consumption, away from product ownership (i.e. access-based consumption offered by rental companies and online platforms in the "sharing economy"), are environmentally beneficial while satisfying consumer needs

In the rest of this chapter on influencing sustainable consumer behavior with information, we will discuss nudging, an approach to behavioral change from the economics discipline.

Nudging

The concept of "nudge" became popular in 2008 when Richard Thaler and Cass Sunstein published the book *Nudge: Improving Decisions about Health, Wealth, and Happiness*. Thaler and Sunstein (2008, p. 6) defined their concept as:

> A nudge is any aspect of the choice architecture that alters people's behavior in a predictable way without forbidding any options or significantly changing their economic incentives. To count as a mere nudge, the intervention must be easy and cheap to avoid. Nudges are not mandates. Putting fruit at eye level counts as a nudge. Banning junk food does not.

Nudges thus aim to improve health, increase welfare, and make people happier – not by forcing alternatives upon consumers but by improving information and making it possible for consumers to make good decisions. In the sustainability context, nudging is a method attempting to make consumers choose the most environmentally friendly option. However, for consumers, it is difficult to make environmentally friendly choices when the information regarding the environmental impact of various options is scant. The advantage of nudging is that "bad options" are not prohibited; rather, it is the consumer's free choice that results in a more environmentally friendly alternative being selected.

Most areas in a consumer's life such as traffic, school, and healthcare have rules regarding what can or cannot be done. In terms of shopping decisions, however, most behaviors are allowed. Today, we have great freedom when it comes to what, how, and when we consume. Nevertheless, if consumers are increasingly interested in sustainability issues, organizations should offer consumption alternatives that have a lower environmental impact than their traditional counterparts. From the perspective of the consumer, it is important to consider freedom of choice and transparency to get consumer confidence and trust.

In Denmark's capital Copenhagen, a litter-prevention program called "Pure Love" was implemented between 2012 and 2015, which has enabled the city to claim the title of cleanest city in Europe by nudging its inhabitants to keep their environment clean. The problem was that although about 90% of Danes claim to be concerned with littering, studies have shown that 30% of the population occasionally leave their trash in the streets or in parks. The Pure Love program was thus about making bins highly visible and easily accessible where and when litter was likely to occur throughout the city, using bright green footsteps leading to bright green bins with a slogan referring to pure/clean love for Copenhagen with a heart logo (see Figure 2.8). The origin of this initiative is found in a study from Roskilde University: first, the researchers gave free caramels to pedestrians, and they counted the number of wrappers thrown out on the street and those in garbage cans. They then replicated the scenario, while also placing green footprints leading to the bins. The result was a startling 46% decrease in wrappers ending up on the streets (Webster 2012). The footprints are a visible reminder for people who litter unconsciously, by habit, that they should recycle and responsibly dispose of trash.

However, all nudging might not work as intended. For instance, in 2010 Chile installed a new system for organ donation that meant by default everybody's organs were donated when they died – instead of the old system where people had to "opt in" for organ donation. However, the results of this presumed consent were actually fewer organ donations rather than more. The reason was that people felt that the state was trying to take their organs, and the number of people who deregistered exceeded the number of people who had registered in the old system. Even if one decides to become an organ donor, their families frequently have the

Figure 2.8 Litter-prevention program in Copenhagen (the cleanest city in Europe) to nudge people in keeping their environment clean. Although 90% of Danes claimed to be concerned with littering, 30% occasionally leave trash in the streets/parks! The campaign "Pure Love" made bins highly visible and easily accessible where and when litter was likely to occur, using bright green footsteps leading to bright green bins with a slogan that meant pure/clean love for Copenhagen with a heart logo.
Source: Roland Magnusson/Adobe Stock.

last word. So, when the government presumes that someone should donate their organs without their explicit consent, families may overturn this decision after their death. Similar results have occurred in France and the United Kingdom (BBC News 2017; Robitaille 2019).

In his doctoral thesis, Hagman shows that the acceptance of a nudge can be affected by its aim (Hagman 2018). For instance, if we sympathize with the idea of a better environment, we accept recycling. But acceptance is affected by who benefits from the nudge. If we ourselves gain from it, we are more prone to accept it than if it is society in general that benefits. Nudges that deliver individual benefits are viewed as less detrimental to one's freedom of choice (Hagman 2018). Furthermore, people's attitudes about the source of the nudge are important in how the nudge is assessed. We are more likely to accept a nudge if it comes from a political party we like (Hagman 2018). For instance, Swedes would be more favorable toward carbon offsetting if proposed by the Green Party, compared to, say, the Sweden Democrats.

Next, we present a checklist for effective nudging design Hagman's (2018):

- *Conscious or unconscious?*
  Is the nudge intended to influence an intuitive behavior or to get the person to reflect upon their behavior? An intuitive nudge requires fewer mental resources, but it is sometimes necessary to make people consider something more actively
- *Technique that prevents or encourages mental deviations?*
  To help people achieve their goals, do you want to prevent or encourage the mental deviations they tend to make?
- *Transparent or not?*
  Nontransparent nudges may be perceived as manipulation
- *Socially, are you acting like your peers?*
  A nudge can use norms or group affiliations to highlight or influence a behavior, such as pointing to a norm in order to show that a behavior is more common than most people think. One example would be "70% of those in your age group save for their retirement" to show that someone is outside the norm
- *Is it easy to use?*
  Otherwise, people are less likely to act on the nudge
- *What's the aim?*
  Acceptance of a nudge is determined by its aim
- *Who will benefit?*
  Acceptance is more probable if the individual benefits from the nudge than if society benefits
- *Detrimental to freedom of choice?*
  Nudges seen as adversely affecting freedom of choice are less accepted. Nudges that deliver individual benefits are seen as less detrimental to our freedom of choice
- *Who is the nudge recipient?*
  Get to know the recipient of the nudge. For instance, trying to use social norms without understanding what is important to the target group can result in the nudge having unintended results

Other scholars focused on consumer reactions to plastic bag restrictions in Chile (the first South American country to ban the use of plastic bags in 2018, much before European Union's ban of single-use plastics in 2021) where they observed negative reactions to the ban since consumers felt more responsible and it caused unsettling emotions in them due to a change of practice (Gonzalez-Arcos et al. 2021). They discovered that consumers refuse to accept and resist such a sustainability intervention, because using disposable plastic bags for shopping was embedded in social practices.

Social practices are activities, materials, and meanings that are similarly understood and shared by a group of people, like eating, cooking, shopping, driving, and reading. These practices determine people's way of life and, to a large extent, who they are.

From this perspective, a behavior such as using a plastic bag to carry groceries is simply a performance of the socially shared, habituated practice of shopping.

- An intervention like banning plastic bags triggers change in the social practice of shopping, as plastic bags are one of the materials that constitute this practice
- To plan and design a practice-based intervention, they recommend to the following:
  1. Identify the practice being targeted (e.g. shopping),= and how it is likely to be disrupted (e.g. material will be eliminated – plastic bags).
  2. Distribute responsibility for change among those involved in the practice (e.g. consumers, retailers, bag manufacturers, government).
  3. Determine potential emotions that may manifest (positive to leverage and negative to placate).
  4. Identify links between the targeted practice and other social practices (e.g. the plastic bags used in shopping are also used for garbage and waste management).

Eventually, Richard Thaler's contribution about nudging to the field of *behavioral* economics was recognized when he received the 2017 Nobel Prize in economic sciences – 15 years after his colleague Daniel Kahneman (2002) who was also awarded the Nobel Prize in economic sciences. In other words, the historical view that people rationally act according to their preferences is outdated (we have already seen this with the attitude-behavior green gap). In contrast to the classical approach that economic decisions are guided by a rational process, the now-established academic field of behavioral economics concerns the study of decision-making influenced by psychological, cognitive, emotional, cultural, and social factors. In short, people do not take all the available information into account when making a decision – in some cases not even their own preferences. Instead, they use mental shortcuts when making everyday judgments. These are called *judgment heuristics*. For example, we usually assume that something expensive is of high quality, although that is not necessarily the case. But people are very lazy; they save cognitive effort whenever possible. So, instead of investigating all product attributes and comparing different options, it is easier and faster to assume that something more expensive equals a better choice. And it actually works out well most of the time.

References

Albinsson, P.A. and Perera, B.Y. (2009). From trash to treasure and beyond: the meaning of voluntary disposition. *Journal of Consumer Behaviour: An International Research Review*, 8(6), 340–353.

BBC News (2017). Organ donation opt-out plan: What do people waiting for transplants think? https://www.bbc.com/news/uk-41513961 (accessed 1 May 2024).

Belz, F.-M. & Peattie, K. (2012). *Sustainable Marketing: A Global Perspective*. (2nd ed.). Chichester: Wiley.

Chan, S. S., Van Solt, M., Cruz, R. E., Philp, M., Bahl, S., Serin, N., . . . Canbulut, M. (2022). Social media and mindfulness: from the fear of missing out (FOMO) to the joy of missing out (JOMO). *Journal of Consumer Affairs*, 56(3), 1312–1331.

Cialdini, R. (1984). *Influence: The Psychology of Persuasion*. Harper Business.

Cialdini, R. (2016). *Pre-Suasion: A Revolutionary Way to Influence and Persuade*. New York, NY: Simon & Schuster.

Dunning, D. (2007). Self-image motives and consumer behavior. *Journal of Consumer Psychology*, 17(4), 237–249.

Ellen, P.S., Wiener, J.L. & Cobb-Walgren, C. (1991). The role of perceived consumer effectiveness in motivating environmentally conscious Behaviors. *Journal of Public Policy & Marketing*, 10(2), 102–117.

Evans, J. S. B. (2008). Dual-processing accounts of reasoning, judgment, and social cognition. *Annual Review of Psychology*, 59 (1), 255–278.

Goldstein, N. J., Cialdini, R. B., & Griskevicius, V. (2008). Room with a viewpoint using social norms to motivate environmental conservation in hotels. *Journal of Consumer Research*, 35, 472–482.

Gonzalez-Arcos, C., Joubert, A.M., Scaraboto, D., Guesalaga, R. and Sandberg, J. (2021). "How do I carry all this now?" Understanding consumer resistance to sustainability interventions. *Journal of Marketing*, 85(3), 44–61.

Guyader, H., Ottosson, M. & Witell, L. (2017). You can't buy what you can't see: retailer practices to increase the green premium. *Journal of Retailing and Consumer Services*, 34 (January), 319–325.

Hagman W. (2018). *When Are Nudges Acceptable? Influences of Beneficiaries, Techniques, Alternatives and Choice Architects*. Linköping University, Department of Behavioural Sciences and Learning, Psychology. Faculty of Arts and Sciences.

Kahneman, D. (2002). Maps of bounded rationality: A perspective on intuitive judgment and choice. *Nobel Prize lecture* at Aula Magna, Stockholm University (8 December 2002).

Kahneman, D. (2011). *Thinking, Fast and Slow*. Macmillan.

Kinnear, T.C., Taylor, J.R., & Ahmed, S.A. (1974). Ecologically concerned consumers: who are they? *Journal of Marketing*, 38(2), 20–24.

Kormos, C., Gifford, R. and Brown, E. (2015). The influence of descriptive social norm information on sustainable transportation behavior: a field experiment. *Environment and Behavior*, 47(5), 479–501.

Kotler, P. & Armstrong, G. (2023) *Principles of Marketing*, Global Edition. Pearson

Lord, KR. & Putrevu, S. (1998). Acceptance of recycling appeals: the moderating role of perceived consumer effectiveness. *Journal of Marketing Management*, 14(6), 581–590.

Nestlé (2019). Why does Nestlé support Nutri-Score in Europe? https://www.nestle.com/ask-nestle/health-nutrition/answers/nestle-nutri-score (accessed 1 April, 2024).

Pham, M.T. (2013). The seven sins of consumer psychology. *Journal of Consumer Psychology*, 23(4), 411–423.

Pichert, D. & Katsikopoulos, K.V. (2008). Green defaults: information presentation and pro-environmental behavior. *Journal of Environmental Psychology*, 28(1), 63–73.

Ray Chaudhury, S. and Albinsson, P.A. (2015). Citizen-consumer oriented practices in naturalistic foodways: the case of the slow food movement. *Journal of Macromarketing*, 35(1), 36–52.

Robitaille, N. (2019). A little nudge goes a long way in increasing organ donor registrations. *The Conversation.* https://theconversation.com/a-little-nudge-goes-a-long-way-in-increasing-organ-donor-registrations-115051 (accessed 1 May 2019).

Shao, W., Lye, A. & Rundle-Thiele, S. (2008). Decisions, decisions, decisions: multiple pathways to choice. *International Journal of Market Research*, 50(6), 797–816.

Sokolova, T., Krishna, A, a& Döring, T. (2023) Paper meets plastic: the perceived environmental friendliness of product packaging, *Journal of Consumer Research*, 50(3), 468–491.

Thaler, R.H. & Sunstein, C.R. (2008). *Nudge: Improving Decisions about Health, Wealth, and Happiness.* New Haven: Yale University Press.

Wästlund, E., Otterbring, T., Gustafsson, A. & Shams, P. (2015). Heuristics and resource depletion: eye-tracking customers' in situ gaze behavior in the field. *Journal of Business Research*, 68(1), 95–101.

Webster, G. (2012). Is a "nudge" in the right direction all we need to be greener? *CNN.* https://edition.cnn.com/2012/02/08/tech/innovation/green-nudge-environment-persuasion/index.html (accessed 15 May 2024).

Webster, F.E. Jr. (1975). Determining the characteristics of the socially conscious consumer. *Journal of Consumer Research*, 2(3), 188–196.

White, K., Habib, R. & Hardisty, D.J. (2019). How to SHIFT consumer behaviors to be more sustainable: a literature review and guiding framework. *Journal of Marketing*, 83(3), 22–49.

Chapter 3

Is There Such a Thing as Sustainable Consumers?

This chapter builds on Chapter 2 as we continue to discuss consumer behavior and sustainable consumption. Using a global view, the content presents various factors affecting consumption patterns and enabling sustainable consumption. We also discuss how a group of consumer researchers have shifted from the unbalanced view of acquisition and consumption by also considering the social impact of their work. This shift to focus on consumer well-being and social impact had its beginnings in the leadership of the Association for Consumer Research and has been named Transformative Consumer Research. The chapter also introduces the attitude-behavior gap, also referred to the *green gap*, that exists in the marketplace. Different ways of exerting influence over consumption and what the individual consumer can do to contribute to sustainability is also discussed.

Learning Objectives

- Define sustainable consumption from three perspectives (economically, environmentally, and socially)
- Understand the importance of consumer well-being and social impact from various contexts

- Understand the "attitude-behavior" or "green-gap" between pro-environmental attitudes and consumer behaviors
- Critically suggest how consumers can act more sustainably

Introduction

Consumption has many functions – it is crucial for the growth of society and constitutes a key part of the activities of companies, government agencies, and households. The global retail sector is valued at c.a. $30 trillion USD, employs hundreds of million people (Statista 2024), and makes up an essential part of the gross national product (GNP) in each nation, meaning that issues relating to how households choose to spend their money, how consumption patterns change, and how this impacts various industries and products are key for a number of major actors in developed economies. The worldwide retail sector sales are expected to grow by another two trillion dollars by 2026 (Statista 2024).

However, consumption gives rise to economic, social, and environmental problems. Thus, it is no exaggeration to argue that consumers play a key role in the journey toward a more sustainable society. Consumers are arguably the ones creating demand for products and influencing companies' business models, product development, and choice of distribution channels.

Consumption also has many more functions than just meeting the basic needs discussed by the Brundtland Commission. For instance, consumption is for many people an ongoing identity-creating activity that contributes to self-fulfillment, which is often impacted by emotions to a high degree (e.g. Warde 1994; Ahuvia 2005; Shankar et al. 2009).

To understand how consumption relates to sustainability, one must first understand what constitutes a consumer and consumption. Answering the question "What makes a consumer's consumption sustainable?" is not as easy as one may think. As we will illustrate in this chapter and we already discussed in Chapter 2, multiple factors influence consumers' purchasing decisions that may change from context to context. Therefore, a more correct way of stating a question on sustainable consumers would be "Under what circumstances, for what reasons, and in response to what offering might different types of consumers adopt more sustainable consumption behaviors and lifestyles (Belz and Peattie 2012, p.103)?

One of the most influential factors in consumer behavior is attitude. Sometimes, consumers can have a positive attitude toward a product, but it may not transfer into a purchase. Likewise, a consumer can be supportive of sustainable products and practices but may not actually buy sustainable products or engage in sustainable practices. This so-called green gap will be discussed later in the chapter.

Attitude has had a strong impact on consumer behavior, and previous research findings could be partially invalidated, which is why this chapter is informed by contemporary literature. Note that the term *customer* refers to the buyer or decision-maker of a purchase, while the term *consumer* usually refers to the ultimate user of goods and services consuming the product. For example, a mom or dad grocery-shopping for breakfast cereals is often called the consumer as they purchase the products even though it is their children who eat what is purchased – that is, children are the ultimate users consuming the product.

Definition of Sustainable Consumption and the "Sustainable Consumer"

Let us start by pointing out that consumer behavior research originated in the discipline of marketing in the 1950s, when business schools engaged in a shift from teaching marketing management (i.e. firm focus on the business applications of marketing principles, taught by managers and consultants) to understanding consumers as buyers from a more theoretical perspective (i.e. consumer behavior research). As such, research on consumer behavior was defined as "the study of consummation": this not only includes acquisition but also includes usage and disposition activities of products as well as more intangible services, ideas, and events: "consumer research encompasses almost all human activities, regarded from the viewpoint of consummation" (Holbrook 1987, p. 131).

This research specialization in the study of consumption emphasizing a broad scope of behaviors and influencing factors focuses on people in their role as consumers, which includes making decisions and judgments based on cues (Deighton 2007). For instance, thinking of oneself as part of a buyer–seller relationship is likely to influence how we interact with others. By identifying what is unique about being a consumer, researchers can better understand the range and limitations of human behavior. In the 1970s, scholars founded the US-based Association for Consumer Research (1969) and the *Journal of Consumer Research* (JCR, 1974). One of the influential past editors, John Deighton, of this journal argues that consumer behavior is "an applied discipline relative to psychology, economics, statistics, sociology, or anthropology but a fundamental discipline relative to marketing or management" (Deighton 2007, p. 279). Moreover, this shift away from strategy topics in marketing advances public policy and societal focus promoting an agenda for consumer protection and social welfare (MacInnis and Folkes 2010). Since the JCR inception, additional Consumer Research–oriented journals have entered the field, e.g. British-based *Journal of Consumer Behaviour*, which published its first issue in 2001 and *Journal of Consumer Marketing* (first volume in 1984) and many others.

The American Marketing Association (AMA) dictionary defines *consumer behavior* as

> "the dynamic interaction of affect and cognition, behavior, and the environment by which human beings conduct the exchange aspects of their lives,"

emphasizing the multitude of influences (psychological, social, cultural, etc.) and activities performed by people in their role of consumers. Moreover, considering societal and ecological issues introduced earlier, consumer researchers have reaffirmed their focus on the "real world problems" of consumers, particularly aiming to improve well-being, such as financial well-being, access to food, youth-related issues, and sustainable consumption (Mick et al. 2012; Davis et al. 2016; Ekpo et al. 2022; Zeng and Botella-Carrubi 2023; Albinsson and Ross 2024). This perspective of consumer research that focuses on consumer well-being and quality of life focuses on social impact and is referred to as *transformative consumer research.*

Transformative Consumer Research

Transformative consumer research (TCR) was initiated by an academic conference theme on consumer welfare, which was intended as a call for action against ineffectual research regarding social and personal well-being. "By transformative research we mean investigations that are framed by a fundamental problem or opportunity, and that strive to respect, uphold, and improve life in relation to the myriad conditions, demands, potentialities, and effects of consumption" (Mick, 2006). The most pressing research topics were environmentally protective behaviors, as well as vulnerable consumer groups (e.g. the poor, children, the illiterate), tobacco, alcohol, and drug consumption, gambling, nutrition and obesity, violence in movies and computer games, financial and medical decision-making, product safety, and organ donations.

The six defining qualities and commitments ofTCR are as follows (Mick et al. 2012):

- Improving well-being
- Employing rigorous theory and methods
- Highlighting socio-cultural and situational contexts
- Forming partnerships with consumers and their caretakers
- Disseminating valuable findings to relevant stakeholders
- Affiliating with the Association for Consumer Research and affirming the value of paradigmatic diversity

In a conversation with Dr. David Glen Mick, who has been attributed to the birth of the TCR movement, we asked him to share his insights on the development of the TCR movement and where he thinks it's heading.

Very humbly Dr. Mick gives credit to Dr. Liza Peñaloza for coming up with the name for TCR as a way to brand the initiative, which focuses on well-being. He gives further credit to 45 leaders in the consumer research community who participated in a short survey on how to make the initiative successful. Some of the ideas were to have bi-annual dialogical conferences and a journal special issue dedicated to the research outcomes from the conference. The first TCR conference was held in 2007, with the 10th planned for 2025. In the last 20 years, TCR has raised and disseminated more than $300 000 to scholars in support of their research on various consumer well-being research projects. As the first book on TCR came out in 2012, Dr. Mick says it may be time for another book to update the field on the most pressing issues that are facing today's consumers and communities. Stay tuned!

Source: Mick et al. 2012; Personal communication with Dr. David Glen Mick, March 30, 2024.

One way to define sustainable consumption has traditionally been to focus on the environmental aspect of sustainability. For instance, sustainable consumer behavior is defined as

> "actions that result in decreases in adverse environmental impacts as well as decreased utilization of natural resources across the life cycle of the product, behavior, or service"

(White et al. 2019, p. 25). In other words, the focus is on environmental sustainability, arguing that this, in turn, will improve both social and economic conditions.

Interestingly, over time much of the scholarship in consumer research has started to include not only purchasing behavior but the user/consumption experience, as well as anti-consumption, voluntary simplicity, disposition, repair, reuse, etc. (Albinsson et al. 2010). Some of these topics show an increasing consumer interest in more sustainable-oriented consumption activities and practices such as voluntarily buying and owning less, and follow a minimalist lifestyle (Oliveira de Mendonca et al. 2021), substituting traditional products for sustainable counterparts (e.g. eco-friendly appliances), conserving energy, water, and products during the use phase of the consumption process (e.g. driving slower, taking shorter showers), and recycling (i.e. sorting out waste according to the material composition, such as organic leftovers, glass, paper, cardboard, plastic, etc.) as well as practices extending a product's lifetime (e.g. sharing, exchanging, donating, recycling, re-furbishing; Albinsson and Perera 2009). Interestingly, when visiting the website of *Journal of Consumer Marketing*, one of the earlier mentioned consumer research–oriented journals, two of the most downloaded articles and top-cited articles in 2023 are on the way social media influence sustainable behaviors in Gen Z consumers e.g. those born between 1996 and 2010, so called digital natives (Confetto et al. 2023), and how to encourage mindful consumption (Gupta et al. 2023).

Three Types of Sustainable Consumption

Following the Brundtland report and its three categories of sustainable development, we might also view sustainable consumption as consisting of three different types, i.e. economically, environmentally, and socially sustainable consumption. In the following sections we discuss all three.

Economically Sustainable Consumption

Households with an economically unsustainable level of consumption are generally less able to function in a socially sustainable way. This relates to their health or the risk of social marginalization. Another factor possibly affecting consumers' ability to engage in economically sustainable consumption includes accessibility. Vulnerable consumer groups such as people with disabilities, the unbanked, the unhoused, etc. can thus be excluded from certain types of consumption, which runs the risk of leading to less choice and higher prices for this group. However, not only disabilities can exclude consumers from various consumption activities. Lack of access to technology such as smartphones, payment apps, bank accounts, etc. can prevent people from fully participating in the marketplace. The so-called platformization of payment systems where corporations asks consumers to download their own ordering and payment app e.g. Starbucks, Grubhub, Uber, or payment apps such as Venmo (US), Swish (Nordic countries), and many others have shown to not only monetize from customer data but also keep track of consumers purchasing records and whereabouts, which may negatively affect consumers' financial well-being (Ekpo et al. 2022; Albinsson and Ross 2024).

In principle, as all consumption entails an environmental impact, reduced consumption can generally entail a more sustainable level of consumption, both economically and environmentally. Typical examples of such win-win situations include reduced energy consumption at home and reduced car travel. It is important, however, to consider the so-called rebound effects (i.e. defined in the energy sector as the benefits from increased efficiency being offset by increased usage; which also includes cost-savings from one sector, leading to increased consumption in another sector, like lower costs of diesel fuel are canceled out by driving more), which are counterintuitive. Later in Chapters 5 and 8, we discuss various service and product sharing systems related to the Sharing Economy, which utilizes peer-to-peer provided resources such as idle cars and homes via collaborative consumption has shown to have both positive and negative effects in terms of consumer safety, resource utilization, waste, and pollution (e.g. Griffiths et al. 2019; Griffiths et al. 2024).

Bearing in mind that different types of consumption have different impacts on the environment, the overall environmental impact may increase even though the overall level of consumption falls. It is thus crucial that consumption goes down in the right areas (i.e. areas with a high environmental impact). Goods with a long life span, high quality, good functionality, and not too much of an environmental impact during manufacturing are beneficial from an environmental sustainability perspective (Holmqvist and Kowalkowski 2023). Such goods can be more expensive to purchase, but the higher initial cost usually results in a lower overall cost for the consumer as the goods may not have to be replaced as often. A recent study on durable goods (e.g. refrigerators; see also Figure 3.1) and their environmental impact illustrates the difficulty of evaluating environmental sustainability using life-cycle assessments (Cappelletti et al. 2022). In addition, consumers are often basing their decisions on past brand evaluations, price, and warranty information and costly service contracts, making the durability part only one of many heuristics taken into consideration during purchase evaluation.

Environmentally Sustainable Consumption

The United Nations (UN) Sustainable Development Goal (SDG) number 12, "responsible consumption and production," encourages consumers to reduce their waste and be mindful of purchasing sustainable options when possible (UN 2024).

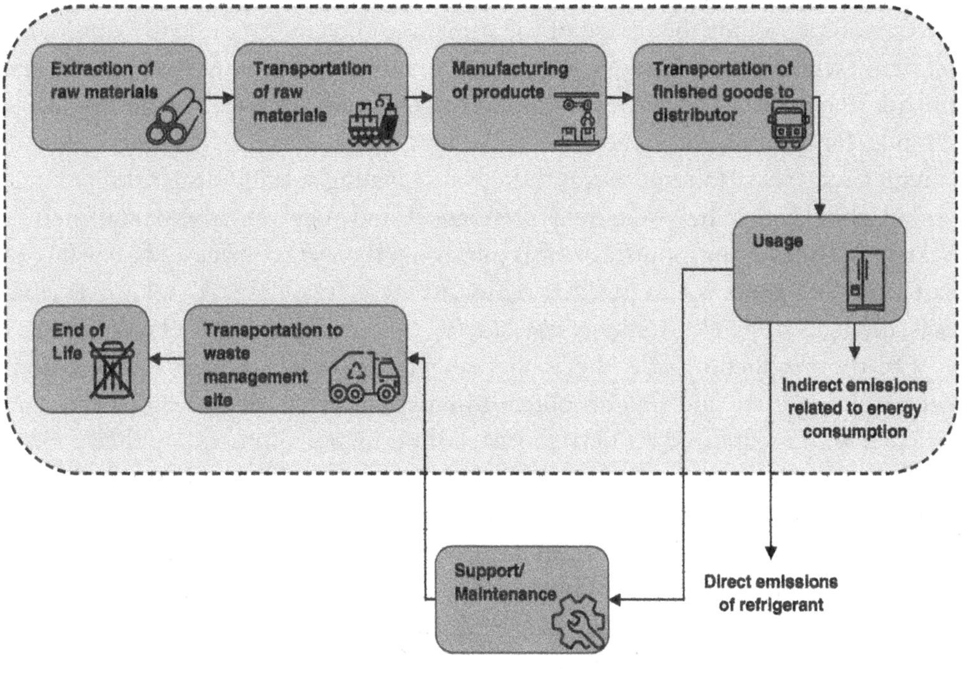

Figure 3.1 System boundaries related to life-cycle assessments.
Source: Adapted from Cappelletti et al. (2022).

While this goal also encourages responsible production such as reducing waste, focusing on circularity, and using design for the environment concepts in product innovation (see Chapters 4 and 8), here we focus on consumer practices.

Environmentally sustainable consumption can, according to the Swedish Consumer Agency, be divided into several main areas: what we eat, how we travel, and how we use energy and take care of our household waste. In addition to these practices, there is also consumption not directly linked to our homes (e.g. resources used for work or holiday journeys). A study shows that private consumption of carbon dioxide equivalents (CO_2-eq, CO_2 hereafter)* can be broken down as follows:

Food – just over 25%
Housing – just over 30%
Travel – just under 30%
Shopping – just under 15%

*For more information on this measure, see the European Commission website: https://ec.europa.eu/eurostat/statistics-explained/index.php?title=Glossary:Carbon_dioxide_equivalent.

In all four areas, there are great opportunities for reducing both emissions and environmental impact. For example, Copenhagen, Denmark, has pledged to be the first carbon-neutral city by 2025 with the help of its many cyclists. Staying ahead of Amsterdam, the Netherlands and other cities, which are also known for their many bikers is also good for the image of the capital, so the city is constantly improving bike lanes while making driving and parking in the city prohibitively expensive and difficult (Robertson 2019). Meanwhile, to reach its carbon-neutrality goal by 2035, Helsinki, Finland, launched the app Think Sustainably to help its citizens decide on activities, transportation options, and shops by toggling specific sustainability filters to find choices that best suit their preferences and meet environmental metrics (Saksala 2019). Goyang, South Korea, is increasing their greenspace and recycling of waste, and Singapore is also greenifying its city by increasing parks, adding cycling trails, and mandating clean-energy vehicles for new car registrations (Puckett 2023).

On the production side, the food that we consume gives rise to emissions that affect air, water, and soil. To obtain improved harvests, fields, and pastures are enriched with natural and artificial fertilizers, but the nourishment supplied cannot always be absorbed by vegetation, instead leaching out of the soil and ending up in the lakes. Over-fertilization (due to run-offs) is thus a major problem affecting many lakes due to the use of artificial fertilizers and the ever-increasing agricultural industry expanding its geographical areas of cultivation. Another problem in the production of food is the emission of carbon dioxide (CO_2). Here, there are marked differences depending on the type of food being produced. The production of meat requires the most resources and also generates most of the CO_2 emissions. In second place, we find dairy products, followed by vegetables, fruit, and grains.

Depending on how calculations are performed (e.g. whether meat production in Brazil had engendered deforestation), values can vary; however, it is obvious that a diet consisting of lots of meat and dairy products is less environmentally sustainable than a diet consisting of vegetables and fruits. Some industry efforts to inform consumers of their food choice and its impact exist. For example, Max Restaurants in Sweden has carbon labeled their menus and introduced their "green family" meals, which consist of falafel, veggie burgers, and other vegetarian options. Panera restaurants in the United States has introduced their "cool foods" menu items that shows consumers the environmental impact of their menu items. Consumer durable goods companies such as LG, Dyson, Nestlé, and others have also started to investigate carbon labeling of their products through Carbon Trust, a UK government initiative that started in 2001. These efforts are made to assist consumers in their decision-making in the marketplace.

Housing accounts for approximately 30% of the individual's personal CO_2 emissions. The categories contributing to the highest emissions here include construction and maintenance, heating, and household electricity. The travel category, similar to the housing category, accounts for about 30% of personal CO_2 emissions. The primary item here is private car journeys – freight traffic is not included in this category. Flights generate high CO_2 emissions. For example, a flight in economy class from Stockholm to New York generates approximately one ton of CO_2 – to be compared with the approximately 1.5 tons generated by a medium-sized family car with a fuel-efficient drivetrain driving a typical annual mileage (i.e. 12 500 km/ 7767 miles). For shopping, which accounts for 15%, the largest categories in this item are clothing and shoes, as well as computers, phones, and TV/electronics. Figure 3.2 illustrates how much Swedes have to reduce their consumption on average to meet the 1.5° Celsius/ 2.7° Fahrenheit goal in the 2015 Paris agreement. A reduction in personal consumption is needed in most countries around the world to meet the reduced carbon emissions goals.

Visit *carbonfootprint.com*, or *footprintcalculator.org*, or *footprint.wwf.org.uk* to compare and contrast your own consumption pattern.

In the United States, as in many other locations, an individual's carbon footprint can vary a lot based on the location and climate, availability of public transportation, and overall lifestyle, as daily car commutes can contribute a lot of carbon emissions.

Many informative resources are available online where different countries' CO_2 emissions can be compared and contrasted in terms of total carbon emissions and per capita emissions. For example, at worldpopulationreview.com enter the search term "carbon footprint per country." However, just looking at one measure can be misleading as countries vary in size, in their population size, in their development stage, etc. For example, Palau, a country consisting of about 340 islands and located about 400 miles east of the Philippines, is attributed with the largest CO_2 emission by person with 59 tons. But it has only 1.28 metric ton emissions in total as their

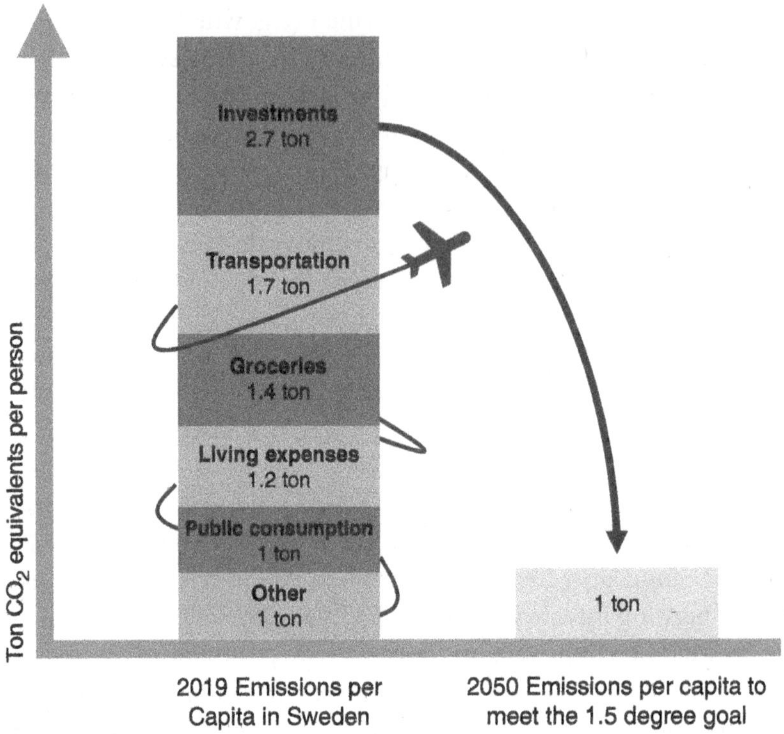

Figure 3.2 Needed per capita CO_2 emission reduction.
Source: Konsumentverket (n.d.).

population is around 18 000 people. In comparison, the United States has about 14.4 tons per person, while the total emissions are about 4853.78 metric tons. China has about 8.85 tons per person and 12 667.43 metric tons as a country. South Africa has about 6.75 tons per person and 404.97 metric tons as a country. What all countries have in common is that every country, and in particular the larger, more populated countries, should aim to lower overall emissions and per capita emissions.

Socially Sustainable Consumption

Socially sustainable consumption, the third category, means that nobody fares badly in connection with the production and consumption of the goods and services we buy. In this context, there are talks of ethical and fair-trade consumption, or ethical consumption. All these terms relate to processes aimed at improving the working conditions of the people producing goods (e.g. by means of a reasonable and fair wage, the right to join a union, the prohibition of child labor) as well as paying attention that production takes its environmental impact into account. Fair-trade goods are, for instance, aiming to benefit small-scale farmers (e.g. coffee farmers) and craftspeople and women in developing countries.

Fairtrade International (fairtrade.net) has established criteria for producing goods fairly. Products certified by Fairtrade can often be bought in normal shops; the organization has developed specific criteria for each product category that must be met before the product can be labeled as such, e.g. fair trade. Fairtrade does not just contribute to social sustainability but also to environmental and economic sustainability, since producers obtain an extra premium for goods that are grown ecologically (e.g. organic food products). It is primarily food that is Fairtrade certified in the marketplace, but also clothing items and handmade craft products.

This focus on fairness must be understood in light of the ever-increasing portion of Western companies' production being outsourced, over the past 30 years, to low-wage countries, usually in Southeast Asia. In principle, not a week goes by without consumers being made aware of the working conditions and wage levels applicable to production in such contexts. When staff costs rise, suppliers often choose to relocate production to countries with lower wages. Wage levels in China have in many cases risen to such levels that Chinese suppliers choose to relocate manufacturing to countries such as Vietnam, Cambodia, and Bangladesh. From a social sustainability perspective, there is a risk that this results in a downward spiral in which such countries are forced to compete against each other with lower wages as their primary factor of differentiation and in which international multicorporations will quickly be able to change conditions related to tax revenues and the labor market by relocating their production when conditions are not deemed satisfactory any longer. A more optimistic attitude is that countries spending less time on producing and more on developing, designing, etc. have lifted themselves out of the worst poverty and increased their power in relation to the prosperous consumers – often in Western countries – who buy the products).

In the 1990s and 2000s, Nike was famously accused of manufacturing its goods in "sweatshops" (i.e. factories in poor countries, with unacceptable conditions for workers: low wages, dangerous and unsafe environments, child labor, etc. (see example in Figure 3.3), which the company denied, arguing it was not responsible as they were not owners of these factories overseas – although Nike was actually responsible for which suppliers they contracted. What is more depressing is the fact that there continue to be child workers, forced marriages, and forced laborers (i.e. modern slavery), which leads to forced production of goods for consumption (International Labour Organization 2022). It is common to hear public revelations about companies that have elements of their supply chain (i.e. manufacturing, transportation) that breach ethical codes of conduct for fair trade. Probably, similar problems apply to many companies with a large portion of their production in developing countries; however, the attention of consumers and the mass media tend to focus on IKEA, H&M, Apple, Walmart, Nike, and other major companies with a multinational market presence.

Figure 3.3 Child workers are still common in many parts of the world, such as in Southeast Asia. Are you aware of such things when you shop?
Source: Shutterstock 2159430215.

Socially sustainable consumption also means that we, as consumers, should not get injured when using products. For example, the goods and services we buy must not be dangerous to use or harmful to our health. To ensure that products maintain a good level of quality, government agencies and independent actors, which publish information aimed at consumers, each year conduct thorough tests of different types of products. In other respects, the media also contribute, via TV programs for consumers, as well as (but less systematically) in social media and Internet forums identifying and scrutinizing the presence of unsustainable products.

Overlaps and Goal Conflicts Between Sustainability Dimensions

There are overlaps and goal conflicts between socially sustainable consumption and economically and environmentally sustainable consumption. One example of a goal conflict between environmentally and socially sustainable consumption is product safety. A classic example is the indispensable fireproofing agents such as fire-retardant chemicals in, among others, car upholsteries and TV sets. Some of these have unfortunately turned out to have environmental and health-impairing effects. Here, a goal conflict also arises within the social dimension.

Goal conflicts can also occur between the various sustainability dimensions. For example, organic food, which is more environmentally sustainable, is usually more expensive than conventional food; e.g. organic beef requires much more land usage than industrial cattle ranches. Another example of trade-offs between sustainability dimensions is choosing local food produce over organic produce from far away, such as e.g. buying nonorganic eggs/milk from your neighbor instead of buying organic eggs/milk at the supermarket that come from 10000+ kilometers away. Ozanne et al. (2016) made 16 case studies to better understand such triple bottom line tensions. Let us look at D.Light, a social organization founded in 2008 in the United States but operating abroad. They sell affordable, high-quality off-grid solar systems (e.g. LED lanterns) to people living without access to reliable and clean energy in the developing countries. While their products are cheaper, healthier, and more environmentally friendly as a source of light (compared to the usual kerosene lamps), D.Light also articulates a clear commitment to a private enterprise – they want to make money. Their argument is that to help the poor in a sustainable way, the organization needs to be financially viable. So, the founders of D.Light (and investors who backed up the organization's social mission at the beginning) have a for-profit approach, whereas the engineers are more "passionate about building a product that millions of people will use" (Farr 2013). Another example from D.Light highlighting the tensions at the triple bottom line is that when the organization expanded its operations from Africa into China, investors and employees did not think that all three dimensions could be pursued simultaneously; as a result, they categorized the organization as either a charity or an unsuccessful business.

The complexity inherent in these questions at times makes it difficult to identify and calculate a net effect. On the other hand, this should not prevent a proactive attitude toward developing sustainability initiatives. The better consumers get at assessing these dimensions, the smaller the risk of one-sided arguments gaining the upper hand.

Should the Burden to Consume Sustainably be on the Consumer?

When products are labeled as "green," they usually follow at least one of the 12 tenets of green chemistry, including "safe for the environment," "design for degradation," and "less hazardous chemical synthesis." These claims are rarely ever supported before releasing a product to the market. Therefore, there are concerns associated with these products and how they impact nontarget organisms that may not be considered during development. Mixture toxicity is the effect of different chemical combinations that can result in antagonistic interactions (effects are lower than single exposure), additive interactions (cumulative of single components), or synergistic (effects are magnified being single components) interactions. When chemicals that are considered "green" are combined, these effects may occur once released. Yet, there is no real

(Continued)

(Continued)

understanding of this. A recently published study in *Environmental Toxicology and Chemistry* called "Are Green Household Consumer Products Less Toxic than Conventional Products" found that "green" household consumer products (HCPs) were equally or more toxic than their conventional counterparts before and after degradation when exposed to sensitive freshwater and marine organisms (Gray et al. 2022). Their results demonstrate that the end-product formulations of green products were not necessarily less toxic before or after degradation treatments, suggesting that consumer skepticism over manufacturer claims is justified. One of the green products tested (dish detergent) had received the USEPA's Design for the Environment certification. For consumers, these concerns are not always at the forefront, and the purchase of these products comes with the trust that they will have a less detrimental impact on the environment. It is imperative that rigorous screening is conducted, as seen in the EPA Design for the Environmental certification, to ensure that what consumers buy truly lives up to its classification as "green" and to help establish trust and quality science.

Source: Personal communication with Austin Gray, Assistant Professor of Biological Sciences, Virginia Tech University; Gray et al. (2022).

Sustainable Customer Segmentation

Marketing research has focused on socio-demographic segmentation (e.g. educated, middle-class, married female consumers with children at home) and psychographics (such as environmental consciousness, perceived consumer effectiveness, altruism, and collectivism) to identify the characteristics of the "green consumer" in developed markets (Laroche et al. 2001; Diamantopoulos et al. 2003; Sharma 2021). Recent research has begun to look at consumers in emerging markets such as India (Jaiswal et al. 2020).

Focusing on the US market, Gleim et al. (2013) categorize American consumers into four clusters based on satisfaction with, and purchase intentions toward, "green products" and personal norms, perceived consumer effectiveness, value, quality, awareness, availability, expertise, advertising trust, organizational trust, and social norms. The authors use a color-code to help us remember what these segments are:

The "Greens": Very knowledgeable consumers regarding sustainability issues, who think that their consumption choices (i.e. to buy "green products") can have a positive impact on the planet. They feel that eco-friendly products are of good value and high quality, and they trust the brands behind them.

The "Yellows": Slightly less sustainability-savvy consumers, although they also feel that ecological products and "green companies" are generally good and trustworthy and that sustainable consumption can have a positive impact on the planet.

The "Oranges": Not very knowledgeable regarding eco-friendly products, as they believe that they are not comparable to traditional products in terms of quality and value-for-price. They also lack trust in so-called sustainable businesses, and their perceived consumer effectiveness (i.e. the impact of their consumption) is ridiculous.

The "Reds": Price-sensitive consumers with zero expertise regarding sustainability, who feel that "green products" are not of good value or high quality and that it is basically a hassle to buy them. They do not trust sustainable businesses, and they tend to believe that they cannot make a positive impact on the planet through their consumption – they do not feel responsible (Figure 3.4).

With regard to Swedish consumers and sustainability, a segmentation study shows that they can be separated into the following four groups (Algehed 2015):

Seven percent of Swedes are "Dedicated," representing the "Greens": This group is the smallest part of the population but by far the most devoted to sustainability – whatever they have to buy and wherever they are, sustainability attributes take center stage. They constantly seek information (e.g. they are likely to contact companies to ask specific questions) and learn about sustainability, and they gladly talk about it in their social circles – to a high extent offering and receiving information about sustainability. Despite this pro-environmental attitude, they sometimes lack funds to walk the talk, since this is a lower-income group compared to the others.

Figure 3.4 Separating groups of customers based on segmentation criteria has a long tradition in marketing and has even been called the holy grail of marketing. Market segmentation is visible in supermarkets where for example, low-priced products can be positioned together, organic products elsewhere, etc.
Source: Stock-ID: 1906987540.

Seventeen percent of Swedes are "Smart," representing the "Yellows": These consumers are typically women. They are interested in and aware of which products are "good for body and soul" – they buy purposefully, but consciously. Price is not the primary consideration, since they are willing to pay for the right content and they can actually afford it. They are curious about and interested in sustainability and gladly discuss it with others – they are considered quite knowledgeable regarding sustainable products in their social circles, as they know which information to look for before making purchase decisions.

Fifty percent of Swedes are "Moderate," representing the "Oranges": Half the Swedish population thinks sustainability "is interesting" (i.e. they are aware of the sustainability debate), but they prioritize price as well as general demands concerning durability, quality, and functionality.

Twenty-six percent of Swedes are "Ego," representing the "Reds": mainly oriented toward price. They are also more concerned with functionality, perceived quality, and durability than sustainability as product attributes. These Swedes are characterized by short-term thinking – they seek simple solutions, choose whatever product or service fulfills their needs, and care only about what is best for themselves.

How Can We Start Becoming More Sustainable?

In the best of worlds, we as consumers should aspire to buy only sustainable products and, above all, avoid unnecessary consumption. This is a normative attitude, but one necessary to comply with if future generations are to be able to live and consume. Consumers who really want to make a difference in their everyday lives are recommended by Belz and Peattie (2012) to concentrate on the following three areas:

Sustainable alternatives concerning choices of food and drink: The reduced consumption of red meat (e.g. beef, pork, goat, and sheep) will lead not only to reduced greenhouse gas emissions like CO_2 but also to improved public health, since red meat in general can increase risks of diabetes, cardiovascular disease, and processed red meat (like cured meats) and can increase the risk of some cancers (Wein 2012). The recommendation is thus to mainly eat food from the vegetable kingdom (i.e. fruit and vegetables), as well as lots of leguminous plants such as peas, lentils, broad beans, chickpeas, soybeans, peanuts, and whole grains such as amaranth, spelt, wild rice, oats, rye, brown rice, quinoa, millet, bulgur. Besides these foods being rich in fiber, vitamins, and minerals, they are, relatively speaking, considerably cheaper than animal products. Moreover, they also have a considerably lower environmental impact during production.

Sustainable alternatives regarding household-related consumption: We spend a large part of our lives at home, where we consume large volumes of energy and natural resources. Trying to reduce our energy consumption at home by means of insulation, water-saving taps, low-energy lighting, and energy-efficient appliances can make a major difference in our environmental impact. Energy rationalization at home saves money and thus also increases the economic sustainability of households.

Sustainable alternatives regarding travel and transportation: Travel accounts for a major portion of the emissions of CO_2 that we consumers give rise to. Sharing car travel with other people (e.g. family, friends, colleagues), using small cars (rather than large SUVs), and choosing to go by bike or public transport can achieve great environmental benefits. The same applies to limiting air travel: we have seen earlier that air travel constitutes a major share of CO_2 emissions, so taking the train has become increasingly popular among supporters of the "flight-shaming" movement (*flygskam* in Swedish) with advocates such as Greta Thunberg (Sidkvist et al. 2019; Swedish Society for Nature Conservation 2024). Thunberg is an environmental activist who gained international recognition in 2018 when, at the age of 15, she started skipping school on Fridays to protest outside the Swedish Parliament. Her School Strike for Climate, which led to the global Fridays for Future movement has made her known for raising awareness about climate change and advocates for urgent action to address the climate crisis (Perera et al. 2022). For example, Greta refuses to fly. In 2019, emphasizing her commitment to reducing CO_2 emissions, Greta sailed across the Atlantic Ocean in a zero-emissions yacht to attend the UN summit in New York.

These three areas in consumers' lives are where, with relatively little sacrifice, we can make a major difference in relation to the environmental impact of consumption. The purpose of emphasizing this is to point to examples where individuals can make a difference. Naturally, as a consumer, you can always go even further in your consumption choices, such as choosing to live in a passive (e.g. fully insulated and airtight for energy efficiency) house or using an electric vehicle; however, realistically, these are not feasible alternatives for all consumers today. Moreover, believing that individual consumers alone will be able to push the whole of society in a more sustainable direction is naive. The burden on the consumer to be an informed consumer by reading labels, trusting labels, understanding labels, ingredients, etc. and their impact on the environment is unfair (Gray et al. 2022).

Here, supranational organizations such as the UN and the European Union, as well as government agencies, companies, and civil society organizations, also have a great responsibility in influencing more sustainable consumption.

The Attitude-Behavior Gap, or Green Gap

Despite many consumers saying they care for the environment, the share of eco-friendly products in shopping baskets is not equivalently high. Sales of organic food and other eco-friendly goods represent only 9.6% of groceries bought in Swedish supermarkets (2018), a country with a high climate change awareness. In the United States, organic food sales amount to only 6% of total food sales – mostly meat products and yogurts, since the main purchase motive is that these products contain no artificial ingredients or pesticides (Statista 2023). Australia is the number-one country for organic farming with about 53 million hectares (Shahbandeh 2024). So, even though consumers express widespread pro-environmental attitudes, they do not purchase products accordingly. This attitude-behavior *green gap* is due to the trade-offs that pro-environmental products frequently force upon their users: for example, higher prices, lower quality, and/or reduced performance. For each choice, consumers balance environmental issues with other important factors, such as price, performance, convenience, and quality. But there are many others (see Figure 3.5 for instance).

Many studies show that consumers find sustainability issues important. However, the values people say they have do not necessarily reflect the way they act. An increasing number of consumers view health and lifestyle aspects as key when making buying decisions. The acronym LOHAS – lifestyles of health and sustainability – is used for describing this segment of consumers. Many studies identify the values and attitudes that are believed to influence how consumers choose products

Figure 3.5 If you praise the idea of cycling to work instead of driving your car but never do it, you may have an attitude-behavior gap. Photo by Elchino portrait.
Source: Pexels 20471042.

(e.g. Gatersleben et al. 2002, 2014; Diamantopoulos et al. 2003; Bouman et al. 2020; Sharma et al. 2023). Gatersleben et al. (2019) explored whether higher-order motives, beyond morality, may be important for understanding pro-environmental behavior, by studying consumer identities. Frugal and moral consumer identities were most salient and were the strongest predictors of pro-environmental behaviors, but in different ways. Frugality was particularly important for behaviors associated with waste reduction of any kind, including money. Moreover, people were found to adopt the same behavior for different reasons, in ways consistent with their consumer identities. Hence, consumers manage multiple consumer identities simultaneously, and environmental policy is more effective if it addresses these multiple identities.

Even though consumers claim to possess increasingly sustainable values, Bask et al. (2013, p. 381) argue that "[. . .] there is a lack of academic literature on how consumers view or value the sustainable features of a product or service [. . .]."

A number of explanations have been put forward to explain the attitude-behavior gap. For example, Belz and Peattie (2012) provide the following examples of factors influencing this inconsistency in the consumer:

- *Value*: Which value does a sustainable product offer in relation to a traditional one? Here, we can speak of both value-in-use and the product's contextual value (e.g. second-hand value). It may, for instance, be unclear to the consumer which (added) value a more expensive ecological product has
- *Frequency*: Many purchases are frequently made without the consumer reflecting upon them. This can be a matter of, for instance, milk and bananas. Ecological products can be rejected for this reason – we buy what we usually buy without reflecting upon this
- *Visibility*: It may be unclear (e.g. on the packaging) that an offer is sustainable
- *Complexity*: Sustainability issues can create increased complexity around the purchase – for instance, there are more factors to consider besides price and quality. The increased level of complexity can entail the consumer rejecting the sustainable product in favor of a traditional one
- *For me or for others*: Depending on whom we buy things for, our will to choose sustainable alternatives may be affected. Many parents, for instance, eat standard foods themselves while being happy to buy eco-friendly baby food for their children in the hope that this baby food contains fewer chemicals
- *Necessity or enjoyment*: Whether the purchase is low-involvement in nature (taking place routinely) or high-involvement in nature (based on extensive information retrieval) may influence the role of sustainability issues in the mind of the consumer. Maybe the consumer feels that an eco-friendly beer from a microbrewery on a Friday night is a luxury that she is happy to pay a bit extra for, while the banana eaten during each coffee break is a boring necessity

Only asking consumers in surveys if they would like to buy sustainable products can thus be criticized for disregarding the complexity of current consumers' purchasing behavior. Critics have claimed, for example, that companies instead of chasing the "green consumer" on the basis of criteria such as age and gender should focus on consumer behavior in certain situations (Peattie 2001). When a person who is favorable to environmental consumption makes an actual purchase, it is not just the sustainable aspects of the good or service that trigger the purchase. A study by Fraj and Martinez (2006) highlights that a majority of consumers are positively inclined toward environment-friendly purchases but that other factors governed the purchase-triggering decision (e.g. traditional and competing non-eco-friendly products). More recently, a Swedish study simply asked consumers what are the main barriers for them not to buy more sustainable food, which yield very similar results: price is still number one (40% think price are unreasonably expensive, 30% say they can't afford it), lack of knowledge comes second (26%), then lack of availability in supermarkets (24%), lack of trust in labels (16%) or sustainability claims made by companies (15%) and lack of time to actually read what these labels/claims mean (15%), and last come disappointing product attributes like bad taste (8%), worse quality (5%), or boring design (3%) (Krav 2021). From the supply side, a recent US study of consumer goods showed that goods marketed as sustainable represent 17% of what's available in store.

In summary, explanations as to why there the green gap persists include the following (cf. Kronthal-Sacco and Whelan 2024):

- Lack of "green products" or availability
- Perceived high prices or low willingness to pay (see further discussion in Chapter 10)
- Low perceived product quality
- Social norms
- Insufficient knowledge or lack of understanding
- Low perceived consumer effectiveness
- Skepticism/lack of trust
- Confusion among labels
- Lack of incentives
- Perceived time (effort)
- Routines and habits

References

Ahuvia, A.C. (2005). Beyond the extended self: loved objects and consumers' identity narratives. *Journal of Consumer Research*, 32, 171–184.

Albinsson, P.A. and Perera, B.Y., 2009. From trash to treasure and beyond: the meaning of voluntary disposition. *Journal of Consumer Behaviour: An International Research Review*, 8, 340–353.

Albinsson, P.A., Wolf, M. and Kopf, D.A., 2010. Anti-consumption in East Germany: Consumer resistance to hyperconsumption. *Journal of Consumer Behaviour*, 9 (6), 412–425.

Albinsson, P.A. & Ross, S.M. (2024). Mobilizing for cash-in-use: addressing the gap in neoliberalism caused by disruptive innovations, *Journal of Association For Consumer Research*, 11, 303–315.

Algehed, J. (2015). Sustainable consumption: a knowledge base. *MISTRA – Swedish foundation for strategic environmental research*. https://www.mistra.org/wp-content/uploads/2018/01/ReportKnowledgebaseSustainableConsumptionAug2015-1.pdf (accessed 3 February, 2024).

Austin Gray (2024). Personal communication with Austin Gray, February 27, 2024

Bask, A., Halme, M., Kallio, M. & Kuula, M. (2013). Consumer preferences for sustainability and their impact on supply chain management: the case of mobile phones. *International Journal of Physical Distribution and Logistics Management*, 43, 380–406.

Belz, F.-M. & Peattie, K. (2012). *Sustainable Marketing: A Global Perspective*. (2nd ed.). Chichester: Wiley.

Bouman, T., Verschoor, M., Albers, C. J., Böhm, G., Fisher, S. D., Poortinga, W., . . . & Steg, L. (2020). When worry about climate change leads to climate action: how values, worry and personal responsibility relate to various climate actions. *Global Environmental Change*, 62, 102061.

Cappelletti, F., Manes, F., Rossi, M., & Germani, M. (2022). Evaluating the environmental sustainability of durable products through life cycle assessment. The case of domestic refrigerators. *Sustainable Production and Consumption*, 34, 177–189.

Confetto, M. G., Covucci, C., Addeo, F., & Normando, M. (2023). Sustainability advocacy antecedents: how social media content influences sustainable behaviours among generation Z. *Journal of Consumer Marketing*, 40 758–774.

Davis, B., Ozanne, J. L., & Hill, R. P. (2016). The transformative consumer research movement. *Journal of Public Policy & Marketing*, 35 (2), 159–169.

Deighton J. (2007). The territory of consumer research: walking the fences, *Journal of Consumer Research*, 34(3): 279–282.

Diamantopoulos, A., Schlegelmilch, B.B., Sinkovics, R.R. & Bohlen, G.M. (2003). Can sociodemographics still play a role in profiling green consumers? A review of the evidence and an empirical investigation. *Journal of Business Research*, 56, 465–480.

Ekpo, A.E., Drenten, J., Albinsson, P.A., Anong, S., Appau, S., Chatterjee, L., Dadzie, C.A, Echelbarger, M., Muldrow, A., Ross, S.M. Santana, S., & Weinberger, M.F. (2022). The platformed money ecosystem: digital financial platforms, datafication, and reimagining financial well-being. *Journal of Consumer Affairs*, 56, 1062–1078.

Farr C. (2013). Want to make money & change the world? An idiot's guide to "social entrepreneurship," *Venture Beat*. https://venturebeat.com/2013/05/24/want-to-make-money-change-the-world-an-idiots-guide-to-social-entrepreneurship (accessed 15 March, 2024).

Fraj, E. & Martinez, E. (2006). Environmental values and lifestyles as determining factors of ecological consumer behaviour: an empirical analysis. *Journal of Consumer Marketing*, 23(3), 113–144.

Gatersleben, B., Steg, L. and Vlek, C. (2002). Measurement and determinants of environmental relevant consumer behavior. *Environment and Behavior*, 34, 335–362.

Gatersleben, B., Murtagh, M. & Abrahamse, W. (2014). Values, identity and pro-environmental behaviour, *Journal of the Academy of Social Sciences*, 9, 374–392.

Gatersleben, B., Murtagh, N., Cherry, M., & Watkins, M. (2019). Moral, wasteful, frugal, or thrifty? Identifying consumer identities to understand and manage pro-environmental behavior. *Environment and Behavior*, 51(1), 24–49.

Gleim, M. R., Smith, J. S., Andrews, D., & Cronin Jr, J. J. (2013). Against the green: a multi-method examination of the barriers to green consumption. *Journal of Retailing*, 89, 44–61.

Gray, A.D., Miller, J.A., & Weinstein, J.E. (2022). Are green household consumer products less toxic than conventional products? An assessment involving grass shrimp (Palaemon pugio) and Daphnia magna. *Environmental Toxicology and Chemistry*, 41, 2444–2453.

Griffiths, M.A., Perera, B.Y., & Albinsson, P.A. (2019). Contrived surplus and negative externalities in the sharing economy. *Journal of Marketing Theory and Practice*, 27, 445–463.

Griffiths, M.A., LaPan, C., & James. C.D. (2024). Negative externalities of collaborative consumption: the cost of exploitation. In *Understanding Collaborative Consumption* ed. Albinsson, P.A., Perera, B.Y, & Lawson, S.J. Cheltenham, UK: Edward Elgar.

Gupta, S., Lim, W.M., Verma, H.V. & Polonsky, M. (2023), "How can we encourage mindful consumption? Insights from mindfulness and religious faith," *Journal of Consumer Marketing*, 40, 344–358.

Holbrook, M.B. (1987). What is consumer research? *Journal of Consumer Research*, 14, 128–132.

Holmqvist, J. & Kowalkowski, C. (2023) Traceability in luxury: harnessing B2B relationships to enhance ethical practices in the luxury industry, *Industrial Marketing Management*, 111, 257–267.

International Labour Organization (2022). 50 million people worldwide in modern slavery. https://www.ilo.org/resource/news/50-million-people-worldwide-modern-slavery-0 (accessed 15 May 2024).

Jaiswal, D., Kaushal, V., Singh, P.K. and Biswas, A., (2020). Green market segmentation and consumer profiling: a cluster approach to an emerging consumer market. *Benchmarking: An International Journal*, 28, 792–812.

Konsumentverket (n.d.). Så kan du minska din klimatpåverkan. https://www.hallakonsument.se/miljo-och-hallbarhet/minska-din-klimatpaverkan (accessed 15 March 2024).

KRAV (2021), Den hållbara maten 2021, en insiktsrapport från KRAV. https://wwwkravse.cdn.triggerfish.cloud/uploads/sites/2/2021/05/krav-den-hallbara-maten-2021.pdf (accessed 3 June 2024).

Kronthal-Sacco, R. & Whelan, T. (2024). Sustainable Market Share Index, New York: The NYU Stern Center for Sustainable Business, https://www.stern.nyu.edu/sites/default/files/2024-05/2024%20CSB%20Report%20for%20website.pdf (accessed 3 June 2024).

Laroche, M., Bergeron, J. & Barbaro-Forleo, G. (2001). Targeting consumers who are willing to pay more for environmentally friendly products. *Journal of Consumer Marketing*, 18(6), 503–520.

MacInnis, D.J. & Folkes, V.S. (2010). The disciplinary status of consumer behavior: a sociology of science perspective on key controversies. *Journal of Consumer Research*, 36, 899–914.

Mick, D.G., Pettigrew, S. Pechmann, C. & Ozanne, J.L. (2012). Origins, qualities, and envisionments of transformative consumer research," in *Transformative Consumer Research for Personal and Collective Well-Being*, ed. Mick, D.G., Pettigrew, S. Pechmann, C. & Ozanne, J.L, New York: Routledge, pp. 3–24.

Mick, D.G., 2006. Meaning and mattering through transformative consumer research. *Advances in Consumer Research*, 33 (1), 1–4.

Oliveira de Mendonca, G., Coelho Rocha, A. R., & Bogéa da Costa Tayt-son, D. (2021). The minimalist process: An interpretivist study. *Journal of Consumer Behaviour*, 20 (5), 1040–1050.

Ozanne, L.K., Phipps, M., Weaver, T., Carrington, M., Luchs, M., Catlin, J., Gupta, S., Santos, N., Scott, K. and Williams, J. (2016). Managing the tensions at the intersection of the triple bottom line: a paradox theory approach to sustainability management. *Journal of Public Policy & Marketing*, 35(2), 249–261.

Peattie, K. (2001). Golden goose or wild goose? The hunt for the green consumer. *Business Strategy and the Environment*, 10, 187–199.

Perera, Y.B., Albinsson, P.A., Ray Chaudhury, S. (2022). Online consumer activism 2.5: youth activism at the forefront of the climate crisis, in *The Routledge Companion to Digital Consumption,* (Belk, R., & Llamas, R., eds.), Routledge: New York, NY, pp. 461–474.

Puckett, J. (2023). These 20 cities were just named the most sustainable, Conde Nast Traveler, November 6, 2023. https://www.cntraveler.com/gallery/most-sustainable-cities-in-the-world (accessed 13 May 2024).

Robertson, D. (2019). Inside Copenhagen's race to be the first carbon-neutral city. The Guardian, 11 October 2019. https://www.theguardian.com/cities/2019/oct/11/inside-copenhagens-race-to-be-the-first-carbon-neutral-city (accessed 6 July 2024).

Saksala, L. (2019). Think Sustainably – The local guide for sustainable Helsinki, https://tourism4sdgs.org/initiatives/think-sustainably-the-local-guide-for-sustainable-helsinki/ (accessed 6 July 2024).

Shahbandeh, M. (2024). Organic agricultural land: leading countries worldwide 2022. https://www.statista.com/statistics/677969/organic-agricultural-land-worldwide-leading-countries. (accessed 15 May 2024).

Shankar, A., Elliott, R., & Fitchett, J. A. (2009). Identity, consumption and narratives of socialization. *Marketing Theory*, 9, 5–94.

Sharma, A.P., (2021). Consumers' purchase behaviour and green marketing: a synthesis, review and agenda. *International Journal of Consumer Studies*, 45, 1217–1238.

Sharma, K., Aswal, C., & Paul, J. (2023). Factors affecting green purchase behavior: a systematic literature review. *Business Strategy and the Environment*, 32(4), 2078–2092.

Sidkvist, A. Elfors, S. Andersson, P. J. Rosen, M. Robèrt, M. Lystrand, C. Crona, J. Klint, M. Werngren, J. (2019) Från flygskam till tågskryt. *Aktuell Hallbarhet*. https://www.aktuellhallbarhet.se/miljo/klimat/fran-flygskam-till-tagskryt/ (accessed 15 March 2024).

Statista (2023). Organic share of total food sales in the U.S. 2008–2022. https://www.statista.com/statistics/244393/share-of-organic-sales-in-the-united-states/ (accessed 15 March 2024).

Statista (2024). Total retail sales worldwide from 2021–2026. https://www.statista.com/statistics/443522/global-retail-sales/ (accessed 15 March 2024).

Swedish Society for Nature Conservation (2024). Vanliga frågor om flygets klimatpåverkan. *Naturskyddsföreningen*. https://www.naturskyddsforeningen.se/artiklar/hur-paverkar-flygresor-klimatet/ (accessed 15 May 2024).

UN (2024). Sustainable Development Goals. https://www.un.org/sustainabledevelopment/sustainable-consumption-production/ (accessed 15 May 2024).

Warde, A. (1994). Consumption, identity-formation and uncertainty. *Sociology*, 28, 877–898.

Wein, H., 2012 Risk in red meat? NIH Research Matters. https://www.nih.gov/news-events/nih-research-matters/risk-red-meat (accessed 1 March 2024).

White, K., Habib, R. and Hardisty, D.J., 2019. How to SHIFT consumer behaviors to be more sustainable: A literature review and guiding framework. *Journal of Marketing*, 83 (3), 22–49.

Zeng, T. & Botella-Carrubi, D., 2023. Improving societal benefit through transformative consumer research: a descriptive review. *Technological Forecasting and Social Change*, 190, 122435.

Chapter 4

Sustainable Marketing Practices

This chapter initiates an exploration into research concerning the sustainable operations of companies, which many perceive as not only beneficial but also obligatory. Historically, companies have often been viewed as unsustainable entities, but a notable shift has occurred due to the growing emphasis on sustainability. For example, sustainability-oriented companies may use biomimicry, design for the environment (DFE), or cradle-to-cradle design concepts when developing new products. Within this chapter, we highlight examples of companies embracing sustainability. We examine the potential benefits these sustainable companies can gain in the market and delve into various reasons why certain companies may resist transitioning toward a more sustainable approach.

Learning Objectives

- Understand design concepts such as biomimicry, DFE, and cradle-to-cradle
- Describe and identify companies' approaches to sustainability: defensive, reactive, and proactive
- Understand the principles of the "circular economy" and the diverse practices that many companies engage in to promote circularity (i.e. considering waste as a resource)
- Leverage the "R" nomenclature (reduce, reuse, recycle, etc.)
- Explain how companies can improve their sustainability endeavors

Introduction

Companies operating without sustainability in their sight are being increasingly noticed by all society stakeholders. Critical consumers and consumer activists who organize in movements, such as the environmental movement, which spread on social media, and later traditional media as well, are important elements when it comes to pushing companies to adjust their agenda toward sustainability. Glaring media headlines about how workers making Apple iPhones in China are working and living under unsustainable conditions, or how those making clothes for H&M in factories in Cambodia are experiencing sexual harassment and termination of employment during pregnancy, reach today's critical consumers. When multinational profitable companies such as Apple and H&M act in a manner that does not correspond with their code of conduct, respect human rights, or follow ethical working conditions, this becomes a prominent subject to write about. Even though various defenses and excuses are often offered, the public tends to despise multinational corporations that are revealed to be exploiting cheap labor opportunities developing countries.

The trend of grassroots-generated information is pushing companies into working toward sustainability. Other factors affecting companies include the ever-increasing costs that governments are placing upon companies to make it more expensive to act unsustainably. Examples of such costs include carbon dioxide (CO_2) tax and tax on electricity consumption. The need to monitor the number of natural resources and energy used in production processes, ethically-sound working conditions, etc., is thus becoming increasingly important.

Scandals related to poor sustainability efforts may also cost multinational companies billions. Case in point: in 2010 British Petroleum (BP) faced severe criticism for its handling of the Deepwater Horizon oil spill in the Gulf of Mexico, which resulted in extensive environmental damage and raised questions about BP's commitment to safety and environmental responsibility. Fines, settlements, compensations, and cleanup costs totaled more than $65 billion (Vaughan 2018).

Hence, a key point of departure in this chapter is discussing the relationship between production (manufacturing) and sustainability. Indeed, many brands have taken sustainability initiatives worldwide, though not all are equivalently efficient in terms of reducing greenhouse gas emissions, or in terms of impact on their brand image and equity. First, it is important to know where brands stand (e.g. a tire manufacturer does not pollute equally to a plastic bottle manufacturer), and many develop initiatives related to measuring or tracking emissions (35% of 350 companies sampled).

Many brands also invest in the different ways to improve manufacturing efficiency themselves (39%), but most brands work on initiatives where the main actor of sustainability is the customers and not themselves, such as allowing customers to easily recycle products (46%), distancing from unsustainable partners (36%), and offsetting emissions (23%), where they compensate their sustainable impact by planting trees or funding actions that are not related to their core activity (Tighe 2024). Looking closer at the ways manufacturing can become more sustainable, another survey of C-level executives about their companies' actions report they are using more sustainable material (59%), increasing the efficiency of energy use (59%), using more energy efficient or climate-friendly equipment (54%), and training employees on climate change actions and impacts (50%) (Burgueño Salas 2023).

Sustainable New Product Development

In sustainable new product development, there are several notable concepts related to eco-design, also called nature-inspired design strategies (NIDSs), which we will discuss next. Some of these are biomimicry, cradle-to-cradle, and Design for the Environment (DFE).

Biomimicry

First, biomimicry (i.e. imitating nature) is built on the notion of "learning from nature"; that is, designers look to how nature builds its components as nature is regarded "as the paradigm for sustainability" (De Pauw et al. 2010). This concept can also be defined as innovations inspired by nature (e.g. Kekic et al. 2020). Biomimicry looks at the way natural, circular processes work for plants and trees and studies the way animals, birds, and insects function in terms of balance, shape, and other characteristics. For example, how does a fly or lizard sit upside down or vertically on a wall? How does nature collect dew drops overnight? How does a kingfisher (bird) dive into the water or fly through the sky? Janine Benyus', a biologist and innovation consultant, wrote a seminal book called *Biomimicry: Innovation Inspired by Nature* that introduced nine principles of nature, resulting in an early method for sustainable product design, or designing products that are beneficial to people, planet, and profit (the triple bottom line) (De Pauw et al. 2014). Benyus' (1997) nine principles are as follows:

- Nature runs on sunlight
- Nature recycles everything
- Nature demands local expertise
- Nature only uses the energy it needs
- Nature taps the power of limits
- Nature rewards cooperation
- Nature fits form to function
- Nature operates on the principle of diversity
- Nature does not allow wastage

Other authors condensed these principles into three. These are the principles guiding biomimicry (Stevens et al. 2019):

- *Nature as a model*: Biomimicry assists innovators to come up with new forms, processes, systems, or strategies for creating sustainable solutions to technical problems
- *Nature as a measure*: Ecological standards are just for sustainable innovation
- *Nature as mentor*: Use nature as a knowledge base for learning

One biomimicry example that has been applied to surface materials is the characteristics of the lotus flower, whose leaves are perfectly clean as any impurities do not stay on the leaf. The process that cleans the lotus flower is due to micro- and nanoscopic surface architecture, which prevents dirt particles from sticking. Wilhelm Barthlott, a German botanist and biomimetic materials scientist, discovered the water-repellent nanostructured surface of the lotus flower in the 1970s and protected this process with the "Lotus effect" trademark. The self-cleaning process has been used in awnings, sails, and facades (i.e. Keric et al. 2020).

The design of Japan's 500 Series Shinkansen bullet train is another example of product designers learning from nature. The product designers used the beak of the kingfisher, a bird that dives headfirst into water, a denser medium than air, without making a splash to reduce noise pollution when the trains exit tunnels (see Benyus 1997; Kennedy and Marting 2016).

Cradle-to-Cradle

Cradle-to-cradle follows biomimicry design principles, with a specific focus of no waste in the production process. In nature, everything is food for other organisms or systems. While many corporations run their operations using eco-efficiency that is to minimize waste, lower pollution, and reduce raw material extraction, they may still use a liner model, i.e. cradle-to-grave (Kerik et al. 2020). Instead of wastage at the end of use, cradle-to-cradle focuses on circularity. Cradle-to-cradle, as mentioned, is in alignment with the guiding principles of biomimicry and incorporates the ideas of using waste as food or other resources, using renewable energy sources, and promoting diversity.

Design for the Environment

Another concept in new product development is DFE or green design (see also Chapter 3). DFE uses a matrix to measure the impact of a product's parts and components. For example, product designers study how easy a product can be disassembled so that each part can be recycled or reused after use. For example, office furniture manufacturer Herman Miller has used this design concept in their designs since 2001 (Herman Miller n.d.) when they formed their DFE team. McDonough and Braungart (2002) stated in *Cradle to Cradle: Remaking the Way We Make Things* that the traditional DFE method was not enough. As a result, they re-focused DFE to include the following focus:

- Material chemistry
- Disassembly
- Recyclability

Today, Herman Miller and many other corporations, e.g. L'Oreal, C&A, and Steelcase, work with McDonough Braungart Design Chemistry in their product design.

Defensive, Reactive, and Proactive Approaches to Sustainability

Stakeholders such as the government, customers, competitors, suppliers, organizations in local society, environmental organizations, and trade organizations exert an ever-greater influence on companies. However, exactly how each company reacts to this pressure is highly dependent on the actions of corporate management. Moreover, in corporations acting reactively or defensively, this stakeholders' pressure will only lead to sustainable changes at a lower rate than that of corporations that are proactive in relation to the sustainability issue.

Companies aiming to adapt their business to the sustainable development principles can act in different ways. Different companies in the same industry can choose to act in opposing ways when facing the same external pressure from their stakeholders for sustainability. Here, we can distinguish between three different approaches at the corporate level regarding adaptation to the sustainability imperative (Guyader et al. 2020):

- The defensive approach
- The reactive approach
- The proactive approach (see Figure 4.1)

Defensive Approach

The *defensive approach* to the sustainability imperative is common and is frequently observed in the business press (Guyader et al. 2020). The most common argument put forward by companies in this approach is that the need for integrating

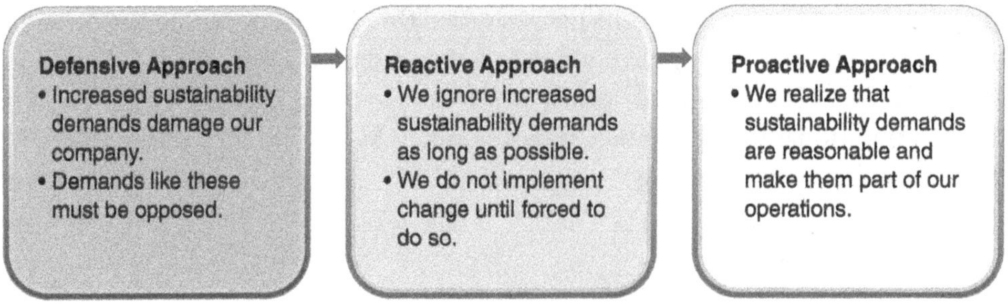

Figure 4.1 Defensive, reactive, and proactive approaches to sustainability.
Source: Guyader et al. (2020).

sustainability concerns would hurt their profitability; frequently, it is even claimed that such adaptation would lead to the elimination of the industry and bankruptcy of companies. Thus, the attitude is that the implementation of more sustainable standards of operation, which may come from the government, through official regulations and laws, or political influences debated by environmental organizations, or other stakeholders, must be opposed. This can be achieved via lobbying by the companies themselves but also via trade associations and employers' organizations.

For example, the South Korean multinational Samsung faced criticism for its environmental and labor practices. It has been accused of using harmful chemicals in its manufacturing processes, contributing to pollution and health risks for workers and communities near its facilities. Despite calls for greater transparency and accountability, Samsung has been slow, to say the least, to adopt more sustainable practices and has faced legal challenges and public backlash for its environmental record. Similarly, in the United States, ExxonMobil has been accused of funding climate change denial campaigns and lobbying against regulations aimed at reducing greenhouse gas emissions, despite increasing pressure from investors and the public to address environmental concerns. In this defensive approach, ExxonMobil has largely maintained its focus on fossil fuel extraction and resisted significant shifts toward renewable energy alternatives.

Oil companies, like ExxonMobil, or Total in France, are known for their lobbying efforts: they involve industry groups and organizations in advocating against environmental regulations or policies that would require them to adopt more sustainable practices. For example, the American Petroleum Institute (API) – a trade association representing the oil and natural gas industry in the United States – lobbies for weakening or blocking environmental regulations aimed at reducing greenhouse gas emissions, such as carbon pricing initiatives or stricter fuel efficiency standards for vehicles. API has argued that such regulations would impose undue burdens on the industry, leading to job losses and economic harm. API lobbying activities include funding political campaigns and advocating for industry-friendly policies. By influencing policymakers and shaping public opinion, API and similar industry groups funded by ExxonMobil, Total, BP, Koch Industries, etc. have sought to maintain the status quo and resist efforts to transition toward more sustainable energy sources and practices, and they represent the defensive approach to sustainability by protecting the firms' interests.

Lobbying efforts take place in other industries and sectors. On several occasions, for instance, the Confederation of Swedish Enterprises (*Svenskt Näringsliv*) has continuously criticized the Swedish government for its CO_2 taxation and for the extensive environmental permits, which is claimed to hurt Sweden's competitiveness. In 2021, for example, it argued that delayed environmental permits cost companies in Sweden billions: "Sweden stands out, 12% of the companies state that they are moving their investments abroad, so for some reason it is easier with permits in other countries" (Söderqvist 2021, np).

McDonald's, one of the largest fast-food chains globally, has made some commitments to improve sustainability (e.g. sourcing of ingredients in some regions), but it has also been accused of lobbying against regulations that would require it to reduce its environmental footprint, such as restrictions on single-use plastics, reductions of packaging waste, or regulations promoting healthier food options. Similarly, Coca-Cola, which owns and operates numerous fast-food chains, such as Costa Coffee, has been involved in lobbying against regulations aimed at reducing plastic waste, such as bottle deposit schemes or bans on single-use plastics, because it could impact its beverage sales and packaging operations (George 2020).

There are several dangers associated with such defensive strategies, like painting a picture of business executives as profit-hungry and basically ignoring socio-environmental concerns in the eyes of the public. The defensive approach also risks forcing companies to put their strategic muscle and energy into counteracting sustainability issues, whereas such resources could be used to proactively adapt to these pressing issues before it is too late and costs them even more. Eventually, from an image perspective, it is strange that some of these defensive companies have nice statements on corporate social responsibility (CSR) and environmental policies on their websites!

Reactive Approach

The *reactive approach* means that companies ignore all the sustainability concerns for as long as possible. Companies choose not to implement any measures until legislation or threats of fines arise. Common reasons for such an approach include companies not perceiving their operations as contributing to socio-environmental problems to a sufficient extent or that their employees have not complained (Guyader et al. 2020).

Reactive means not reacting until something forces a reaction, which often happens when it is too late. Such companies bet that a certain status quo remains although there is evidence that the circumstances will eventually change. For example, preventative working environment measures are not implemented until an accident happens, despite the principal safety representative on-site having pointed out possible deficiencies on several occasions. For companies with a reactive approach, sustainability issues are thus not strategic but primarily operative in nature.

Walmart, one of the world's largest retailers, has faced criticism for its slow response to sustainability issues despite its significant environmental impact. For years, Walmart was criticized for its reliance on fossil fuels, poor labor practices, and contributions to deforestation through its supply chain. Critics argue that Walmart made some commitments (e.g. setting renewable energy targets and reducing greenhouse gas emissions) but that these were reactive rather than proactive. Indeed, Walmart has often made changes only when faced with pressure from stakeholders, including consumers, investors, and regulators.

In the agriculture sector, there has been talks between regulators, farmers, chemical manufacturers, and so on about forbidding the use of glyphosate, the active ingredient that is widely used in many herbicides – most notably Roundup – due to its detrimental health and environmental impacts. For years, Monsanto (now Bayer) marketed Roundup as a safe and effective weed killer with minimal environmental impact. However, concerns began to arise, and glyphosate was classified as a probable carcinogen by the International Agency for Research on Cancer. Despite mounting evidence and public outcry, Monsanto initially resisted calls to reevaluate the safety of glyphosate, continuing to defend the use of Roundup in numerous lawsuits from individuals who claimed to have gotten cancer. For example, in 2018, a California jury awarded a substantial settlement to a groundskeeper who developed non-Hodgkin's lymphoma after using Roundup (Yan 2018). It was only then that Monsanto announced plans to settle thousands of similar lawsuits. Yet, it is not illegal to use glyphosate in herbicides. Despite the controversy surrounding glyphosate and the legal challenges faced by companies like Monsanto, these products remain available for purchase in many markets. It won't be until it is officially banned that herbicide manufacturers will eventually react and remove the chemical from their list of ingredients.

Proactive Approach

Finally, the *proactive approach* involves management realizing that sustainability issues are reasonable, and they should be addressed as best and as soon as possible. Companies adopting this approach try to make sustainability part of their core business. Sustainability thus becomes a strategic issue for them; for example, regulatory changes like environmental taxes (or tax exemption for companies making efforts) in their external environment are seen in a positive light. Companies using a proactive approach can even aspire to more stringent demands than those presently existing – for instance, demands for higher costs in relation to the use of fossil energy resources – as this increases the competitiveness of sustainable companies in the marketplace (Guyader et al. 2020).

Syngenta (a major agricultural chemical company like Monsanto) downplayed concerns against glyphosate and continued to market its herbicides aggressively for years. However, as regulatory scrutiny and public awareness of glyphosate's risks have recently increased, Syngenta has been forced to reassess its approach. In 2020, Syngenta announced plans to phase out its production and sale of glyphosate-based herbicides in Europe by 2023, citing changing market conditions and regulatory developments. This decision reflects a more reactive approach to sustainability, since Syngenta made these changes in response to external pressures from the general public, rather than proactively addressing concerns about glyphosate's safety.

An example of the proactive approach is sustainability champion Patagonia, the outdoor clothing company: it has implemented various sustainability initiatives, including using recycled materials in its products, investing in renewable energy, and supporting environmental activism. Patagonia's commitment to sustainability is deeply ingrained in its corporate culture and business practices, making it a role model for other companies striving to make a positive impact. In the mobility industry, Tesla also exemplifies such a proactive approach to sustainability through its mission to accelerate the world's transition to sustainable energy. Tesla's products (electric cars, solar panels, and energy storage solutions) are designed to reduce reliance on fossil fuels and mitigate climate change. The company's visionary leadership and commitment to innovation have driven advancements in renewable energy technology, inspiring other companies to follow suit. These examples highlight how companies and organizations can take a proactive approach to sustainability by setting ambitious goals, implementing innovative solutions, and integrating sustainability into their core business strategies.

WA3RM Is Building a "Regenergy Project" in Sweden

An interesting example of a company with a proactive circular approach to sustainable development is Swedish firm WA3RM. The 3R stands for the key principles of WA3RM: Responsible, Renewable, and Recyclable. The company designs and finances industrial projects based on regenerating underutilized or discarded resources: surplus heat, waste sludge, or CO_2, for example, which are considered industrial waste. WA3RM manages the projects and provides the legal and financial structures. WA3RM has a "Regenergy project" in the small town of Frövi in Sweden, based on two greenhouses (10 ha) farming 8 000 tons of tomatoes per year. What's great is that the energy needed to grow the vegetables will be recovered from the excess heat from the neighboring pulp and paper mill. The excess heat would otherwise just be

(Continued)

(Continued)

Figure 4.2 Tomatoes growing in a greenhouse similar to the one in Frövi.
Source: Shutterstock 1612292698.

cooled off in a surrounding river. The regenergy greenhouses in Frövi make up the first successful demonstration of WA3RM. This means that about every 10th tomato in Sweden will be produced in Frövi (Figure 4.2). In addition to major environmental gains, more than 100 new full-time jobs have been created. WA3RM's business model is based on circularity: waste becomes a valuable resource. WA3RM earns money by procuring waste streams from the pulp and paper mill, and it leases the regenerating infrastructure bundled with the acquired resources to the operators of the tomato greenhouses. WA3RM has several similar projects planned in Europe: using residual heat from industrial processes (e.g. steel production, data centers) to produce sustainable food.

Source: https://www.wa3rm.com/regenergy-frovi.

The Circular Economy

Today, societies are paying to get rid of our waste through landfill fees and waste incineration. We are wasting perfectly good materials that can be reused. In this regard, the circular economy paradigm is a driver for change. The Ellen MacArthur Foundation, which has been leading such change by working with governments (for regulations) and companies (through consulting work) for more than a decade, defines the circular economy as "a systemic approach to economic development designed to benefit businesses, society, and the environment. In contrast to the 'take-make-waste' linear model, a circular economy is regenerative by design and aims to gradually decouple growth from the consumption of finite resources" (Ellen MacArthur Foundation 2019). Essential in the circular economy is creating more value out of waste – or valuing waste (Guyader et al. 2022).

Our current economic system is based on a linear system; that is, we produce quantities of goods by extracting and utilizing nature's resources, which are then used and disposed of to finally become waste. Since the industrial revolution, economic growth has gone hand in hand with an increased use of energy and natural resources and increasing amounts of waste. It is not possible to continue eroding the earth's resources in the same way as today. Sweden, the European Union, and the United Nations are promoting the circular economy paradigm among their goals for development and growth. This means working to ensure that as little as possible of the products used go to waste. The resources will instead be collected and recycled to be included in new production – sometimes called *upcycling*. Moreover, the goods that are produced should be usable as long as possible. But these goals are not particularly easy to achieve. For an economy to become circular, major changes in society are required.

The so-called butterfly diagram is a popular visualization of the circular economy made by Ellen MacArthur Foundation (see Figure 4.3). It represents circularity in two categories: biological materials and technical materials that have a set of loops for materials to circulate in (see also Chapter 8).

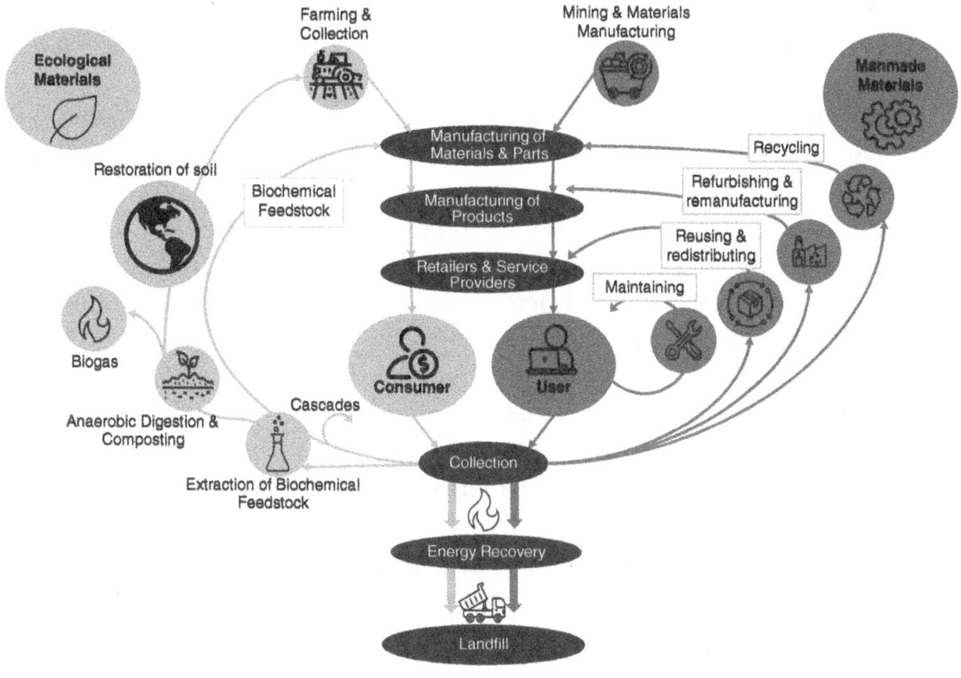

Figure 4.3 Circular Economy System.
Source: Based on Ellen MacArthur Foundation's (2019) butterfly diagram and McDonough and Braungart's (2002) cradle-to-cradle framework.

4Rs (or Even 9Rs) to Reach Sustainability

The following four activities increase circularity and commonly occur in literature (Kirchherr et al. 2017):

1. Reduce
2. Reuse
3. Recycle
4. Recover

Multiple versions of the 4R framework exist in literature today; one alternative is the 9R framework (van Buren et al. 2016), which is a more expanded version

1. Refuse: Preventing the use of raw materials
2. Reduce: Reducing the use of raw materials
3. Reuse: Product reuse (second-hand, sharing of products)
4. Repair: Maintenance and repair
5. Refurbish: Refurbishing a product
6. Remanufacture: Creating new products from (parts of) old products
7. Repurpose: Product reuse for a different purpose
8. Recycle: Processing and reuse of materials
9. Recover energy: Incineration of residual flows

Despite adding five extra activities, there are a lot of overlaps between the 4R and 9R frameworks and the loops in the Ellen MacArthur foundation butterfly diagram. The "maintain" activity, for example, includes "refuse" and "reduce" by keeping resources and products in use for longer life-cycles instead of manufacturing new ones. Both frameworks also lack the need to design new products that have a longer life-cycle, which we add here when discussing the five most important steps for an economy to be circular:

1. Reduce consumption of new things
2. Reuse more
3. Design products and packaging for a longer life-cycle
4. Recycle more material
5. Recover the resources that cannot be recycled

Reduce the Consumption of New Products

Although knowledge exists that we need to reduce the extraction of the earth's resources, consumption is increasing everywhere in the world. Reducing consumption in society represents a difficult challenge. The environmental impact of consumption is crucial for our future opportunities to live and consume. As the consumer society evolves, the wear-and-tear mentality has increasingly been replaced by a buy-and-throw-out mentality. That is to say that fully functional products are thrown away for reasons such as being outdated or not being the latest model. Kitchens are rebuilt and bathrooms are renovated even though they are fully functional.

For consumption to be reduced, the goods that are produced need to be of good quality so that they can be used for a long time and sometimes by several people. These days, objects are rarely repaired but are thrown away when they break. One reason is that it is often more expensive to repair than to buy new ones. Labor costs have increased, objects have become cheaper, and the ability to repair has diminished as well as specialist knowledge. Products must be able to be repaired and upgraded to a greater extent so that they become more durable and have a longer life. This requires changes in all parts of the economy.

Reuse More

Waste is the most important link between population, consumption, and climate change. The most important aspect is to identify and do something about waste that generates greenhouse gases. It is a challenge that deserves to be taken seriously. This requires commitment from consumers, but also from companies, organizations, and public authorities. Everyone has a responsibility to change direction. In a society where sustainability is emphasized, knowledge about repairing, reusing, and recycling will be valued higher than in a society that promotes consumption patterns with an emphasis on buy-and-throw-out.

For example, if a garment is used three times longer, its environmental impact decreases by as much as 70%. Recycling may, for example, be about sewing clothes. This was more common in the past, either by hiring a seamstress or by sewing yourself. Today, there are fewer seamstresses and tailors, and, in many cases, it is cheaper to buy new clothes than to repair torn clothes. The environmental impact of products can also be reduced if several people share things, by owning them together, or by borrowing or renting. Besides saving the environment, it is typically also cheaper.

Design Products and Packaging for a Longer Lifecycle

It is sometimes difficult to use some recycled material, as it is not clear what the products contain. Many products are composed of a variety of materials and additives. This means that hazardous chemicals risk being recycled together with the materials. Products containing hazardous chemicals need to be phased out and safely destroyed, and all new products that are produced must be able to be recycled in a safe manner.

Many products presently are also of poor quality. What is even worse is that these products are manufactured to prevent a longer life-cycle – that is called *planned obsolescence* and further discussed in Chapter 7. Manufacturers simply want you to buy new products instead of servicing existing products. Smartphones are one such example, as it is often impossible to just change their battery, which means the entire phone is discarded when simply a battery change could prolong the service life.

Recycle More Material

In large parts of the world today waste is just put in landfills. Such landfills, however, create severe environmental problems such as leakage of greenhouse gases and toxic substances, fires, alteration of the fauna and smell, and reduction of the value of surrounding land. Sweden is an exception internationally.

Sweden as a Global Leader in Waste Management

Since 2002, it has been prohibited in Sweden to deposit combustible waste, and in 2005, the ban was extended to include all organic waste. Sweden has developed a national system for sorting and recycling newspapers, glass, paper, metal, and plastic. Eighty-nine percent of the aluminum cans, 86% of the glass, and 82% of aluminum (including cans subject to deposit) and iron-based metal (steel) ended up in material recycling. Material recycling of plastic packaging was less successful; only 35% of plastic packaging, including plastic bottles with a deposit, went to material recycling. The proportion of recycled paper packaging was 78%, and the proportion for PET bottles with a deposit was 81% (SCB 2022).

There is currently no similar system for clothing and textiles, despite that cotton production generates large CO_2 emissions and uses massive amounts of water. This is however about to change since by 2025 at the latest, textile waste must be collected separately according to the European Union's new waste directive.

Visits to recycling centers testify to the fact that many people are willing to get rid of things after holidays when they have been off work, such as after Christmas, Easter, or Ascension Thursday. The country's approximately 590 recycling centers receive 26 million visits annually. In total, Swedish households hand in almost 5 tons of raw waste each year, which corresponds to approximately 466 kg per person.

At these recycling centers, people are expected to sort their waste, such as separating electronic equipment and building materials. Some municipalities have a secondary market in connection with the recycling center where people are offered the chance to buy what someone else no longer wants. One example is the "ReTuna Recycling Mall" in Eskilstuna, close to Stockholm. It is located next to the recycling center and enables consumers to leave things to be reused at ReTuna and other things (i.e. actual waste that nobody else would want) at the recycling center for recycling or incineration. Things can also be repaired to be sold again at ReTuna. In the shopping mall where ReTuna is located, there are a number of shops, a restaurant, an adult-learning, conference rooms, and an exhibition space. ReTuna is an example of the circular economy. Waste is not seen as a problem but as a resource, and products should be designed so that they can be reused.

Recover the Resources that Cannot be Recycled

According to the Food Waste Index Report of the United Nations Environment Program (UNEP 2024), one-third of all food produced is lost or wasted – around 1.3 billion tons of food per year – costing the global economy close to $940 billion each year. Up to 10% of global greenhouse gases come from food that is produced, but not eaten. The total food waste in the world could be used to feed 48% of the global population. Food waste is caused by low prices, ignorance, habits, and lifestyle factors, such as poor planning, curiosity regarding testing new food products, and various targeting options for different family members.

Thus, it is necessary to prevent food waste from occurring in the first place, and the food that nevertheless is wasted should be used in the best possible way. Much of the nutrition and energy that is present in the food waste can be used as a resource. All governments' goals should be to increasingly sort out organic waste from households, catering, shops, and restaurants and to process it biologically. If food waste is collected and converted into biogas in so-called digestive power plants, that waste becomes valuable as a source of energy! Biogas is formed naturally when food waste is broken down by microorganisms in an oxygen-free environment. Food waste will become biogas that can replace petrol and diesel in vehicles, and the leftover sludge from the transformation process can be used as a nutritious and eco-friendly fertilizer in agriculture. Then, the local cycle is closed, and we both reduce CO_2 emissions and return nutrients to our fields.

Reducing food waste is thus important internationally (Figure 4.4). On a global level, there is the United Nation's Sustainability Development Goal 12, target 12.3, on reducing food loss and waste by 2030 (One Planet Network 2024) and in the European Union, there are targets to reduce food waste by 2025.

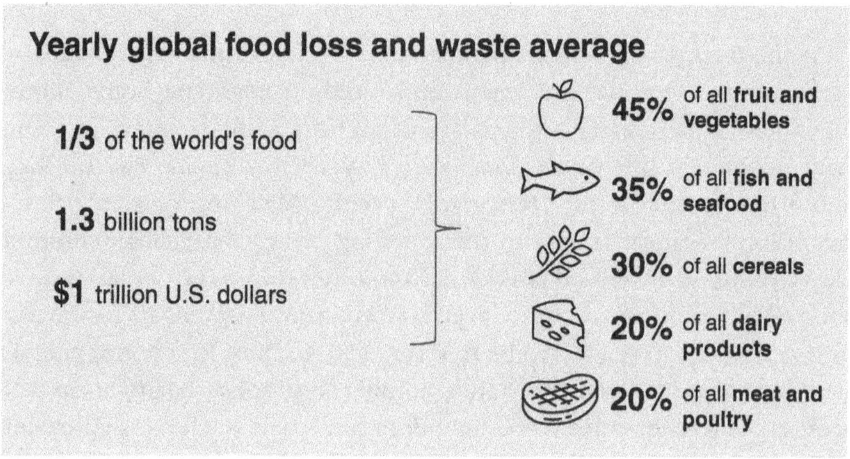

Figure 4.4 Yearly average global food loss and waste.
Source: Rezaei and Liu (2017).

Scope 1, 2, and 3 Emissions

Today it is common to talk about different types of emissions that relate to companies' activities. In sustainability reporting it is often referred to Scopes 1, 2, and 3. Scope 1 emissions are direct greenhouse gas emissions that occur from factories or buildings that are controlled or owned by the company. This might be emissions from fuel combustion in boilers or from company vehicles. Scope 2 emissions are indirect greenhouse gas emissions due to purchase of electricity, steam, heat, or cooling from suppliers. Scope 3 emissions are the result of activities not owned or controlled by the company but that are indirectly affected by the company. Scope 3 activities are thus found downstream in the company's value chain and can, for example, be emissions from transport and distribution as well as disposal and recycling (Figure 4.5).

Life-Cycle Analysis

Life-cycle analysis (LCA) is a method for analyzing products' socio-environmental performance over time. A product's life cycle encompasses all stages from raw material extraction, manufacturing, distribution, and usage to waste management. Calculations also include all intermediaries during distribution (e.g. wholesalers and retailers). LCA has a clear environmental focus, with economic and social sustainability dimensions considered only when the environment is somewhat affected. LCA, too, has been standardized by the International Organization for Standardization (ISO) through several different standards (i.e. the ISO 14040 series).

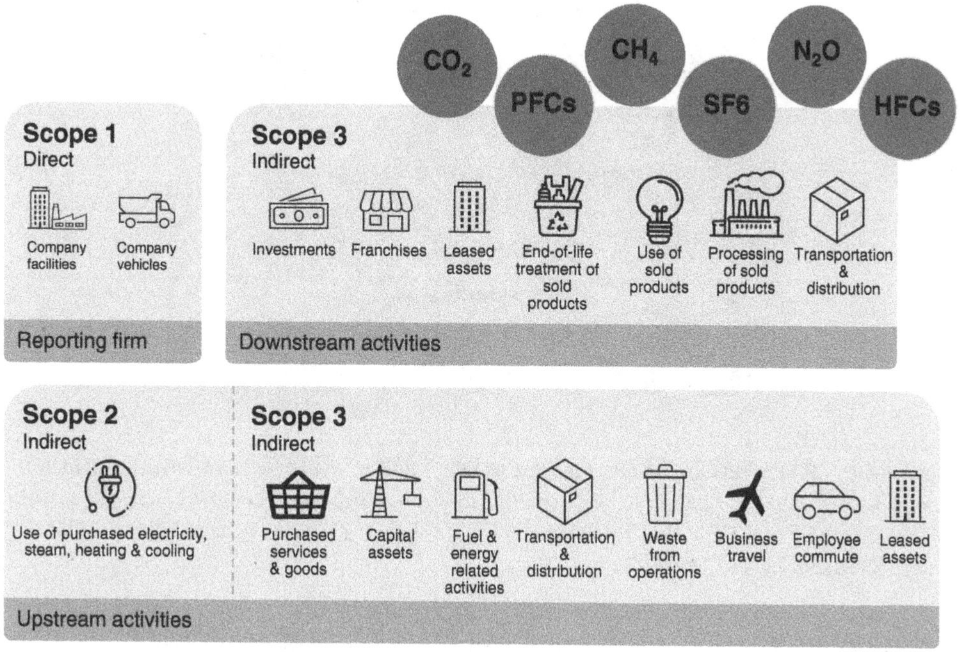

Figure 4.5 Scope 1, 2, and 3 emissions.
Source: Adapted from Bernoville (2022).

An LCA specifies which quantities of various natural resources have been consumed and which pollution has occurred in the air, soil, and water. This can be a matter of, for instance, emissions of CO_2. The compilation of such an analysis is usually called the LCA inventory data. This inventory data is then followed by an analysis of the environmental impact, in which factors such as climate impact, acidification, and resource depletion (among others) are analyzed. After having conducted an LCA, it may still be difficult to evaluate whether one product is more environmentally friendly than another, since it depends on how a certain environmental impact (e.g. air pollution) is evaluated in relation to another type of impact (e.g. biodiversity loss). However, an LCA provides companies with the opportunity of having actual data that can inform strategic decisions. LCAs are also being used increasingly by companies in their marketing communication.

An Example of LCA: Evaluating the Environmental Impact of E-Scooters

E-scooters have been spreading throughout the world since Lime and Bird were launched in the United States in 2017 and expanded to Europe in the summer of 2018. Competition between the different actors is tough (Blixt 2020). Glyde, a Swedish company, gave up the Stockholm market only three months after its launch! Despite the publicity e-scooters have received over the last few years, these

Figure 4.6 E-scooters are convenient but unsafe – and may not be as sustainable as many people assume. They are certainly contributing to cleaner air in city centers compared to vehicles running on fossil fuel – but their very short life span is a serious sustainability problem. *Source:* Shutterstock 1612292698.

companies have quite a few problems to solve to ensure that they become and remain an integral part of the shared mobility ecosystem – notwithstanding their financial viability. Many companies launched before 2020 no longer exist due to unsustainable business models, e.g. the costs of maintaining a fleet of free-floating e-scooters are higher than revenues from infrequent users (Figure 4.6).

These electric dockless kick scooters are available in major cities for short-term rentals – for anybody with a smartphone. They are marketed as "smooth" and "cool" but also "emissions free" or "climate-friendly." For instance, Lime argues that riding e-scooters reduces society's dependence on private car ownership and "leaves future generations a cleaner and healthier planet." Bird claims that e-scooters enable users to "cruise past traffic and cut back on CO_2 emissions – one ride at a time" (Temple 2019). VOI, in Sweden, asserts to offer a "clean, convenient, cost-friendly, car-shrinking alternative." But is that really true?

Several reports show that such environmentally friendly statements are unfounded: the lifetime of the first generation of e-scooters was only 40–60 days (i.e. five to eight weeks). This means for example that 8 000–12 000 e-scooters in Stockholm alone could end up the junkyard in one year. Facing these allegations, VOI says that most of the time, their e-scooters can be fixed – without giving any figures). Considering the fact that it takes about 10 weeks (at approximately $30 per week) for e-scooter companies to cover the acquisition costs of an e-scooter ($300) – which is almost twice as long as their lifetime – it is definitely a problem worth investigating for all market actors!

According to Hollingsworth et al. (2019), who conducted a study based on an LCA, the actual environmental impact of e-scooters is heavily dependent (at 50%)

on how they are manufactured – most often in China, and then shipped internationally, how they are replaced or recycled – especially the lithium-ion battery and the aluminum frame and the length of their lifetime. Moreover, e-scooters are also collected, charged, and moved around where needed the most – by car or truck – which altogether can greatly contribute to global warming (approximately 43% impact), rather than mitigating it.

Hollingsworth et al.'s (2019) study shows that e-scooters actually produce more CO_2 emissions per passenger than a bus, an electric moped, and an electric bicycle, as well as, of course, a normal bike or just walking. To be precise, e-scooters produce half the emissions of a standard car – 202 g versus 415 g of CO_2 per mile. The study also found that if e-scooters did not exist, only 34% of customers would have used a private car or ride-hailing service (e.g. Uber), 49% would have biked or walked, and 11% would have taken the bus, whereas 7% would not have traveled at all (Hollingsworth et al. 2019).

However, some claim that the LCA was not properly executed as the assessments of CO_2 emissions per trip were made without considering the total environmental impact of a mobility option (HaveAGo 2019). Such a total LCA should have included how private cars are manufactured and maintained, but also the infrastructure necessary for their use and the various externalities of driving cars, such as deaths and injuries due to traffic. Besides, the LCA study did not take car ownership into their calculations either, which may eliminate sources of emissions such as wear and tear by 50%. Eventually, one has to note that benefits (i.e. increased use of public transit thanks to riding e-scooters) are not addressed in such an LCA.

Hollingsworth et al. (2019) conclude their study by stating that emissions from e-scooters could be reduced by 30% (to 142 g CO_2 emission) if their lifetime was extended to two years, instead of a couple of months. The researchers also advised cities to enforce policies to reduce vandalism of e-scooters and advised companies to act to make e-scooter collection, charging, and distribution more efficient. For consumers, the most environmentally friendly mobility option will always be walking.

Getting Companies to Walk the Talk

Market solutions, public instruments of control, and collaboration between the private sector and public actors, or between private and public actors, are three different ways of exerting influence on companies, organizations, and consumers (Eriksson and Bonnedahl 2009).

Market Solutions

In recent years, market solutions have gained increased acceptance, based on the insight that they can be a cost-effective way of swaying people's consumption in a more sustainable direction. The *pricing mechanism* holds a unique position here and is based on the logic that prices increasingly internalize (include) the negative (and possibly positive) sustainability effects of consumption.

Over the years, a lot of criticism has been leveled at market solutions and the pricing mechanism as a solution to consumption problems. For the pricing mechanism to optimally work, a functioning and effective market is required, as well as consumers who are informed about benefits and prices and who thus act rationally. When the market mechanism works, it is without a doubt a quick and effective way of altering consumption; however, at the same time, different types of transaction costs can undermine its effectiveness (Eriksson and Bonnedahl 2009). It has also turned out to be very difficult to include the future costs of sustainability aspects. Above all, the difficulty relates to the size of the discount factors used to value current and future assets. In practice, this may entail us depreciating future assets in relation to present-day consumption (Stern 2006). Nor may future generations plead their case. Consequently, present generations tend to underestimate the value of future generations' access to water and other necessities.

Policy Instruments

Market-based policy instruments can be related to market failures (i.e. the fact that consumption and production do not fully take into consideration the socio-economic costs consumption gives rise to). Nonsustainable costs should thus be internalized into calculations and into economic supporting data with the aim of making the polluter pay (Eriksson and Bonnedahl 2009). Examples of policy instruments applying such an approach include charges and taxes. In Sweden, a number of taxes and charges of this type are imposed by the government to balance unsustainable consumption behaviors, such as energy taxes on engine fuels and heating oil, as well as congestion charges upon entering and leaving Stockholm and Gothenburg by car. The idea behind environmental taxes and charges is that the cost of, for example, driving a car must be visible in the price, thus exerting influence on the choices made by consumers.

A key question in this context is which level of taxes or charges is required in order to exert influence on this behavior. In the case of too low a price being attached to pollution, no meaningful change will be achieved. Too high a price may, on the other hand, be deemed unfair from an economic sustainability perspective, as this will mean that richer people can afford to pollute while poorer people will, for instance, be forced to leave their cars at home (Eriksson and Bonnedahl 2009, p. 68). In practice, however, this is actually already the case on a global scale due to the major income gaps that exist between various regions of the world.

Environment-related subsidies also occur. France and many other European countries use environmental car bonus systems. Tax reductions are also used in some countries to reduce costs when installing green technology. Other policy instruments include administrative policy instruments such as licensing and prohibition.

Subsidies often encounter criticism from various actors, something that is not particularly surprising since they naturally relate to interventions into market mechanisms. Norway has had a very comprehensive support system for electric cars resulting in almost 80% of all sold cars in 2022 being electrical cars. These electric cars are exempt from value-added tax (VAT) and are also not subjected to an extra car tax at the time of purchase – something that cars with a combustion engine are subject to. These electric cars also have extra benefits (e.g. they are allowed to drive in bus lanes and charging and parking are in many cases free). This support scheme, however, has been costly for the Norwegian state and a research study stated "Intriguingly, more than half of the households owning battery electric vehicles had three or more of these vehicles in 2022, indicating an unbalanced ownership distribution concentrating on the wealthiest" (Qorbani et al. 2024, p. 1).

Several different types of policy instruments are used in different countries. For companies not complying with laws or other stipulations in the fields of natural or working environment, governments have the possibility to, via its agencies and courts, bring sanctions to bear in the form of, for instance, fines and levies. Legal instruments of control are thus usually referred to as mandatory or "hard" instruments of control.

Economic instruments of control are not mandatory, instead aimed at "correcting" incorrect pricing signals in markets. They either work as carrots (e.g. tax relief, contributions, and support) or sticks (e.g. taxes and levies) guiding companies' or consumers' actions in a more sustainable direction.

Collaboration to Promote Sustainability

Looking at collaboration as a form of influence, Eriksson and Bonnedahl (2009) consider different types of collaboration between, for example, consumer and industry interests and the government. One such example is the collaboration between the automotive industry and the government regarding CO_2 emission limits (Eriksson and Bonnedahl 2009, p. 70). This may also concern voluntary agreements that take place under, for example, the threat of legislation on the part of politicians. Other examples include sector agreements, training endeavors, environmental management systems, standards, and eco-labeling. These types of initiatives normally aim to be informative, enlightening consumers with regard to their impact on sustainability.

In the increasingly polarized society today, collaboration is however often getting more and more difficult even in industry associations. For example, Houdini, the Swedish outdoor brand known for being at the forefront of sustainable performance design (e.g. down-free jackets, free service of broken zippers) announced in 2023 that they don't longer want to be a part of the Confederation of Swedish Enterprises due to the Confederation's defensive approach toward climate change in general and specifically its support of right-wing think-tank Timbro (Ternby and Stiernstedt 2023, p. 13).

References

Benyus, J. (1997). *Biomimicry: Innovation Inspired by Nature.* William Morrow & Co, New York.

Bernoville, T. (2022). What are Scopes 1, 2 and 3 of Carbon Emissions? *Plan A.* June 12, 2022. https://plana.earth/academy/what-are-scope-1-2-3-emissions (accessed 8 February 2024).

Blixt, T. (2020). Voi-grundaren tror på masslakt bland scooter-boolagen. Breakit. January 7, 2020. https://www.breakit.se/artikel/23164/voi-grundaren-tror-pa-masslakt-bland-scooter-bolagen (accessed 3 June 2024).

van Buren, N., Demmers, M., van der Heijden, R., & Witlox, F. (2016). Towards a circular economy: the role of Dutch logistics industries and governments. *Sustainability* 8(7), 647.

Burgueño Salas, E. (2023). Leading sustainability actions taken up by companies globally 2022. *Statista.* November 8, 2023. https://www.statista.com/statistics/1323546/major-global-sustainability-actions-by-companies (accessed 8 February 2024).

De Pauw, I., Kandachar, P., Karana, E., Peck, D., & Wever, R. (2010). Nature inspired design: Strategies towards sustainability. In *Knowledge Collaboration & Learning for Sustainable Innovation: 14th European Roundtable on Sustainable Consumption and Production (ERSCP) conference and the 6th Environmental Management for Sustainable Universities (EMSU) conference, Delft, The Netherlands, October 25–29, 2010.* Delft University of Technology; The Hague University of Applied Sciences; TNO.

Ellen MacArthur Foundation (2019). The Circular Economy in Detail. https://www.ellenmacarthurfoundation.org/the-circular-economy-in-detail-deep- (accessed 3 February 2024).

Eriksson, J. & Bonnedahl, K.J. (2009). *Hållbar konsumtion: (Hur) är det möjligt?* In: P.Braunerhjelm (ed.), *Entreprenörskap och innovationer för hållbar utveckling.* Swedish Economic Forum Report 2009. Örebro: Entreprenörskapsforum

George, S. (2020). 'Hypocrisy': Consumer goods giants accused of covert lobbying against stronger plastics legislation. September 17, 2020. https://www.edie.net/hypocrisy-consumer-goods-giants-accused-of-covert-lobbying-against-stronger-plastics-legislation (accessed 3 April 2024).

Guyader, H., Ottosson, M. and Parment, A. (2020) *Marketing & Sustainability: Why and how Sustainability Is Changing Current Marketing Practices.* Lund: Studentlitteratur. ISBN 9789144139869.

Guyader, H., Ponsignon, F., Salignac, F. and Bojovic, N. (2022). Beyond a mediocre customer experience in the circular economy: the satisfaction of contributing to the ecological transition. *Journal of Cleaner Production,* 378, 134495.

HaveAGo (2019). How a simplistic life cycle analysis completely misrepresented scooter emissions and caused a media flurry of bad science. https://haveago.city/life-cyle-analysis-analysis (accessed 3 May 2024).

Herman Miller (n.d.). https://www.hermanmiller.com/better-world/sustainability (accessed 1 May 2024).

Hollingsworth, J., Copeland, B., & Johnson, J. (2019). Are e-scooters polluters? The environmental impacts of shared dockless electric scooters. *Environmental Research Letters,* 14(8), 084031

Kekic, A. Stojanovic Bjelic, L. & Noskovic Markic, D. (2020). Nature-inspired design: biomimicry and cradle to cradle. *Quality of Life,* 11, 58–66.

Kennedy, E.B., & Marting, T. A. (2016). Biomimicry: streamlining the front end of innovation for environmentally sustainable products. *Research-Technology Management,* 59, 40–48.

Kirchherr, J., Reike, D., & Hekkert, M. (2017). Conceptualizing the circular economy: an analysis of 114 definitions. *Resources, Conservation and Recycling*, 127, 221–232.

McDonough, W., Braungart, M., 2002. *Cradle to Cradle: Remaking the Way we Make Things*. North Point Press, New York.

One Planet Network (2024). Target 12.3 food loss & waste. https://sdg12hub.org/sdg-12-hub/see-progress-on-sdg-12-by-target/123-food-loss-waste (accessed 7 April 2024).

de Pauw, I. C., Karana, E., Kandachar, P., & Poppelaars, F. (2014). Comparing biomimicry and cradle to cradle with EcoDesign: a case study of student design projects. *Journal of Cleaner Production* 78, 174–183.

Qorbani, D., Korzilius, H.P.L.M. & Fleten, SE. (2024). Ownership of battery electric vehicles is uneven in Norwegian households. *Communications Earth & Environment*, 5, 170.

Rezaei & Liu (2017). Food loss and waste in the food supply chain. NutFruit. July 2017. https://www.fao.org/save-food/resources (accessed 26 March 2024).

SCB (2022) https://www.scb.se/hitta-statistik/sverige-i-siffror/miljo/atervinning-av-forpackningar-i-sverige (accessed 11 March 2024).

Söderqvist, N. (2021). Notan för miljötillstånden: 50 miljarder kronor. November 18, 2021. https://www.svensktnaringsliv.se/sakomraden/hallbarhet-miljo-och-energi/notan-for-miljotillstanden-50-miljarder-kronor_1177481.html (accessed 11 March 2024).

Stern, N. (2006). *Stern Review on the Economics of Climate Change*. Cambridge: Cambridge University Press.

Stevens, L., DeVries, M. M. Bos, M.M., & Kopnina H. (2019). Biomimicry design education essentials. In *Proceedings of the Design Society: International Conference on Engineering Design*, 1, 459–468.

Temple, J. (2019). Sorry, scooters aren't so climate-friendly after all. *MIT Technology Review*. August 2, 2019. https://www.technologyreview.com/2019/08/02/646/electric-scooters-arent-so-climate-friendly-after-all-lime-bird (accessed 4 April 2024).

Ternby, L. & Stiernstedt J. (2023) Omställningen skapar kaos hos branschorganisationer. *Dagens Industri*. March 26, 2023. https://www.di.se/nyheter/omstallningen-skapar-kaos-hos-branschorganisationer (accessed 7 March 2024).

Tighe, D. (2024). Global: most common sustainability initatives by brands 2021–2022. *Statista*. March 11, 2024. https://www.statista.com/statistics/1305916/main-sustainability-initiatives-by-brands-worldwide (accessed 5 April 2024).

UNEP (2024). Food Waste Index Report. https://www.unep.org/resources/publication/food-waste-index-report-2024 (accessed 5 April 2024).

Vaughan, A. (2018). BP's Deepwater Horizon bill tops $65bn. *The Guardian*. January 16, 2018. https://www.theguardian.com/business/2018/jan/16/bps-deepwater-horizon-bill-tops-65bn (accessed 16 March 2024).

Yan, H. (2018). Jurors give $289 million to man they say got cancer from Monsanto's Roundup weedkiller. CNN.com. August 11, 2018. https://www.cnn.com/2018/08/10/health/monsanto-johnson-trial-verdict/index.html (accessed 16 March 2024).

Chapter 5

Sustainability by Service Provision

Much of the early work regarding companies and sustainability focused on manufacturing firms and their emissions to air, water, and soil. In this chapter we introduce service research, which increasingly has started to analyze how service provision could become more sustainable. We uncover innovative ways to reduce environmental impacts within the service sector, which plays a crucial role in modern economies. Additionally, a deeper understanding of sustainability in service provision can drive the development of new practices that support long-term ecological balance and social well-being.

Learning Objectives

- Differentiate service marketing from goods marketing
- Explain what the rental paradigm and access-based services are
- Understand the concept of sustainable service
- Explain what sustainable service ecosystems are
- Understand the sharing economy paradigm and peer-to-peer (P2P) services

Introduction

The inception of the subdiscipline of service marketing (i.e. the marketing of services) started when the characteristics of services were established to differentiate them from pure tangible goods in the late twentieth century, and then these characteristics were debated, critiqued, and expanded upon in the early 2000s (Sasser et al. 1978; Lovelock and Gummesson 2004; Moeller 2010). Over time, the premise that goods are part of service provision, that they are merely a vehicle for service delivery, and, hence, that services should be the basis for economic exchange vis-à-vis goods, took hold. This view is the basis of what we can call the service economy – which can be considered the ancestor of the more recent sharing paradigm. We will see that offering services can reduce the environmental impact of consumption through better resource efficiency (compared to the traditional commerce of goods). Yet as service sectors dominate the world (e.g. consider all services related to logistics and transportation), these firms need to pay attention to how their diverse value-creation and delivery processes influence sustainability.

The Development of Service Marketing and Service Research

Marketing was established as a discipline with the exchange of goods at its core. That made sense in the early twentieth century (1900s–1940s), as the global economy was primarily agrarian and industrial. However, as industrialization progressed and urbanization increased, the demand for services such as transportation, finance, and retail began to grow. By the mid-twentieth century (1950s–1970s), the services sector experienced significant growth – banking, healthcare, education, and tourism – driven by technological advancements, increased consumer spending, and the expansion of the middle class. In academia, marketing scholars began to criticize manufacturing firms for suffering from *marketing myopia* (i.e. only preoccupied with converting merchandize into cash) instead of satisfying customer needs (Levitt 1960; Judd 1964; Berry and Maricle 1973). Services were defined at the time as anything "other than the transfer of ownership of a tangible commodity" (Judd 1964, p. 59). Thus, a goods versus services debate arose (Johnson 1969) and eventually focused on service firms (Shostack 1977) with an adapted marketing nomenclature (Grönroos 1978). Since then, four defining characteristics have been regularly applied to services: intangibility, heterogeneity, inseparability, and perishability (IHIP; Sasser et al. 1978). It is these IHIP characteristics that differentiate service provision from goods:

- *Intangibility:* Services cannot be directly observed or evaluated prior to delivery. Intangibility is assigned to the service offering. For example, a haircut can't be seen before it's done
- *Heterogeneity:* Service outputs vary widely depending on the customer and service provider. For example, a haircut varies for each customer (due to their hair) but also for each hairdresser (due to their specific skills)
- *Inseparability:* Production and consumption are simultaneous. For example, a haircut can't be done before the customer and hairdresser meet
- *Perishability:* Services cannot be stored. For example, a haircut can't be stored and sold on a supermarket shelf

The concept of marketing mix based on the 4Ps of marketing (i.e. Product, Price, Place, and Promotion) is one of the core concepts of marketing theory (McCarthy 1964). However, the 4Ps have increasingly come under attack with the result that different marketing mixes have been put forward for different marketing contexts (e.g. the 4Cs, the 4Es). While numerous modifications to the 4Ps framework have been proposed, the most concerted criticism has come from the service marketing scholars: Booms and Bitner (1982). They proposed to extend the traditional McCarthy (1964) 4Ps with three additional Ps to make up the 7Ps of service marketing:

- *Process:* Services are process-like and require interaction with customers; this process needs to be designed. For example, Starbucks is a chain of cafés that use the same process worldwide, which enables the provision of the same sophisticated experience/ambiance everywhere. The supply chain from the procurement of coffee beans to the delivery of coffee and other products in any Starbucks store is well-managed and uses the highest technology to maintain premium standards. Starbucks also offers automated kiosks and machines in a few locations
- *People:* Many services are delivered by employees whose skills and behavior affect service outcomes and customer satisfaction. For example, Starbucks is a customer-centric company, where baristas write the names of every individual differently on the coffee cups. Starbucks claims the way they hire, develop, and advance their employees is fundamental to their commitment to create a place of belonging. Baristas are key links in Starbucks' value chain
- *Physical evidence:* Physical evidence is often still necessary to make immaterial services more concrete and tangible. For example, Starbucks' stores, ambiance, coffee mugs/glasses with the logo printed, paper napkins, etc. all come under the physical evidence of the brand
- *Material signs:* To make intangible services more concrete, material signs are often still required

Meanwhile, the importance of service sectors in the global economy (like telecommunications, information technology, and financial services) continued to increase in the late twentieth century (1980s–1990s) due to globalization, deregulation, and advances in information and communication technologies (ICT) like the Internet. Around that time, Johnson et al. (1998) explored shared usage and access-based consumption (i.e. the core ideas of the sharing economy) when they conceptually differentiated product-sharing services from conventional ownership, leasing, and renting modes. Such services offer new commercial opportunities because multiple "customers have the opportunity to use the same product at different times during the same contract period" (p. 169). Their empirical study of car sharing (a service we present later along with other shared mobility services) showed that customers perceive rental costs, period of advance booking notice, return options and location flexibility, distance to parking lot, and opening hours as the most important service attributes. Johnson et al. (1998, p. 172) wrote that "although each vehicle is theoretically 'shared' by between three and five people, the goal is to guarantee the availability by having a vehicle stock (as long as the demand is predictable)." Hence, product-sharing services offer flexibility and convenience compared to ownership, and firms should use them to expand their portfolio of offerings and to grow and expand their market. Other than cars, goods that can be potentially shared are those that are expensive, are infrequently used, and where access can be predicted/contracted (Johnson et al. 1998), like an apartment, sports gear, or high-tech equipment – all available to rental by diverse service firms nowadays.

From Ownership to Access

Similarly, Lovelock and Gummesson (2004) argued that services offer the benefits of product ownership but without actual ownership. They criticized the contemporary paradigm that differentiated services from goods based on the historic four IHIP dimensions of services for being flawed. Instead, they argued for an *access paradigm*, or *rental paradigm*, in which "services offer benefits through access or temporary possession, instead of ownership, with payments taking the form of rentals or access fees" (p. 20). As such, Lovelock and Gummesson (2004) focused on the lack of transfer of ownership in services as the basis for the access paradigm – this is fundamentally different from secondhand market sales where goods change hands and owners. They also identified five access-based service categories to illustrate their point (Lovelock and Gummesson 2004):

- Rented goods services (e.g. renting a machine)
- Place and space rentals (e.g. manufacturing facilities)

- Labor and expertise rentals (e.g. hiring a lawyer)
- Physical facility access and usage (e.g. renting admission to a conference site)
- Network access and usage (e.g. telecommunications)

Lovelock and Gummesson (2004) dusted off the concept of *nonownership* (first conceptualized by Berry and Maricle 1973), which they defined as "marketing transactions that do not involve a transfer of ownership" (p. 34), and they used this definition as the basis of the access paradigm. These articles so far emphasized how firms can leverage material assets to sell a service to customers instead of goods – in other words, new opportunities to satisfy customers and provide them with the benefits of ownership through rental services.

In the twenty-first century, the services sector continued to dominate the global economy: more than 50% of GDP in average in the world, 70–80% in developed and high-income economies (e.g. U.S., UK, France, Japan, etc.), and around 20–40% in developing and low-income counties (Global Economy 2023). See Figure 5.1 for example of the growth of the share of services in the gross domestic product (GDP) in the United States. Technological innovation, digitalization, and the rise of the knowledge economy have further accelerated the growth of service industries such as software development, e-commerce, digital media, and professional services. In sum, the share of services (versus manufacturing and

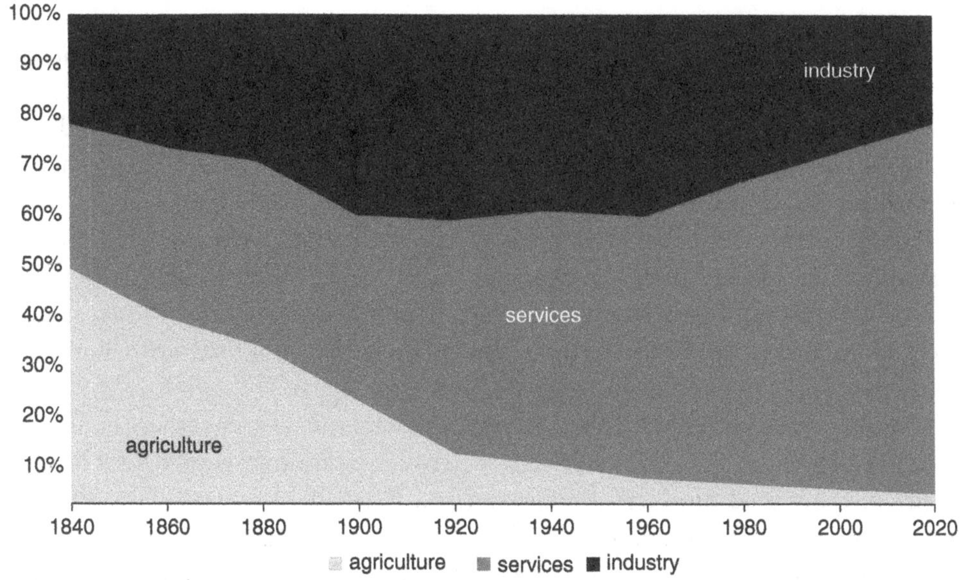

Figure 5.1 The growth of the share of services (and agricultural and industrial sectors) in GDP (US).
Source: Authors' own.

the production of goods) has steadily increased over the past century, reflecting the ongoing transition from agriculture and industrial economies to service economies – which the "access economy" or "sharing economy" are embedded in, as we will discuss shortly.

Early research on sharing systems looked at the grassroots and community levels, such as shared community networks that focus on the recirculation and reuse of goods such as clothing exchanges (Albinsson and Perera 2009), community building through toy libraries (Ozanne and Ozanne 2011), and recirculation in alternative marketplaces (Albinsson and Perera 2012). Another research stream concentrated on more formalized so-called plentitude economies where consumers bartered, exchanged, and shared goods and services. These were some of the precursors to access-based consumption (Bardhi and Eckhardt 2012) and product-service systems (PSSs) (e.g. Mont and Tukker 2006). For example, Moeller and Wittkowski (2010) built on the concept of "nonownership" and proposed that the *burdens of ownership* can be alleviated by rental services. They argued that the importance of possessions (i.e. attachment to ownership), trend orientation (i.e. trying new things), convenience orientation, experience orientation (i.e. looking for fun in consumption), price consciousness, and environmentalism would influence consumers' decision to rent goods rather than buy and own them (Moeller and Wittkowski 2010). They showed that only possession importance (negative influence) and trend and convenience orientations (positive influence) had significant effects on the adoption of nonownership services.

Lamberton and Rose (2012) conceptualized what they called *commercial sharing programs* as market-mediated systems (i.e. based on monetary exchanges) that offer consumers a sustainable and profitable alternative to ownership. People would participate in such commercial sharing programs because of the cost savings that can be realized, but also for their self-interest and for utilitarian motives (rather than hedonic motives). Schaefers et al. (2016a) and Bardhi and Eckhardt (2012)'s car-sharing studies (of Car2Go and Zipcar customers, respectively) also found the same. On the other hand, Lamberton and Rose (2012) found that people would not be likely to participate if they value possessions or if they hold strong materialism values (like Moeller and Wittkowski's 2010 study of apparel rental). It is important to note that these commercial sharing systems are based on business-to-consumer (B2C) relationships, "[...] characterized by between-consumer rivalry for a limited supply of the shared product" (Lamberton and Rose 2012, p. 109). For example, two customers can be in competition to rent and use the same vehicle offered by a car sharing firm. These two customers cannot use the vehicle at the same time, but only sequentially. In essence, customers would pay a fee for the time they use the shared goods, but an additional membership fee can be added (e.g. one needs to be a member of a car-sharing firm and pay a small monthly fee, to benefit from a lower usage cost).

Access-Based Services

Service research eventually adopted the term *access-based services* (see also Figure 5.2), defined as

> "market-mediated transactions that provide customers with temporally limited access to goods in return for an access fee, while the legal ownership remains with the service provider. At the core of an access-based service is thus an asset that is successively used by multiple individuals (i.e. shared) over time"

(Schaefers et al. 2016a, p. 571). While the term *access-based consumption* was used by Bardhi and Eckhardt (2012), the term *access-based services* first appeared in services research that investigated motives behind commercial car-sharing participation (Schaefers 2013a). He showed that not only utilitarian motives (cost-saving and convenience) but also affective motives (environmentalism and lifestyle trends)

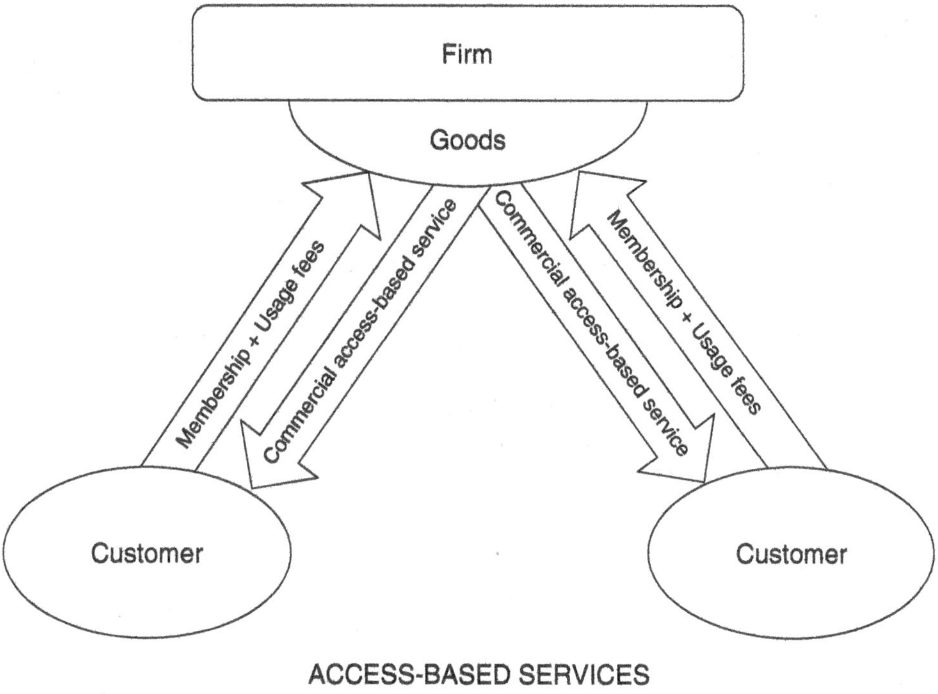

Figure 5.2 Access-based services business model.
Source: Authors' own.

were driving the acceptance and usage of car sharing (Schaefers 2013b). In line with this, Hazée et al. (2017) redefined access-based services by emphasizing the "unique technology-based service innovations," which they characterized as follows:

- High customer involvement with minimal supervision from the service provider (e.g. using a smartcard or a mobile phone app to access a car-sharing vehicle without talking to a representative of the firm)
- Substantial interpersonal anonymity
- Temporal access to goods – without permanent transfer of ownership

In another study, Schaefers et al. (2016b) showed that customer misbehavior in the context of access-based services is contagious but not if people feel part of a community. Importantly, communal identification reversed the contagious effect. Hazée et al. (2017) also argued that the participation motive in access-based services is to alleviate the burdens of ownership (Berry and Maricle 1973; Moeller and Wittkowski 2010), but they further showed that customers encounter the *burdens of access* constituted by the barriers themselves (i.e. complexity, reliability, contamination, responsibility, compatibility, and image barriers), as well as the practices that customers engage in to attenuate those barriers. That is, firms commercializing access-based services where multiple customers sequentially share usage of the same goods encounter different challenges than traditional firms selling goods on B2C markets or traditional rental services (due to the short duration of rental period). It is also interesting to note that Lawson (2010) was among the first consumer researchers to look at this paradigm shift that she called *nonownership consumption*. She defined participants in such access-based consumption as "transumers": they are driven by experience (i.e. based on value-in-use) instead of ownership (i.e. based on value-in-exchange) by living a transient lifestyle away from possessions. Today these transumers intentionally living with few things are called *minimalists*. The minimalist lifestyle is a philosophy centered around simplifying one's life by focusing on what is essential and letting go of excess possessions, distractions, and commitments. It emphasizes the pursuit of intentional living, where individuals prioritize experiences, relationships, and personal growth over material possessions. Made popular by Japanese Marie Kondo (in her book and a popular Netflix show), minimalists aim to "declutter" their physical spaces, digital environments, and schedules to create room for what truly matters to them, what makes them happy, and what "sparks joy" (DeVries 2019). This lifestyle encourages mindfulness, sustainability, and financial freedom by fostering a deeper appreciation for the things that add value to one's life while reducing the burden of unnecessary clutter and consumerism.

Another term and lifestyle put forth by consumer research scholars is *liquid consumption*, which is conceptualized in opposition to the traditional *solid consumption*, which is ownership-based, enduring, and tangible stuff (Bardhi and Eckhardt 2017; Eckhardt and Bardhi 2020). As such, liquid consumption is characterized by more fluid, ephemeral (i.e. temporal), access-based, and dematerialized consumption patterns (Bardhi et al. 2012; Bardhi and Eckhardt 2017). This perspective underscores consumption values like flexibility, adaptability, fluidity, lightness, detachment, and speed. Thus, liquid consumption is particularly relevant in digital contexts. For example, Atanasova et al. (2024) studied "digital nomads" for four years, during turbulent times that call for agility and adaptability (like pandemics or economic recessions we've experienced since 2020), and they found that they benefit from *liquid consumer security*, defined as "a form of felt security that stems from avoidance of solid consumption and its risks and responsibilities" (p.1244) – contrary to solid consumers who are more vulnerable. Liquid consumer security is characterized by a lack of ownership, attachments, or rootedness, contrasting with the temporal demands, financial liabilities, and commitments associated with solid consumption, which pose risks. This security is attained through three strategies: minimizing solid risks, reconstructing security through the liquid marketplace, and ideological legitimization. Ultimately, this concept of liquid consumption has implications across various domains, including attachment and appropriation, the importance of use value, materialism, brand relationships and communities, identity, prosumption, big data, quantification of the self, and surveillance (Bardhi and Eckhardt 2017).

In summary, "everything is a service" in the *Age of Access* (Rifkin 2000). The future of business activities is based on the provision of access-based consumption, through service, since consumers find using goods on a short-term basis through service provision (e.g. rental) more convenient, flexible, and cost-efficient than acquisition and private individual ownership. The access paradigm has become a nonownership lifestyle (popular among millennials) that is focused on service experience instead of material possession. For example, the function of possessing the car as a status-signal for adulthood and autonomy has shifted to value-in-use (Rifkin 2000) rather than value-in-ownership or its inventory-value (e.g. Houston and Gassenheimer 1987).

The conceptualization of service as value cocreation between customer(s) and provider(s) further enabled the development of service marketing as its own discipline (see Figure 5.3).

Sustainable Services

As the service sectors dominate the world's economies, how these services are provided account for a large environmental impact, but they also represent a great potential for improving resource efficiency when making use of goods more efficiently. Gummesson (1993) was the first to introduce the notion of "green service quality" at a marketing conference in Sweden. He then emphasized "[...] that services have just as much impact on the environment as goods" (Gummesson 2000, p. 122). In other words, "greening" service firms and their value propositions should

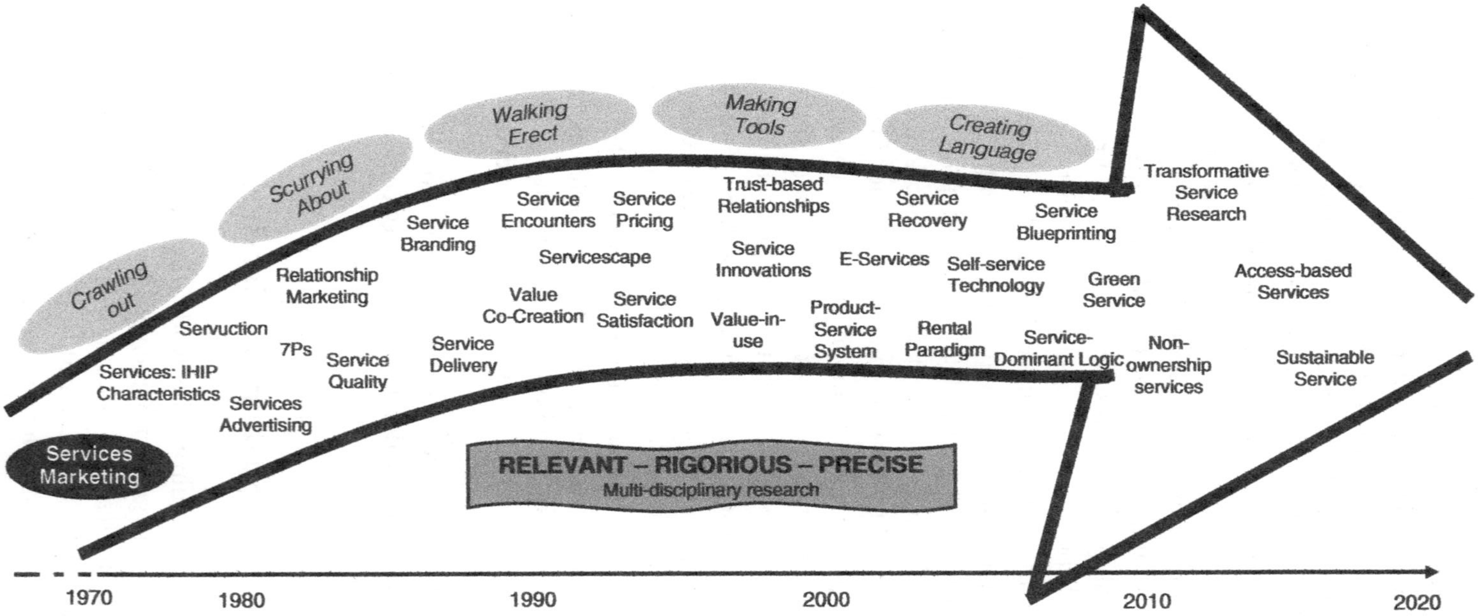

Figure 5.3 Evolution of service research as a discipline.
Source: Adapted from Guyader et al. (2019).

be pursued while providing excellent customer experiences (Grove et al. 1996; Graedel 2003). To provide a *sustainable service* can be defined as service provision aimed at improving the well-being of the natural ecosystem in order "to better the quality of life of present and future generations" (Guyader et al. 2019, p. 840). Hence, sustainable services are not only service provision focused on satisfying customer needs (i.e. reducing the environmental impact of consumption), but also focused on improving environmental benefits.

Today, developing sustainable services is at least as important as designing eco-efficient products. At a time when natural resources risk being depleted, sustainable services may in fact increase the resources of the natural ecosystem to preserve humanity. That is, it is time to take a step further: we must concentrate not only on reducing the negative impact on the environment but should also work to strengthen and expand the ecosystem. This is not a case of doing the same thing with fewer resources, but rather doing more with fewer resources. What does this mean in practice? For example:

- Transportation firm A wants to reduce its negative impact on the environment and thus takes a number of measures to reduce fuel consumption. The drivers drive more gently and keep the speed limits, the company purchases new vehicles with modern engines that conform to stringent emission limits, etc
- Transportation firm B invests in biogas-powered vehicles and not only reduces its own carbon footprint but also contributes to increasing the demand for renewable biogas, which, in turn, stimulates the collection and sorting of organic waste. In addition to fuel, the production provides high-quality biological fertilizer that returns important nutrients to neighboring arable land. In this way, transportation firm B has contributed to increasing the amount of sustainable resources

Sustainability in service provision aims to ensure that services, even those without tangible products, meet present needs while safeguarding the prospects of future generations (Keiningham et al. 2024). Hence, service sustainability entails the strategic fusion of diverse disciplines such as policymaking, engineering, environmental economics, and resource management, among others. Central to this approach is the harmonization of these disciplines to continually enhance services while respecting the socio-cultural, environmental, and economic intricacies of our global context.

Koskela-Huotari et al. (2024) conceptualized *sustainability in service* "as the focal system's (e.g. a service firm's) ability to sustain the broader system(s) that contains it; it is, thus, depended upon." It emphasizes that the sustainability of a firm, a household, or an entire industrial ecosystem, is based on its capacity to meet the needs of other systems it is part of and relies upon over time. For instance, the long-term success of a service firm hinges on its capability to support the welfare of the community it operates within and, most importantly, the health of the ecological systems it interacts with. Hence, sustainability in services necessitates acknowledging the varied interests of multiple stakeholders and striking a balance to maximize societal benefits, recognizing that equitable outcomes may not always be immediate or uniform. For instance, during the transition to renewable energy, fossil fuel suppliers may encounter challenges, emphasizing the importance of inclusive strategies that prioritize the common good.

Services in the Sharing Economy

In recent years, there has been a growing trend toward a so-called sharing economy. However, this is not a new phenomenon. The term *share economy* appeared already in an economics book in the 1980s but was at that time more focused on the labor market. Weitzman (1984) argued that full employment and social welfare could be achieved if workers were paid a "share" of the firm revenues. Nowadays, the sharing economy is related to a plethora of activities, practices, or trends related to consumption and production, such as the following:

- The use of peer-to-peer (P2P) services facilitated by online platforms, like ride-sharing, ride-hailing, or accommodation rental. These practices coordinated and regulated through mobile apps are ever-more convenient (closer, faster, cheaper) than access-based and rental practices based on B2C relationships previously mentioned
- The recirculation of goods and material resources that are not used or wanted by one entity to another that can put them to further good use; for instance, donations to charity thrift stores that refurbish and resell secondhand goods, swapping unwanted items for something else, but also functional recycling and creative upcycling practices. Such practices are driven by a wish to cease the accumulation of unnecessary goods, not by throwing them away but by putting them back in circulation through redistribution systems to increase their overall utilization. There is also an anticapitalistic ideology behind using alternatives to traditional marketplaces
- Sharing skills, knowledge, and information (e.g. massive open online courses, P2P file sharing, collaborative encyclopedias). These practices also rely on online platforms to produce or consume a variety of intangible resources (i.e. not material goods)
- New ways to find financing (e.g. crowdfunding, P2P loans, collective purchasing for joint ownership) and exchange monetary funds (e.g. Bitcoin, mobile payments). These practices enable people to collaborative more efficiently
- Sharing productive assets (e.g. fab-labs, makerspaces, hackerspaces, farmers' cooperatives) when ownership and, most importantly, the benefits of ownership are shared collectively – whether it is a 3D printer or an agricultural tool

- Distributed governance (e.g. based on blockchain technology) that organizations rely on to operate with more transparency and democracy

In a nutshell, the sharing economy phenomenon is mostly about sharing the usage of goods through service provision. Some of this sharing is collaborative and simultaneous (e.g. sharing a ride with other people going in the same direction when carpooling), some of it is sequential (e.g. car-sharing customers accessing a fleet car one after another), and some of it is a mix of rental services facilitated by platforms (i.e. for-profit motives) and collaborative lifestyles (e.g. Airbnb, an online marketplace that allows people to rent out their properties or spare rooms to guests for short-term stays).

Increased Resource Efficiency by Reduced Ownership

One important aspect of the sharing economy is that it can increase resource efficiency through service provision – using goods that would not have been utilized to their full extent otherwise. For example, a car can be rented out instead of staying parked 90% of the time, and a lawnmower and a power drill are tools that many people possess but rarely use. Basically, people want the services of using these tools, not particularly owning them. The sharing economy paradigm represents a great potential for the dematerialization of consumption, as embraced by advocates of a minimalist lifestyle: owning as little as possible. People realized they do not have to own material things that can be accessed via a company or a neighbor (or stranger) through rental services – or for free (i.e. borrowing). In terms of capital-intensive activities, such as transportation and housing, these can even generate revenue if they are rented out or used to provide further services through online platforms such as Airbnb or Uber. For society, the sharing economy may result in fewer resources being used through a more efficient utilization of dormant resources, in addition to reduced energy consumption.

Over time, the interest in sharing possessions has thus increased. Possessions and property used to be considered symbols of wealth and status – but today, owning things is increasingly questioned (e.g. minimalism is a growing lifestyle trend in developed countries). In Germany, almost a quarter of consumers are so-called socially innovative co-consumers, according to a study from the University of Lüneburg (Boeing and Lubbadeh 2013). Younger consumers are particularly prone to such trends. According to PwC (2015), more than 80% of Germans under the age of 30 have shared and exchanged goods and services instead of buying. Among people over the age of 60, the same number is only 25%. Nearly half of the study participants find it difficult and cumbersome to own things, 64% think that the regulation that is carried out through others in the sharing community is more important than the regulation carried out by state, and 69% think that recommendations from someone you trust are essential for whether or not you are willing to share (PwC 2015). Digitization results in new services and solutions that simplify the sharing economy and reduce transaction costs.

Peer-to-Peer Services for Collaborative Consumption

In their seminal book *What's Mine is Yours*, Botsman and Rogers (2010) use the term *collaborative consumption* to describe

> "traditional sharing, bartering, lending, trading, renting, gifting, and swapping, redefined through technology and peer communities. [. . .] enabling people to realize the enormous benefits of access to products and services over ownership, and at the same time save money, space, and time; make new friends; and become active citizens once again"

(p. xv–xvi). Botsman's TEDx Talks in 2010 and 2012 had a strong impact on the popular debate and academia. Her conceptualization of collaborative consumption included most practices referred to as part of the sharing economy phenomenon today. The book summarizes the four underlying principles of the sharing economy as idling or excess capacity of unused goods, a critical mass of people, a belief in the common good, and social trust. The P2P Foundation also identify two main societal drivers of the sharing economy based on collaborative consumption: community dynamics in conducting business and the combined effect of digital reproduction and the increasingly "socialized" production of value (Bauwens et al. 2012).

On the one hand, collaborative consumption merely adapted the "rules of shopping" from e-commerce (e.g. eBay's reputation systems and recirculation of goods, PayPal's secured online payment system) to facilitate monetary exchanges between private individuals. On the other hand, collaborative consumption also leveraged social media network technologies (i.e. Facebook profile and contacts) to facilitate social interactions and the emergence of communities (Guyader 2019).

Uber and Lyft – Two Transportation Network Companies (TNC)

Uber was founded in California in 2009 (originally as "UberCab") and provides a ride-sourcing service to professional drivers (i.e. UberBLACK, UberSUV, UberLUX, UberTAXI) or private individuals/amateur drivers (UberX launched in 2012 and UberPOP in Europe) and a private transportation service (i.e. ride-hailing) to passengers via a mobile application. Since 2014, UberPOOL and Express Pool enable passengers to be matched with other passengers, thereby sharing portions of their hailed ride and splitting the bill (which is not yet truly carpooling – but "ride-splitting" – as drivers are paid to provide a shuttle service to multiple passengers).

Uber also diversified its mobility services into UberBOAT for crossings in the Mediterranean in 2015, UberMOTO using motorcycles and scooters in Indonesia in 2016, and in UberAIR (UberELEVATE, UberCHOPPER among others) aiming to transport passengers using flying vehicles. In other sectors, UberEATS and UberRUSH were launched in 2014 as a food delivery service and in 2015 as a package delivery service, respectively.

In 2018, UberRENT was launched in partnership with GetAround to enable P2P car rental from its app, and UberBike was launched after acquiring bike-sharing firm JUMP. There are also services dedicated to specific customer segments: UberPET, UberKIDS, UberWAV, and UberHEALTH. Uber went public in 2019 and was then valued at $75 billion (May 2019) (e.g. Perera and Albinsson 2020), which is the most valuable startup worldwide – for reference, Ferrari was valued at $10 billion in 2015.

Lyft is offering a ride-hailing service launched in 2012 in California by Zimride. The mobile app Zimride Instant (later renamed Lyft in 2013) was initially launched to enable ride requests from passengers to be matched on-demand with drivers from Zimride's ride-sharing community. Ride-sharing turned into ride hailing when unlicensed drivers (i.e. individuals in their private vehicles) were invited to sign up as drivers to compete with taxis (and UberBLACK). Zimride's founders were fully dedicated to turning their startup into a transportation network company. However, compared to Uber, Lyft did not fix prices but let passengers pay "a suggested donation" to drivers until 2013. The "suggested donation" argument is a regulatory trick adopted by Heetch (which a TNC launched in France in 2013) to replace UberPOP (closed in 2015), which closed down in 2017. In practice, ride-hailing drivers get compensated for their labor (not only car ownership costs), which means that TNCs facilitate remunerated work.

Lyft also enabled tipping from the outset. LyftLine was launched in 2014 to enable passengers to split a ride with others on the route (before Uber-POOL). LyftCarpool was launched in 2016, offering an actual ride-sharing service to commuters by inviting drivers to register their recurring itinerary (i.e. a trip they would have made anyway, even without passengers) to be matched with other people (i.e. passengers), especially from city suburbs into city centers and longer distances. LyftCarpool was closed due to lack of drivers' registration in 2016. Lyft also launched Express Drive in 2016, a program for drivers to rent a General Motors vehicle, which evolved into a partnership with LeasePlan in 2018. Until 2018, Lyft operated only in the United States

(Continued)

(Continued)

(contrary to other TNCs), where it has a roughly 30% market share of the ride-hailing sector and was valued at $11.5 billion in 2017.

While ride-sharing may offer some societal benefits in terms of providing rides to areas where public transportation may not serve and for using cars more efficiently, it has been criticized for creating many negative externalities for drivers so called gig workers, but also for users (safety), cities (increased idling and pollution), and reduced public transportation usage (e.g. Griffiths et al. 2019).

Sources: e.g. Perera and Albinsson (2020); Uber.com; Lyft.com.

Critics of the Sharing Economy

The sharing economy is both an ideological and practical criticism of the branded society or the consumer society in general. It thus represents a threat to traditional companies that do not embrace the sharing economy. For instance, Zervas et al. (2017) show that the rapid growth of Airbnb in Texas (from approximately 450 listings in 2010 to more than 8500 listings in 2014) has had a negative impact (8–10%) on local hotel room revenue. But there are critics of the sharing economy as well.

Several voices in the popular debate have been raised against "we-washing," "co-washing," or "share-washing" practices, where the words and ideas of community, belonging, and genuine sharing have been associated with for-profit companies with self-interested activities (e.g. Kalamar 2013; Huang 2015; Kessler 2015). Bardhi and Eckhardt – having had a great impact on consumer research on access-based consumption with their 2012 study – were the first to point out that "'sharing' is just a fancy word for 'rental'" (Fournier et al. 2013, p. 2702) and that "the sharing economy isn't about sharing at all" (Eckhardt and Bardhi 2015). For instance, Zipcar (on-demand car rental service) users are motivated by increased convenience, and they seek to maximize the outcomes of their participation (as in traditional marketplace exchanges) to serve their own self-interest with no sense of commonality between the parties involved (Bardhi and Eckhardt 2012; Lamberton and Rose 2012). That is, it has nothing to with the collaborative and communal nature of sharing. One manager of a shared mobility platform explained that their P2P car rental business is more about rental than peers: "With the rapidity, without paperwork, with the flexibility of the pick-up location and a lower price, we're doing the same thing as Avis or Hertz, just cheaper." For-profit platforms want to be associated with the positive associations with the word *community* (i.e. social belonging, collective well-being, solidarity, support networks), which describes an existing set of (warm) relationships where members (a collective body of people) express a sense of common identity and characteristics (Williams 1976, p. 76).

"This new economy is not really about sharing at all" is also a recurrent affirmation in the *platform-coop* movement. Further critics in the popular debate target the "big sharing unicorns" and their profits (e.g. Uber, Airbnb) that subordinate their users to market forces, "extending the deregulated free market into previously private areas of our lives" (Scholz 2016, p. 3). Some might have dubbed the era of the sharing economy as the "age of market triumphalism" (Sandel 2012), where the "financialization of life" has been facilitated by technology (Iaconesi 2017). For-profit platforms have brought on the monetization of resources that were previously outside the market (e.g. personal cars, homes, private time) through corporate platforms matching people "who offer services and others who are looking for them, thereby embedding extractive processes into social interactions" (Belk 2014; Slee 2015; Scholz 2016, p. 4; Munger 2018). The potential for monetization is emphasized to a greater extent compared to the *true sharing* aspect (i.e. collaboration, social exchange, community) of this new economy.

Schor (2014) also considers the economic, social, and ecological arguments put forth by sharing economy advocates and finds little support. For instance, due to platform transaction fees (e.g. 20–30% for P2P car rental), collaborative consumption alternatives are not necessarily cheaper. Munger (2018) also explains that the sharing economy is very much a middleman economy in that what is reduced are transaction costs and not the production costs. Such cuts in transaction costs (due to ICT developments) are the cause behind the disruption of traditional businesses (e.g. in the taxi and hotel industries).

Therefore, the "renting economy," "reselling economy," and "gig economy" might be better names for what is today referred to as the sharing economy (Herbst 2014; Hern 2015; Roberts 2015). Owyang (2015) also remarks that the term *collaborative economy* provides the "right scope and is most accurate for this growing movement," while the term *sharing economy* is "just a subset of the overall movement of P2P commerce" (such as PayPal and Amazon). Meanwhile, the European Parliament (2015) defines the sharing economy as "a new socio-economic model that has taken off thanks to the technological revolution, with the internet connecting people through online platforms on which transactions involving goods and services can be conducted securely and transparently" – but there is no mention of business model, employments, or profits in that definition, which was not useful in terms of regulating platforms such as Uber or Deliveroo. More helpful for us is the definition of the sharing economy as

> "an economic system in which assets or services are shared between private individuals, either for free or for a fee, typically by means of the internet"

(Oxford English Dictionary 2015).

Frenken and Schor (2017) emphasize that "the notion of sharing of idle capacity is central to the definition of sharing economy, because it distinguishes the practice of sharing of goods from the practice of on-demand personal services," similarly to Muñoz and Cohen (2017) who write: "Unlike the Instacart platform, BlaBlaCar relies on the availability of under-utilized resources (i.e. under-utilized seats) to operate." That is, Zipcar, Uber, and BlaBlaCar facilitate different consumption modes in relation to how and who provides the service. For the *Special Issue* editorial from the *1st International Workshop on the Sharing Economy*, Frenken and Schor (2017) "put the sharing economy into perspective" (i.e. an economic-historic perspective) and raised their concerns regarding the ambiguity of definitions and the resulting confusion surrounding this phenomenon. Thus, they argued that there are three defining characteristics of the sharing economy: P2P interaction, temporary access, and underutilized physical goods (Frenken et al. 2015; Frenken and Schor 2017). This resonates with Botsman and Rogers' (2010) systems classification, while being more accurate in taking previous and simultaneous paradigms into account. Moreover, these characteristics of the sharing economy constitute broader economic trends than what is commonly referred to (see Figure 5.4):

- The P2P or platform economy
- The access economy
- The circular economy (Frenken 2017)

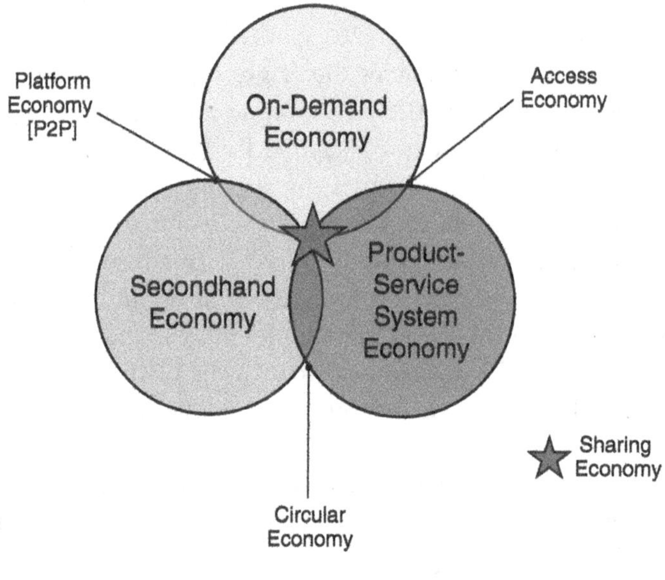

Figure 5.4 The sharing economy and its related paradigms.
Source: Adapted from Frenken et al. (2015); Frenken (2017); and Frenken and Schor (2017).

Inversely, these characteristics enable situating and distinguishing the sharing economy from other economic trends starting before the Internet:

- *The second-hand economy*: "Consumers selling goods to each other" with a permanent change of ownership and sometimes without payment
- *The PSS economy, based on business-to-consumer (B2C) relationships*: "Renting goods from a company rather than from another consumer," such as Hertz
- *The on-demand or gig economy*: "P2P service delivery instead of P2P good sharing," such as a handyman

CouchSurfing versus Airbnb

Bucher et al. (2016) exemplify a segmentation of "Internet-mediated sharing" consumers with the two platforms:

- Noncommercial sharers (e.g. CouchSurfing platform users) score higher on volunteering and sociability and have higher moral and social-hedonic participation motives
- Commercial sharers (e.g. Airbnb platform users) score higher on materialism and have higher monetary motivations

In a *Wired* article titled "Before Airbnb, there was Couchsurfing" (Mitroff 2012), one can read that on CouchSurfing, "[p]ictures of hosts far outnumber pictures of their accommodations, reinforcing the idea that you're not staying with someone for their questionable couch or lumpy twin bed, you're camping out with them for the experience they can offer. [. . .] CouchSurfing's business is more like a social network that charges for certain benefits, rather than a vacation rental service like Airbnb."

In a Ouishare article (Marin 2018), it is explained that CouchSurfing did not succeed the way Airbnb did, since the former required a high level of trust in strangers, whereas the latter did not:

Couchsurfing forced you to become somewhat intimate with a stranger. "Oh, you want me to sleep on your couch. . .? What's wrong with you? Are you trying to sleep with me? Are you just creepy?" There were lots of young people in particular willing to do it, really forward-thinking who liked the ideas behind this model and felt safe to do it. Airbnb made it a more transactional relation, by bringing money into the system, it made it easier to understand. "Well, of course, she's letting me sleep on her couch, I'm paying

(Continued)

(Continued)

her 60 bucks!" That shift made it so that people who wouldn't have thought of sleeping on a stranger's couch or in their guest room, all of a sudden were willing to try that. So once they had that experience, and felt it was great, it opened their minds to whole new business models, a whole different way of seeing the world that had been only visible to the people who had been participating in Couchsurfing, but they wouldn't have crossed that threshold otherwise.

In a nutshell, CouchSurfing's network members prefer an authentic cultural exchange and the feeling of belonging to a community of like-minded travelers (thought of as friends), while Airbnb guests are willing to pay more for the convenience, certainty, and efficiency of an online booking system and prefer to pay with money instead of with conversation.

Environmental Effects of the Sharing Economy

Environmental concerns and a sustainability mindset have become prominent in society, and people want to reduce the ecological impact of their daily life by reducing waste and using existing resources more efficiently – that is what the sharing economy is aiming to promote. Consumers (and thus firms) are cautious of the environmental performance of products and services, even if it costs a little more. They pursue a more efficient use of what is available to them. By increasing the use of existing resources, reducing waste and surplus, refurbishing products, making donations, using other recirculation systems, and discouraging new acquisitions through rental services, the sharing economy promises to enable a more sustainable consumption.

However, there may be more cost-conscious consumers than pro-environmentalists who try sharing things on collaborative consumption platforms. After all, "sustainability is often an unintended consequence of collaborative consumption [. . .] in the sense that the initial or driving motivation for a company or the consumer may not be about 'being green'" (Botsman and Rogers 2010, p. 74). Hartl et al. (2018) refer to the environmental benefits as a "nice bonus" but not the core participation motive. For Wilhelms et al. (2017), it is also an "indirect consequence" for people offering their cars for rent to others: "environmental concerns were not part of their participation decision, but that environmental benefits are rather perceived as a byproduct" (p. 45).

Eventually, the environmental benefits of sharing can easily become challenges: "use rather than own" schemes can contribute to a more efficient use of material goods only if certain framework conditions are observed by, for instance, using durable products or enhancing device utilization (Leismann et al. 2013). That is, it is important to note that whereas car sharing and collaborative consumption are practices oriented toward reducing the environmental impact of driving/consuming, P2P car rental offers a mitigated potential from a sustainability perspective. Indeed, when compared to using public transportation or trains, renting and driving a car have a greater environmental footprint. Moreover, compared to traditional car-sharing where cars are new, electric, or with a superior fuel economy, private cars (though already in the road system) are more likely to be older and pollute more. Both forms of car sharing eventually facilitate mobility, which engenders a series of behaviors and consumption practices that make the environmental impact of car sharing on society difficult to evaluate. Schor (2014) also raises concerns for the actual risks of increasing the environmental footprint of consumption due to more access (e.g. mobility services enable people to go places and consume more than they would without access to mobility) and the recirculation of polluting goods (e.g. old cars are used more than they would otherwise). Yet, many argue that the sharing economy is a potential pathway to sustainability (e.g. Heinrichs 2013).

The Lift Group

The Lift Group started as a simple Facebook group in Sweden in 2007 (*Skjutsgruppen*) as a way to attenuate the necessary leap in trust to participate in ride-sharing with strangers by checking their personal page, social network connections, and other personal aspects of their life. This Facebook initiative was nothing more than a group of people with a shared feeling of responsibility regarding the environmental impact of driving and a list of destinations. In other words, the Facebook group was the equivalent of an online notice board, a tool to help people organize ride-sharing on an ad hoc basis, without central coordination from the Lift Group, and hosted on an external social media network.

As a grassroots movement, the Lift Group community relied exclusively on social media networks until 2012, when the movement crowdfunded ($10 000) the development of a platform with more functionalities than Facebook groups. This embeds the sharing logic of a cooperative group of people who self-organize to redistribute resources (Belk 2010). It also shows that social media networks (only) are a valuable source of trust for P2P exchanges without a reputation system – since 2016 Facebook Marketplace is a digital market where Facebook users can buy/sell items, essentially what eBay

(Continued)

(Continued)

stands for. In other words, the key to the development of the ride-sharing practice for the Lift Group was to overcome barriers of trust between drivers and passengers, which social media networks adequately support.

To inspire feelings of trust, the Lift Group does not rely on the peer-review systems typical of e-commerce websites. However, the platform displays the "degrees of separation" between users by showing how many other relationships separate them. Since Milgram's small world experiment (1967), it is assumed that everyone on Earth can be connected to each other through six other individuals or fewer. While the exact number of friends of friends separating two platform users decrease with how "well-connected" one is (Milgram 1967; Watts 2004), the Lift Group relies on these Facebook friend connections (as well as its own platform friends when members add each other as such) to emphasize that ride-sharing participants are not complete strangers when considering the extension of their social network.

The founder of the Facebook group explains why the Lift Group is particularly engaging its community – not only through crowd-financing and crowdsourcing – but also by calling their members to be actors within the ride-sharing movement: "We call ourselves a civil society movement. None of our users are customers, we are all participants." This "participatory culture" separates the Lift Group from other ride-sharing platforms, such as BlaBlaCar that offers mobility solutions rather being an environmental movement. New members in the Lift Group community are asked to agree to a statement, reading as an engagement: "We are friends and friends of friends. Friends don't make money off friends." From a legal point of view, it is actually forbidden to make profits from driving people around without declaring it a (taxi service) business. In other words, the Lift Group promotes a genuine idea of ride-sharing to its members based on sharing the costs of driving among car occupants, with a strong environmental orientation. BlaBlaCar users must also accept the "Member's Agreement" as a statement of good conduct.

There are more than 80 000 people affiliated the Lift Group movement on its website or platform.

Source: https://skjutsgruppen.se.

Shared Mobility Services

Private cars are on average used for an hour a day – they are parked more than 90% of the time, which is far from efficient. With car-sharing services, it is possible to save ownership costs and still enjoy the comfort and convenience represented by having access to a car when needed (and thus mobility), while creating a more sustainable society since moving away from individual car ownership frees up parking space in the streets and reduces traffic jams. Here, we also find P2P services, meaning that consumers rent a car from their neighbors and share a ride via carpooling platforms. The shared mobility sector includes a range of practices and business models based on sharing the use of cars. Yet there are significant differences between the various modes of transportation, and this terminology is used in marketing communication as well as regulation. For instance, although Uber argues that it is a ride-sharing platform, it is not really – compared to BlaBlaCar or the Lift Group (mentioned earlier in this chapter). Here are useful definitions and examples of these shared mobility practices (Guyader et al. 2021) we note these terms are sometimes mixed up or used interchangeably such as ride-sharing and ride-hailing:

- *Hitchhiking* (also known as *auto-stop* and *thumbing*) is the unorganized (ad hoc) way to travel by getting free rides in passing vehicles. It means to hitch oneself onboard a moving vehicle or otherwise hike along the road. In practice, hitchhikers signal (i.e. the almost universal thumbs up) to drivers to stop, so they can inquire about their destination and hop on to share a portion of their journey. From being a necessity for people with no access to transportation during the Great Depression and early twentieth century, Kerouac's *On the Road* (1957) popularized hitchhiking as a lifestyle, inspired by hobos illegally traveling for free on merchandize trains in the United States
- *Slugging* is when people informally queue at strategic positions to hitch a ride in a car with empty seats, enabling drivers to use high-occupancy vehicle (HOV) lanes. This practice that created "slugging lines" along highways began to form in the late 1970s in the United States
- *Ride-sharing* (also known as *carpooling* in the United States and *liftsharing* in the United Kingdom) is about adding passengers to an already planned car trip. Such an arrangement provides additional transportation options for riders while letting drivers fill otherwise empty seats in their vehicles. Examples include BlaBlaCar, the Lift Group, and Kangaride
- *Commute ride-sharing* (or short-distance daily carpooling) is about regularly sharing a car trip to/from work or school. This practice is organized through informal networks (e.g. family, friends, employees) or facilitated by an online platform. As its name indicates, short-distance carpooling refers to sharing regular short trips (20–80 km). Examples include https://Carpoolworld.com, Share the Ride, and BlaBlaLine
- *Ride-hailing* (also known as *E-hail*, *ride-sourcing*, and *ride-splitting*) is a practice based on apps (on smartphones with location-based services) enabling on-demand mobility services provided by drivers for remuneration (e.g. professionally trained and licensed drivers). Ride-splitting is when TNCs that facilitate ride-hailing further offer their customers to split their itinerary and fare with other customers from the same sourced ride. Examples are Uber and Lyft

- *Car-sharing* is a membership-based service offered by car-sharing organizations (CSOs) providing access (without ownership) to a fleet of eco-friendly cars conveniently located in city centers. CSO members pay per use, which is cheaper than traditional car rental organizations (e.g. AVIS, Hertz)
  - *Return car-sharing* (also known as *round-trip*) is the most common model of car-sharing operation. It requires customers to borrow and return vehicles at the same location. Examples include Zipcar and HyreCar
  - *One-way car-sharing* (also known as *point-to-point*) is enabled by Global Positioning System (GPS), network communication, and smartphone technologies, and cars (typically electric) can be picked up and dropped off at different parking locations or charging stations (e.g. similarly to bike-sharing docking stations) in city centers. An example is ShareNow
  - *Free-floating car-sharing* is essentially the same as one-way car-sharing but without the dedicated parking spots. Instead, the fleet of vehicles is spread out within a predefined geographic region (i.e. city centers), and customers can geolocalize (and unlock) each car from a smartphone app. An examples is ShareNow
  - *P2P car rental* (also known as *personal car-sharing*) is privately owned vehicles made temporarily available to rent for members of a platform. P2P car rental is a return mode of car-sharing. Examples are GetAround, Turo, and Snappcar

Figure 5.5 Keyless technology in car-sharing refers to the use of digital or electronic methods (e.g. a keycard, a smartphone) to access and start vehicles, eliminating the need for physical keys, which thus enhances the convenience and efficiency of car-sharing services by allowing P2P car rental customers to access vehicles without needing to meet and physically exchange keys (e.g. Lync & Co).
Source: Shutterstock 2259903855.

References

Albinsson, P.A. & Perera, B.Y. (2009). From trash to treasure and beyond: the meaning of voluntary disposition. *Journal of Consumer Behaviour: An International Research Review*, 8(6), 340–353.

Albinsson, P. A., & Perera, B.Y. (2012). Alternative marketplaces in the 21st century: building community through sharing events. *Journal of Consumer Behaviour*, 11(4), 303–315.

Atanasova, A., Eckhardt, G.M. & Husemann, K.C. (2024). Liquid consumer security. *Journal of Consumer Research*, 50(6), 1243–1264.

Bardhi, F. & Eckhardt, G.M. (2012). Access-based consumption: the case of car sharing. *Journal of Consumer Research*, 39(4), 881–898.

Bardhi, F. & Eckhardt, G.M. (2017). Liquid consumption. *Journal of Consumer Research*, 44(3), 582–597.

Bardhi, F., Eckhardt, G.M., & Arnould E.J. (2012). Liquid relationship to possessions. *Journal of Consumer Research*, 39(3), 510–529.

Bauwens, M., Mendoza, N., Iacomella, F. & Al., E. (2012). "A synthetic overview of the collaborative economy." Orange Labs, P2P Foundation.

Belk, R. (2010). Sharing. *Journal of Consumer Research*, 36(5), 715–734.

Belk, R.W. (2014). You are what you can access: sharing and collaborative consumption online. *Journal of Business Research*, 67(8), 1595–1600.

Berry L.L. & Maricle K.E. (1973). Consumption without ownership: marketing opportunity for today and tomorrow. *MSU Business Topics*, 21(1), 33–41.

Boeing, N. & Lubbadeh, J. (2013). Sharing economy: Meins ist auch deins. *Beobachter*, 5.

Booms, B. H., & Bitner, M. J. (1982). Marketing services by managing the environment. *Cornell Hotel and Restaurant Administration Quarterly*, 23(1), 35–40.

Botsman, R. & Rogers, R. (2010). *What's Mine is Yours: The Rise of Collaborative Consumption*. London: Harper Collins.

Bucher, E., Fieseler, C. & Lutz C. (2016). What's mine is yours (for a nominal fee): exploring the spectrum of utilitarian to altruistic motives for internet-mediated sharing. *Computers in Human Behavior*, 62(September), 316–326.

DeVries, H. (2019). Time to Declutter Marketing That Doesn't Spark Joy Per Marie Kondo. *Forbes*. January 28, 2019. https://www.forbes.com/sites/henrydevries/2019/01/28/time-to-declutter-marketing-that-doesnt-spark-joy-per-marie-kondo/?sh=42facb20316e (accessed 3 March 2024).

Eckhardt, G.M. & Bardhi F. (2015). The sharing economy isn't about sharing at all. *Harvard Business Review*, 39(4), 881–898.

Eckhardt, G. M., and Bardhi, F. (2020). The value in de-emphasizing structure in liquidity. *Marketing Theory*, 20(4), 573–580.

European Parliament (2015). European Parliament resolution of 29 October 2015 on new challenges and concepts for the promotion of tourism in Europe. *European Parliament*. https://oeil.secure.europarl.europa.eu/oeil/popups/ficheprocedure.do?lang=en&reference=2014/2241(INI) (accessed 5 May 2024).

Fournier, S., Eckhardt, G.M. & Bardhi F. (2013). Learning to play in the new "share Economy." *Harvard Business Review*, 91(July-August), 2701–2703.

Frenken, K. (2017). Political economies and environmental futures for the sharing economy. *Philosophical Transactions of the Royal Society A: Mathematical, Physical and Engineering Sciences*, 375, (2095).

Frenken, K. & Schor, J. (2017). Putting the sharing economy into perspective. *Environmental Innovation and Societal Transitions,* 23, 3–10.

Frenken, K., Meelen, T., Arets, M. & van de Glind, P. (2015). Smarter regulation for the sharing economy. *The Guardian*. https://www.theguardian.com/science/political-science/2015/may/20/smarter-regulation-for-the-sharing-economy (accessed 1 May 2024).

Global Economy (2023). Share of services – country rankings. https://www.theglobaleconomy.com/rankings/share_of_services (accessed 1 May 2024).

Graedel, T.E. (2003). Greening the service industries. *The Service Industries Journal*, 23(5), 48–64.

Griffiths, M.A., Perera, B.Y. and Albinsson, P.A., 2019. Contrived surplus and negative externalities in the sharing economy. *Journal of Marketing Theory and Practice*, 27(4), 445–463.

Grönroos, C. (1978). A service-orientated approach to marketing of services. *European Journal of Marketing*, 12(8), 588–601.

Grove, S.J., Fisk, R.P., Pickett, G.M. and Kangun, N. (1996). Going green in the service sector: social responsibility issues, implications and implementation. *European Journal of Marketing*, 30(5), 56–66.

Gummesson, E. (1993). *Green service quality*. 3rd Quality in Services Symposium, Karlstad, Sweden, June 1992.

Gummesson, E. (2000). Evert Gummesson, in Fisk, R.P., Grove, S.J. and John, J. (Eds.), *Services Marketing Self-Portraits: Introspections, Reflections, and Glimpses from Experts*, American Marketing Association, Chicago, IL, pp. 109–132.

Guyader, H., 2019. *The Heart and Wallet Paradox of Collaborative Consumption* (Vol. 763). Linköping University Electronic Press.

Guyader, H., Ottosson, M., Frankelius, P., Witell, L. (2019). Identifying the resource integration processes of green service. *Journal of Service Management*, 31(4), 839–859.

Guyader H, Friman M, Olsson L.E. (2021). Shared mobility: evolving practices for sustainability. *Sustainability*, 13(21), 12148.

Hartl, B., Sabitzer, T., Hofmann, E. and Penz, E. (2018). Sustainability is a nice bonus: the role of sustainability in car-sharing from a consumer perspective. *Journal of Cleaner Production*, 202, 88–100.

Hazée, S., Delcourt, C., and Van Vaerenbergh, Y. (2017). Burdens of access: understanding customer barriers and barrier-attenuating practices in access-based services. *Journal of Service Research*, 20(4), 441–456.

Heinrichs, H. (2013). Sharing economy: a potential new pathway to sustainability. *Gaia* 22/4, 228–231.

Herbst, M. (2014). Let's get real: The "sharing economy" won't solve our jobs crisis. *The Guardian*. https://www.theguardian.com/commentisfree/2014/jan/07/sharing-economy-not-solution-to-jobs-crisis (accessed 3 April 2024).

Hern, A. (2015). Why the term "sharing economy" needs to die. *The Guardian*. https://www.theguardian.com/technology/2015/oct/05/why-the-term-sharing-economy-needs-to-die (accessed 3 April 2024).

Houston F.S. & Gassenheimer J.B. (1987). Marketing and exchange. *Journal of Marketing*, 51(4), 3–18.

Huang, L.-S. (2015). #WeWashing: when "sharing" is renting and "community" is a commodity. *Huffington Post.* May 16, 2015. http://www.huffingtonpost.com/leese-an-huang/wewashing-when-sharing-is_b_6879018.html (accessed 9 February 2024).

Iaconesi, S. (2017). The financialization of life. *Startups & Venture Capital.* https://startupsventurecapital.com/the-financialization-of-life-a90fe2cb839f (accessed 3 March 2024).

Johnson E.M. (1969). *Are goods and services different? An exercise in marketing theory.* Doctoral dissertation. Business School, Washington University.

Johnson M., Herrmann A., & Huber F. (1998). Growth through product-sharing services. *Journal of Service Research,* 2(1), 167–177.

Judd R.C. (1964). The case for redefining services. *Journal of Marketing,* 28(1), 58–59.

Kalamar, A. (2013). Sharewashing is the new greenwashing. *OpEdNews.* http://www.opednews.com/articles/Sharewashing-is-the-New-Gr-by-Anthony-Kalamar-130513-834.html (accessed 1 May 2024).

Keiningham, T., Aksoy, L., & Malthouse, E. (2024). Sustainable service. *Journal of Service Research,* 27(1), 3–5.

Kessler, S. (2015). The "Sharing Economy" is dead, and we killed it. *Fast Company.* http://www.fastcompany.com/3050775/the-sharing-economy-is-dead-and-we-killed-it#1 (accessed 2 February 2024).

Koskela-Huotari, K., Svärd, K., Williams, H., Trischler, J. & Wikström, F. (2024). Drivers and hinderers of (un) sustainable service: a systems view. *Journal of Service Research,* 27(1), 106–123.

Lamberton C.P. & Rose R.L. (2012). When is ours better than mine? A framework for understanding and sharing systems. *Journal of Marketing,* 76(4), 109–125.

Lawson S.J. (2010). Transumers: motivations of non-ownership consumption. *Advances in Consumer Research,* 37, 842–853.

Leismann, K., Schmitt, M., Rohn, H. and Baedeker, C. (2013). Collaborative consumption: towards a resource-saving consumption culture. *Resources,* 2(3), 184–203.

Levitt T.H. (1960). Marketing myopia. *Harvard Business Review,* 38(7/8), 45–56.

Lovelock C. & Gummesson E. (2004). Whither services marketing? In search of a new paradigm and fresh perspectives. *Journal of Service Research,* 7(1), 20–41.

Marin F. (2018). Holochain: The beginnings of a brave new internet. *Ouishare.* https://www.ouishare.net/article/holochain-the-beginnings-of-a-brave-new-internet-vol-ii (accessed 1 May 2024).

McCarthy, J. (1964). The concept of the marketing mix. *Journal of Advertising Research,* 2–7.

Milgram, S. (1967). The small world problem. *Psychology Today,* 1(1), 61–67.

Mitroff, S. (2012). Before Airbnb, there was Couchsurfing. *Wired.* http://www.wired.com/2012/08/before-airbnb-there-was-couchsurfing (accessed 3 April 2024).

Moeller, S. (2010). Characteristics of services–a new approach uncovers their value. *Journal of Services Marketing,* 24(5), 359–368.

Moeller S. & Wittkowski K. (2010). The burdens of ownership: reasons for preferring renting. *Managing Service Quality,* 20(2), 176–191.

Mont, O. & Tukker, A. (2006). Product-service systems: reviewing achievements and refining the research agenda. *Journal of Cleaner Production,* 14(17), 1451–1454.

Munger, M.C. (2018). *Tomorrow 3.0: Transaction Costs and the Sharing Economy.* Cambridge: Cambridge University Press.

Muñoz, P. & Cohen, B. (2017). Mapping out the sharing economy: a configurational approach to sharing business modeling. *Technological Forecasting and Social Change,* 125, 21–37.

Oxford English Dictionary (2015). Sharing Economy. http://www.oxforddictionaries.com/definition/english/sharing-economy (accessed 30 May 2018).

Ozanne, L.K. & Ozanne, J.L. (2011). A child's right to play: the social construction of civic virtues in toy libraries. *Journal of Public Policy & Marketing*, 30(2), 264–278.

Owyang J. (2015), "The collaborative economy defined," *Crowd Companies*. Available at: http://www.web-strategist.com/blog/2015/08/27/the-collaborative-economy-defined/ (accessed 20 July 2024).

Perera, B.Y. & Albinsson, P.A. (2020). *Uber*. Westport, CT: Greenwood.

PwC (2015), "The sharing economy: Consumer intelligence series," *BAV Consulting*. Available at: https://www.pwc.fr/fr/assets/files/pdf/2015/05/pwc_etude_sharing _economy.pdf (accessed 18 May 2018).

Rifkin J. (2000). *The Age of Access: The New Culture of Hypercapitalism, Where all of Life Is a Paid-for Experience*. Tarcer/Putnam, New York, NY.

Roberts, J.J. (2015). As "sharing economy" fades, these 2 phrases are likely to replace it. *Fortune*. https://fortune.com/2015/07/29/sharing-economy-chart (accessed 2 January 2024).

Sandel, M.J. (2012). *What Money Can't Buy: The Moral Limits of Markets*. New York: Farrar, Straus and Giroux (Macmillan).

Sasser W.E. Jr., Olsen R.P., & Wyckoff D.D. (1978). *Management of Service Operations: Text, Cases, and Readings*. Allyn and Bacon, Boston, MA.

Schaefers T. (2013a). Saving time, money, or the environment? Consumers' motives of access-based service use," in Kubacki (ed.), *Ideas in Marketing - Finding the New and Polishing the Old: Proceedings of the Academy of Marketing Science Annual Conference 2013*, p. 652.

Schaefers T. (2013b). Exploring car-sharing usage motives: a hierarchical means-end chain analysis. *Transportation Research Part A*, 47. 69–77.

Schaefers T., Lawson S.J., & Kukar-Kinney M. (2016a) How the burdens of ownership promote consumer usage of access-based services. *Marketing Letters*, 27(3): 569–577.

Schaefers T., Wittkowski K., Benoit S., & Ferraro R. (2016b). Contagious effects of customer misbehavior in access-based services. *Journal of Service Research*, 19(1), 3–21.

Slee T. (2015). *What's yours is mine: Against the sharing economy*. OR Books, New York, NY.

Scholz, T. (2016). *Platform Cooperativism: Challenging the Corporate Sharing Economy*. New York. http://www.rosalux-nyc.org/wp-content/files_mf/scholz_platformcooperativism_2016.pdf (accessed 3 March 2024).

Schor, J. (2014). Debating the sharing economy. *Great Transition Initiative*. http://www.greattransition.org/publication/debating-the-sharing-economy (accessed 5 March 2024).

Shostack G.L. (1977). Breaking free from product marketing. *Journal of Marketing*, 41(2), 73–80.

Watts, D.J. (2004). *Six Degrees: The Science of a Connected Age*. WW Norton & Company.

Weitzman, M.L. (1984). *The Share Economy: Conquering Stagflation*. Harvard University Press.

Wilhelms, M. P., Henkel, S., & Falk, T. (2017). To earn is not enough: A means-end analysis to uncover peer-providers' participation motives in peer-to-peer carsharing. *Technological Forecasting and Social Change*, 125, 38–47.

Williams, R. (1976). Keywords: A Vocabulary of Culture and Society. Fontana.

Zervas G., Proserpio D. & Byers, J.W. (2017). The rise of the sharing economy: estimating the impact of Airbnb on the hotel industry. *Journal of Marketing Research*, 54(10), 687–705.

Chapter 6

How to Communicate Sustainability Initiatives

In recent years, the concept of sustainability has become increasingly important in marketing communication strategies. As consumers become more environmentally and socially conscious, they are demanding that businesses adopt sustainable practices and communicate with them effectively. In this chapter, we will explore various types of sustainable marketing communication strategies and their implications for businesses. Marketing communications and sustainability strongly influence each other: companies with sustainability claims must carry out marketing communications differently, and marketing communications will be different when sustainability is part of the communication. Meanwhile, consumers and other stakeholders are increasingly expecting companies to be sustainable; yet many companies engage in greenwashing. Sustainability requires honesty, transparency, and a societal orientation, and these characteristics must be reflected in messages that are being communicated.

Learning Objectives

- Discover the foundations of sustainability communication
- Understand the concept of "sustainabilization" and the marketing opportunity it constitutes
- Comprehend and harness the grassroots revolution

- Take considerations in designing sustainable marketing communication
- Understand what greenwashing is

Introduction

Sustainability and the strong consumption focus of our society are not compatible in the long run; hence, marketing must change to include sustainability and its social and environmental implications. Marketing communications, therefore, must change accordingly.

In today's world, consumers are becoming increasingly conscious of sustainability and environmental responsibility. As a result, companies are under pressure to integrate sustainable practices into their operations – but the practices must also be communicated effectively to buyers and other stakeholders. The concept of greenwashing and its implications for stakeholders have been extensively explored by researchers. Santos et al. (2023), for example, highlight the prevalence of greenwashing across various industries and the challenges it poses for consumers, investors, regulators, and society as a whole. Furthermore, Montgomery et al. (2023) offers valuable insights into the persistent nature of greenwashing, emphasizing the need for continued attention and action to address this phenomenon effectively.

Marketing communications play a crucial role in this process, serving as the bridge between a company's sustainability efforts and its target audience. Accordingly, sustainable marketing communications could help consumers switch to more sustainable behavior (Lee et al. 2020).

This chapter explores strategies and best practices for effectively communicating sustainability initiatives. Effective communication is essential for maximizing the impact of sustainability initiatives and fostering stakeholder support and engagement. By adopting authentic, transparent, and engaging communication strategies, companies can build trust, enhance brand reputation, and contribute to a more sustainable future while avoiding greenwashing and its negative effects.

Foundations of Communication are the Same

Although sustainability communication is different from traditional marketing communications, the mechanisms and steps that bring a message from the sender to the receiver are basically the same. On its way, many things can happen that result in a message not producing the desired response (see Figure 6.1).

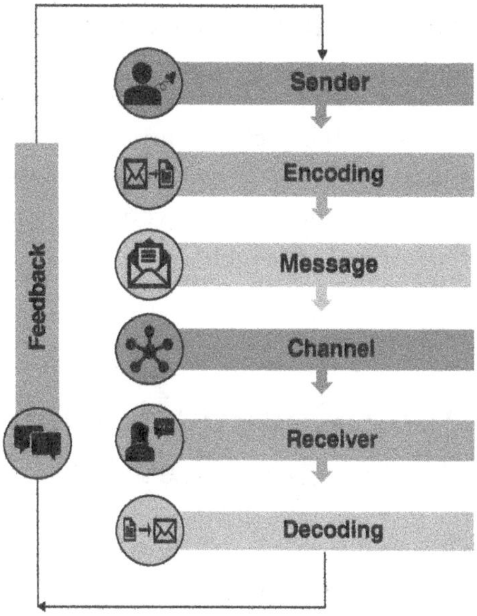

Figure 6.1 Key steps in marketing communications.
Source: Based on Schramm (1954) and Smith and Taylor (2004).

The Increasing Diversity of Marketing Communications Stakeholders

A fundamental change in marketing communications is a shift toward dealing with numerous stakeholders. While the number of stakeholders has increased, transparency throughout the value/supply chain network has increased too, and there are today various stakeholder groups that investigate companies and their communications efforts. The complexity in dealing with many stakeholders could even result in strategic ambiguity and hence put increased tension on running the firm with a clear focus when the interests of numerous stakeholders should be considered (Scandelius and Cohen 2016).

A challenge for companies is to convey consistent messages across various stakeholders and the increasing number of channels. Against the increased interest in companies' sustainability practices, stronger sustainability claims emphasize the sustainability implications of the organization's practices. It puts demands on organizations to keep track throughout their value supply chains and make sure that not only suppliers but also suppliers' suppliers work in sustainable ways. If not, sustainable marketing communication is unlikely to work – sustainability is based on transparency, honesty, and due diligence (i.e. pro-action).

Sustainability Communication

Sustainability communication refers to the strategic dissemination of information about a company's sustainability efforts, goals, and achievements to its various stakeholders. These stakeholders may include consumers, employees, investors, politicians, and the wider community. Effective sustainability communication is transparent, honest, and consistent, aiming to build trust and credibility with stakeholders (see Figure 6.2).

Marketing Communications and Sustainability – Can They Be Combined?

Effective sustainable marketing communication is crucial for companies seeking to establish trust, credibility, and positive stakeholder perceptions. Sustainability communication, hence, can play a crucial role in bridging this gap, as it helps understand how companies can utilize social media effectively in their communication strategies. Sustainable marketing has become a widespread practice and is backdropped by significant theoretical contributions, largely starting with Du et al. (2010), who developed a comprehensive conceptual framework that addresses the key aspects of corporate sustainability communication.

According to an article in the *Economist* that refers to the levels of carbon dioxide in the atmosphere as measured by the Mauna Loa Observatory (Hawaii), the concentration of CO_2 in the atmosphere is 30% higher than it was 64 years ago when measurements began and 50% higher than in pre-industrial times. Marketing communications has contributed to the disastrous effects of greenhouse gas–driven climate change on the lives of people, animals, and plants around the globe through downplaying environmental concerns while embellishing practices. Hence, for firms with sustainability claims, communications must contribute to consumers choosing sustainable products, managers engaging in circular supply chain management, and green consumption choices being an affordable offer for more people (Alden 2023; The Economist 2022).

The stakeholders that are targets of the communication, and the emphasis each of them should be given, varies across companies and industries; however,

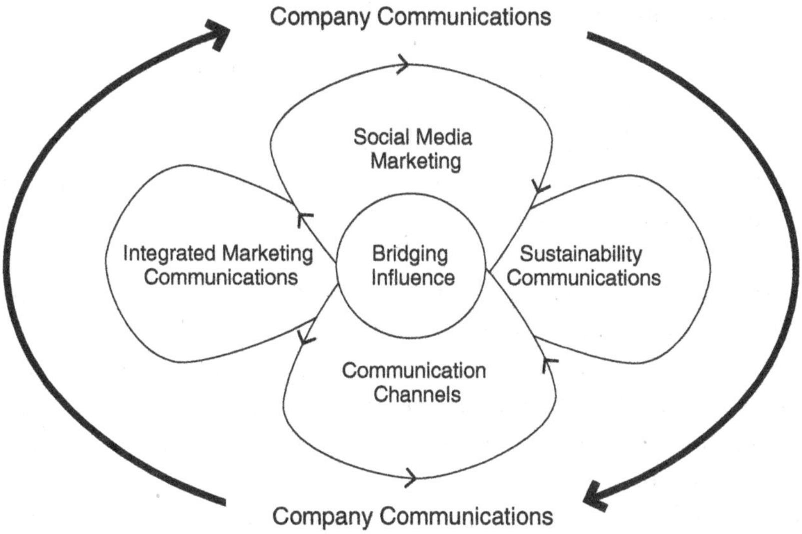

Figure 6.2 Sustainability communications.

three stakeholder groups stand out as they are always important in businesses, something that also holds true for sustainable communications efforts (Vasilieva et al. 2017):

- *Consumers, or business buyers in the case of business-to-business (B2B) markets:* Consumers determine the outcome of any business as they decide whether to buy or not. Here, it's crucial to understand the extent to which consumers are willing to buy for a higher sustainability performance. It's easy to agree on the advantages of fossil-free steel or sustainably sourced energy, but if buyers don't want to pay for the sustainability advantage, success in the marketplace will be difficult to accomplish. Sustainability communications could help convince buyers about the sustainability advantages
- *Employees:* A sustainable company must attract, recruit, and keep employees who understand sustainability and how it could be integrated into the company's practices (Kryger Aggerholm et al. 2011; Yasin et al. 2023)
- *Investors/owners:* Without happy and convinced investors and owners, it's very difficult to become truly sustainable. The advantages of sustainability efforts, for short-term as well as long-term profitability, must be communicated to them regularly unless they are of the not very common breed of people who see sustainable investments as a self-evident choice

Key Functions of Sustainability Communications

Sustainability communications have several key functions for companies with sustainability ambitions; see Figure 6.3 for an overview. Ideally, communication works as a glue that holds the company's sustainability efforts together.

According to Veland et al. (2018), the key components of effective sustainability communication include the following areas:

- *Authenticity* is paramount in sustainability communication. Consumers can quickly discern greenwashing, and increasingly so since the awareness is increasing. The practice of making misleading or unsubstantiated claims about the environmental benefits of a product or service is therefore becoming more difficult. Companies must ensure that their sustainability initiatives are genuine and backed by concrete actions
- *Transparency* involves openly sharing information about a company's sustainability practices, including its successes, challenges, and areas for improvement. Transparent communication builds trust and fosters accountability, as stakeholders can assess a company's performance based on reliable information
- *Education:* There are still consumers who don't understand the environmental impact of their purchasing decisions or the significance of sustainability initiatives. Effective communication should educate consumers and other stakeholders about sustainability issues, helping them make informed choices and encouraging support for sustainable practices
- *Marketing:* Visual communication and other marketing vehicles could amplify the reach and impact of sustainability messaging. Consistent messaging across channels reinforces key sustainability themes and enhances brand visibility

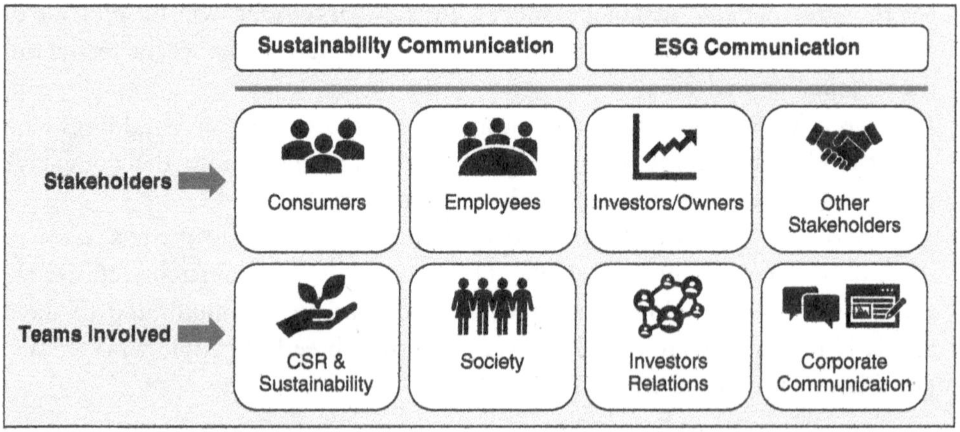

Figure 6.3 Key functions of sustainability communications.

- *Partnerships:* Partnerships demonstrate a company's commitment to collective action and leverage shared resources to drive meaningful change. Collaborating could take place with any organization, nongovernmental organization (NGO), influencer, etc. if it amplifies the reach and credibility of sustainability initiatives. The values of the partners must be consistent with the sustainability efforts of the company
- *Storytelling* might be a powerful tool for compellingly communicating sustainability initiatives. Companies can share narratives that highlight the journey, challenges, and impact of their sustainability efforts, resonating with consumers on an emotional level as a complement to more factual information (Veland et al. 2018)

The Importance of Sustainability in Marketing Communications

Sustainable marketing communications have become increasingly prominent in response to growing consumer demand for environmentally and socially responsible products and brands. This development reflects a broader shift toward sustainability across company practices. Here, marketing communications play a crucial role (see Figure 6.4).

As sustainability has emerged as a paramount concern across various industries, marketing communications has become even more important. In the best case, marketing communications contribute to sharing the company's sustainability concerns across stakeholders. In the worst case, marketing communications work as a megaphone for the company's lack of engagement, moral deficits, and attempts to

Figure 6.4 Communicating sustainable initiatives is very important, but tricky, as we'll see in this chapter.
Source: Shutterstock 2429975793.

greenwash. Accordingly, companies that engage in green advertising, eco-friendly branding, and other communication activities with sustainability claims have to be careful with their marketing communications efforts, which are often used to differentiate the companies and their brands in the market. For instance, the tendency to greenwash is evident in campaigns promoting renewable energy, recycling, and carbon footprint reduction. Multinational corporations like Unilever and Patagonia have launched sustainability-focused advertising campaigns to communicate their commitment to environmental stewardship (Mohr et al. 2019). The more companies engage in sustainability efforts, the more important it is that consumers and other stakeholders use a critical eye when evaluating the communication and the message behind it.

Companies are increasingly recognizing the power of narrative in engaging consumers and are hence incorporating sustainability narratives into their messaging. Patagonia is a successful example of a company that practices this method. By aligning their brand stories with environmental and social causes, companies can foster deeper connections with consumers who prioritize sustainability values (Luchs et al. 2012), such as when outdoor apparel company REI's "Opt Outside" campaign encourages consumers to spend time outdoors while promoting environmental conservation.

Patagonia – Promoting Sustainability in an Unsustainable Industry

Patagonia, a renowned outdoor clothing company, stands out as a trailblazer in using marketing communications to promote sustainability. Through its innovative and authentic approach, Patagonia has effectively communicated its commitment to environmental and social responsibility while engaging consumers and driving business growth. Here's how Patagonia utilizes marketing communications to promote sustainability:

- *Authentic brand storytelling:* The company's founder, Yvon Chouinard, built Patagonia with a strong ethos of environmental activism and sustainability, which permeates every aspect of the company's marketing communications, including campaigns, which often feature narratives that highlight Patagonia's commitment to environmental conservation, sustainable sourcing, and ethical business practices. By sharing stories of real people and initiatives, Patagonia establishes credibility and resonates with environmentally conscious consumers

- *Transparency and accountability:* Patagonia openly shares information about its supply chain, manufacturing processes, and environmental initiatives, allowing consumers to make informed choices. Patagonia's "Footprint Chronicles" initiative, for instance, provides detailed insights into the environmental and social impacts of its products, including information about materials sourcing, production methods, and transportation. By being transparent about its practices, Patagonia fosters trust and credibility among consumers
- *Environmental advocacy:* Patagonia uses its marketing communications as a platform for environmental advocacy and activism. The company frequently engages in advocacy campaigns on pressing environmental issues, such as climate change, biodiversity conservation, and public lands protection. Patagonia's "Vote Our Planet" campaign, launched during the 2016 US presidential election, encouraged citizens to vote for candidates who prioritize environmental stewardship. By leveraging its brand platform for advocacy, Patagonia amplifies its impact beyond product sales and inspires positive change
- *Innovative product design:* Patagonia integrates sustainability into its product design and development process and communicates these. The company invests in innovative materials, such as recycled polyester and organic cotton, to reduce its environmental footprint. Patagonia's "Worn Wear" initiative promotes product longevity and repairability, encouraging consumers to repair and reuse their clothing instead of buying new. Through its marketing communications, Patagonia educates consumers about the environmental benefits of its products and encourages mindful consumption
- *Community engagement:* Patagonia fosters community engagement and collaboration through its marketing communications. The company actively involves customers, employees, and environmental organizations in its sustainability initiatives and campaigns. Patagonia's "1% for the Planet" program, for instance, donates 1% of its sales to environmental nonprofits and encourages other companies to do the same. Through its marketing communications, Patagonia builds a sense of community around shared values of environmental stewardship and social responsibility (see Figure 6.5)

In sum, Patagonia demonstrates how effective marketing communications can be used to promote sustainability authentically and effectively by emphasizing authenticity, transparency, innovation, and community engagement. Patagonia has established itself as a leader in sustainable marketing communications and continues to inspire positive change within the industry and beyond.

(Continued)

(Continued)

Figure 6.5 Patagonia is a popular brand among highly educated and sustainability-conscious consumers – accordingly, the products are often sold in attractive locations. *Source:* Shutterstock 1051543736.

By experience, however, we know that not even well-intended companies are protected from scandals – so Patagonia has to be careful while consumers and other stakeholders continue following the company's communications efforts.

Source: Chouinard (2006), Hollender (2010), Joy et al. (2012), Luchs et al. (2016), and Patagonia (2024).

Companies have explored the role of technology and digital media in advancing sustainable marketing communications. Social media platforms have become instrumental in facilitating dialogue with increasingly environmentally conscious consumers (Polonsky et al. 2016). Companies can leverage social media channels to share updates on sustainability initiatives, respond to consumer inquiries, and solicit feedback on environmental practices.

Although companies face many challenges in accomplishing sustainability, those who successfully succeed in integrating sustainability into their operations stand to gain a competitive advantage by appealing to environmentally conscious consumers and enhancing brand reputation (Hartmann et al. 2015).

Sustainability Claims Differentiate Marketing Communications

Sustainable marketing communications isn't about totally reinventing how companies communicate with their buyers and other stakeholders but rather rethinking about it through a responsible lens looking at the words and language used, meeting the audience where it is, making things relevant and relatable so a story beyond selling stuff can be told, and driving positive change for individuals and society.

An organization with high-sustainability standards aims to minimize the impact on its global and local environments, and this should be reflected in that organization's communication. Products with less environmental impact and a higher fulfillment of environmental goals than other comparable products provide opportunities to communicate via different channels the fact that the company making them is "greener" than its competitors. One conceivable criterion when making decisions is whether a measure or activity meets customer requirements without harming the possibility of future generations having their needs met (cf. Hart & Milstein 2003).

Sustainability communication involves many areas such as the overall approach, the tools used, and the way of thinking about your communications to make consumers support the communication through creating ongoing conversations. Consumers and their increased interest in communications and interesting in being part of marketing communications must be considered. We'll come back to that. And as always, understanding audiences and their buying preferences, and explaining sustainability concepts through clear communication, may be at the core of the organization's marketing communications efforts.

Through the emergence of social media marketing and grassroots marketing, an area that will be explored later in the chapter, contemporary consumer markets are characterized by a more intimate relationship between brands and their customers. Accordingly, the power of consumers is much stronger. In the best case, consumer power promotes the company, its brand, its products, and its sustainability efforts. In the worst case, the company may come under fire for deceptive claims, high-pressure sales, disruptive tactics, or any other deceptive practices (see Chapter 7).

Dieselgate

In April 2019 the European Union proclaimed that Germany's three largest carmakers – Volkswagen, Daimler, and BMW – secretly agreed more than three years prior to equip their vehicles with inferior emissions equipment, a deceptive practice that exacerbated air quality issues across Europe and contributed to 40 000 early deaths annually.

Ironically, while Volkswagen peddled its diesel fleet in the United States under the banner of "clean diesel," consumers were unwittingly subjected to a hazardous deceptive practice (Cremer & Lewis 2015). This deceit extended globally, ensnaring millions of vehicles across Volkswagen's subsidiaries and affiliated brands, including Audi, Porsche, Skoda, and Seat (FAZ). The roots

(Continued)

(Continued)

of this scandal trace back to 2015 when Volkswagen confessed their diesel-powered vehicles had been equipped with software that could detect laboratory testing conditions, where the engine is running but the steering wheel typically is not being used, and adjust emissions to meet standards in such a setting. In real-world driving, these cars spewed significantly higher levels of nitrogen oxide (NOx), with some models emitting up to 38 times the permissible limit (Ewing 2015).

The scandal – dubbed *Dieselgate* – erupted when it was revealed that VW had installed this illegal software in millions of vehicles to cheat emissions tests. Volkswagen had long been known for its diesel engine technology but found it increasingly challenging to meet the standards without sacrificing performance or fuel economy. In response, engineers developed the defeat software.

The scandal came to light when researchers at the International Council on Clean Transportation (ICCT) and West Virginia University discovered discrepancies between emissions levels in real-world driving conditions and those recorded during laboratory tests for certain VW diesel vehicles.

Did everyone involved in powertrain development at Volkswagen know about the cheating? It's still unclear, but the company faced immense public backlash, tarnishing its reputation as a trusted automaker committed to sustainability. VW's stock value plummeted, and 11 million cars had to be rebuilt to avoid buying them back. Several lawsuits have been filed by consumers, regulators, and investors worldwide against VW over various issues related to Dieselgate.

In the years following Dieselgate, Volkswagen embarked on a comprehensive damage control effort. The company issued public apologies, committed to overhauling its corporate culture and compliance processes, and pledged to transition toward electric vehicles (EVs) as part of its long-term strategy to regain trust and mitigate environmental impact. VW also agreed to settlements with various stakeholders, including consumers, regulators, and class-action lawsuits, totaling billions of dollars. Additionally, the scandal prompted greater scrutiny of emissions testing procedures and regulatory oversight in the automotive industry globally. There has been significant evidence that competitors also have engaged in cheating – but in less obvious ways. Yet, Dieselgate was not an isolated incident but symptomatic of a broader malaise within the automotive industry (Ewing and Granville 2019).

The Dieselgate scandal stands as a cautionary tale of corporate misconduct and the repercussions of prioritizing short-term gains over ethical and legal obligations. This flagrant manipulation of emissions tests epitomized a reckless disregard for public health and environmental well-being. Nitrogen oxides, recognized as hazardous pollutants, pose grave health risks, including respiratory ailments and premature mortality. Volkswagen's illicit actions not only inflicted significant financial and reputational damage but also underscored the importance of transparency, accountability, and regulatory compliance. Dieselgate serves as a stark reminder that ethical lapses can have profound and enduring consequences for companies, consumers, and the environment alike.

Sustainabilization as Marketing Opportunity

Sustainabilization is the process of making formerly unsustainable practices sustainable, such as implementing environmentally friendly practices, reducing carbon footprints, promoting social equity, or fostering economic resilience. It has become a pivotal global marketing trend, profoundly shaping strategic decisions across businesses of all sizes. Media frequently highlight instances of sustainability failures, warning of the risks of being perceived as irresponsible. The fear of being involved in a scandal like Dieselgate puts pressure on companies to take sustainability seriously and hence avoid legal repercussions, financial losses, tarnished reputation, and environmental damage. Consequently, businesses are compelled to prioritize sustainability, knowing it directly impacts financial performance and consumer satisfaction in both the short and long term.

In the best case, this sparks a creative revolution, fostering the emergence of innovative sustainable business models and consumption practices. Business models based on sharing usage (e.g. collaborative consumption) or closing resource loops (e.g. circular economy) have gained traction and contributed to redefining the marketing landscape – see Chapters 4 and 8 on circularity and sharing systems. These sustainable opportunities share a common goal: resource and energy economization through reduced consumption and more recycling.

A shift toward valuing brand experiences over ownership reduces the need for excessive product circulation. Sharing economy principles promote shared product usage, challenging traditional notions of ownership. These initiatives must be communicated clearly. It's also about the future position of a company. When car manufacturers such as Toyota, Volvo, or Volkswagen offer car sharing through their car-sharing subsidiaries Kinto Share, Volvo on Demand, and Ubeequo (a subsidiary of car rental giant Europcar, owned by the Volkswagen Group), respectively, it certainly contributes to a transition away from personal car ownership. But if car manufacturers are not at the forefront in the transition, other companies will likely take the lead in offering car sharing (see Figure 6.6).

Figure 6.6 Car sharing gives more people the opportunity to go on vacation or visit relatives and friends by car, while keeping the number of new cars built lower, a procedure that taxes a lot of environmental resources.
Source: Shutterstock 424578970.

Actively embracing sustainable marketing, which involves developing, producing, and bringing to market products and services that benefit consumers, producers, and the environment, is crucial for achieving commercial success. On the contrary, neglecting sustainability poses significant risks for companies.

For a few decades now, sustainability has emerged as a strategic imperative for companies (Lubin and Esty 2010; Rezaee 2017). This has several rationales. First, there's a growing expectation for businesses to operate with goodwill, as consumers increasingly shun associations with entities contributing to environmental degradation and social injustices. Therefore, maintaining a positive sustainable reputation is in the best interest of every business. Transparency regarding the environmental and social impacts of production and consumption is vital for building consumer trust. Patagonia's initiative, the Patagonia Footprint Chronicles, exemplifies this transparency by detailing the origins of their garments and materials (see Figure 6.7). Conversely, failure to uphold sustainable practices can lead to damaging repercussions, as seen in media reports exposing poor working conditions in fast fashion factories and tarnishing the reputations of companies like H&M and Walmart. Greenwashing, or misleading claims about environmental or social benefits, further erodes trust and can be detrimental to a company's image. Sustainability could hence be a business opportunity – consumers are willing to pay a price premium for products from companies that avoid greenwashing.

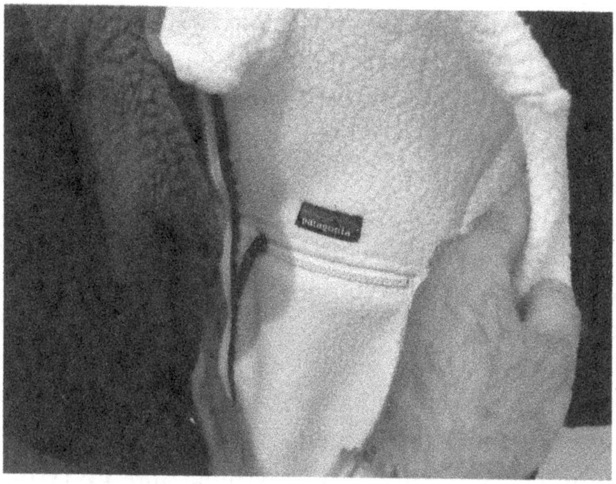

Figure 6.7 Patagonia's garment has become trendy among aware consumers, including those with high purchase power, making the company's sustainable approach a business opportunity.
Source: ifeelstock/Adobe Stock.

Beware of Greenwashing

It is evident that greenwashing remains a pressing issue that warrants further investigation and action. As companies increasingly seek to position themselves as environmentally responsible, the risk of greenwashing persists, necessitating vigilance and scrutiny from stakeholders. By advancing our understanding of greenwashing and its impacts, researchers can inform policies, practices, and consumer behaviors to foster genuine sustainability and mitigate the risks associated with deceptive marketing practices.

The term *greenwashing* is used to describe how companies use marketing communication and, in particular, advertising to claim that products are considerably more environmentally friendly than they really are. Exaggerated claims regarding a product's environmental performance and the like do not impress consumers (Peattie 1999) nor does "much ado about nothing," something that applies to things that are becoming increasingly self-evident: for instance, sorting waste by source, shops donating unsellable food to relief organizations, environmentally oriented travel policies, etc. Greenwashing appears when marketing effort is put in to deceptively promote products as eco-friendly and imply the policies of an organization are sustainable although there is no solid ambition for sustainability. Grant (2007) even argues that pretentious claims with little support can be counterproductive, as the consumer then adopts a questioning stance with regard to whether the company has something to hide since it is indulging in misleading communication about sustainability.

As greenwashing has become such a frequent activity, there is a tendency for consumers to reject all marketing communication in which sustainability claims are made. Instead, they choose brands and products that do not communicate any such arguments at all. Sustainability being communicated for the sake of a company's purposes, and which is not due to any genuine conviction regarding a more sustainable society, thus runs the risk of jeopardizing the reputation and effect of sustainability communication. Since marketing communication regarding sustainable products is aimed at changing consumer behavior, greenwashing runs the risk of threatening all necessary adjustments to move from unsustainable toward sustainable offerings. This is both serious and unfortunate as a large portion of consumers may completely abandon sustainable products and "shut down" their attention to important aspects of sustainability in their consumption choices.

In today's markets, it seems as if anything and everything has become sustainable: airlines, retailers, car companies, restaurants, universities, hotels, and banks. Nonetheless, greenwashing in all these sectors can be harmful for the environment, for consumers, for society and future generations, but also for the business itself since its reputation will ultimately be affected negatively (Torelli et al. 2020). Sustainability ratings reflect a higher transparency and contribute to a worse reputation (Parguel et al. 2011). Greenwashing takes many forms (see Figure 6.8), so consumers have to be attentive.

Figure 6.8 Greenwashing takes many forms.

When an organization spends more resources claiming to be sustainable through marketing than on the actual implementation of business practices that minimize its environmental impact, it engages in greenwashing. A typical example is an energy company that runs an advertising campaign touting sustainable technology but that turns out to represent only an insignificant part of its otherwise not-so-sustainable business. Greenwashing draws upon the expression whitewashing, which is a coordinated attempt to hide unpleasant facts in a political context. Greenwashing is a similar phenomenon, but in an environmental or sustainability context.

A typical practice in hotels – even the ones that call themselves sustainable – is to enable guests to choose to sleep on the same sheets and reuse towels, something that might have sounded appealing in the 1990s (in fact, Hilton hotels promoted this idea in the 1980s) but actually does very little to save water and energy where it counts. The very same hotels may use vast amounts of energy for appliances and lighting, in kitchens, and in their vehicle fleet. Extensive 24/7 lighting and a significant waste of food that is exposed during breakfast and lunch buffets to provide an aesthetically appealing environment contribute to the lack of sustainability. If the bigger picture is considered, reducing towels in the laundry will provide insignificant savings.

On the positive side, organizations claiming to be sustainable do not want to risk being accused of practicing greenwashing. Hence, they are forced to make sure they live up to their promises. Montgomery et al. (2023) provides a comprehensive review of greenwashing practices and proposes a research agenda to guide future studies in this area. Their work underscores the importance of developing robust frameworks for detecting and combatting greenwashing, as well as exploring the motivations behind deceptive environmental claims. Additionally, Montgomery et al. (2023) advocate for ongoing collaboration between researchers, practitioners, policymakers, and other stakeholders to develop sustainable solutions and promote greater transparency and accountability in corporate communications.

Greenwashing Has a Strong Impact on Consumer Attitudes. . .

Studies have examined consumer perceptions of green advertising, highlighting the importance of authenticity and transparency in messaging (Chernev and Blair 2015). For a long time, consumers have been skeptical of greenwashing and expected companies to demonstrate genuine commitment to sustainability (Delmas and Burbano 2011). A lot of studies have dealt with the effects of greenwashing on consumers.

. . .and Contributes to Consumer Skepticism

Studies across industries underscore the necessity for companies to uphold genuine sustainability practices and maintain transparency in their marketing communications. Greenwashing not only erodes consumer trust but also hinders efforts to promote sustainable consumption behavior. Greenwashing, hence, has a number of negative effects that contribute to consumer skepticism: a poor impact on the company's reputation; a negative influence on the purchase intentions; and significant effects on consumers' feelings of betrayal, which have an influence on their purchasing intentions. Environmental responsibility further intensifies the negative effect of greenwashing perception on these intentions, emphasizing the importance of trust and credibility in marketing communications (de Jong et al. 2020; Lu et al. 2022; Setiawan and Yosephani 2022; Sun and Shi 2022).

The Seven Sins of Greenwashing

Greenwashing, the deceptive practice of presenting a misleadingly positive image of a company's environmental efforts, has become a major concern in contemporary marketing communications. Greenwashing represents a betrayal of consumer trust and a hindrance to meaningful progress toward environmental sustainability. By understanding the sins of greenwashing and their implications, stakeholders can work together to promote honesty, transparency, and authenticity in environmental marketing.

The "Seven Sins of Greenwashing" is a framework developed by TerraChoice (now part of Underwriters Laboratories) to identify deceptive environmental marketing claims. These sins highlight common tactics used by companies to mislead consumers into believing that their products are more environmentally friendly than they actually are. The framework helps consumers and other stakeholders identify greenwashing among companies, highlighting greenwashings' detrimental effects on consumer trust, environmental progress, and corporate reputation (see Figure 6.9).

The seven sins according to Manning (2023) are:

- *Sin of the Hidden Trade-Off:* This occurs when companies make an environmental claim about a product based on a narrow set of attributes while ignoring other, potentially more significant environmental impacts. For example, labeling a product as "green" solely because it uses recycled materials while ignoring other negative environmental aspects
- *Sin of No Proof:* This involves making an environmental claim that cannot be substantiated by easily accessible supporting information or by a reliable third-party certification. Claims such as "eco-friendly" or "green" without any evidence or certification fall into this category
- *Sin of Vagueness:* This occurs when environmental claims are so poorly defined or broad that their true meaning is likely to be misunderstood by consumers. For instance, using terms like "all-natural" or "environmentally friendly" without specifying what aspects of the product or production process are environmentally beneficial

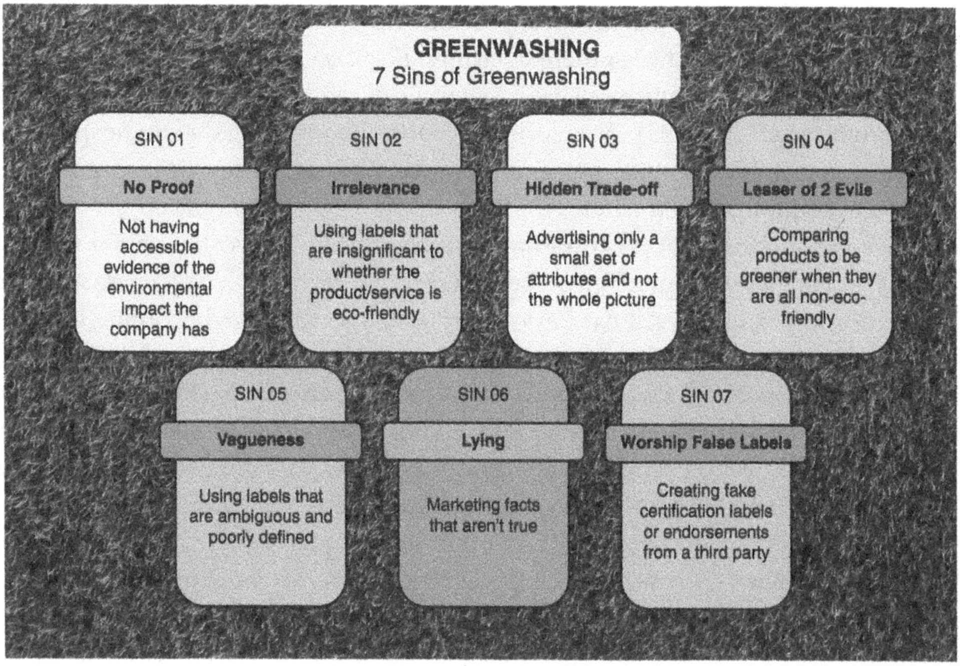

Figure 6.9 The seven sins of greenwashing.
Source: Based on Manning (2023).

- *Sin of Irrelevance:* This happens when an environmental claim is technically true but is ultimately unimportant or irrelevant to the product or its impact. An example would be labeling a product as "CFC-free" when chlorofluorocarbons (CFCs) are already banned by law
- *Sin of Lesser of Two Evils:* This occurs when a company promotes an environmental benefit of a product that is only marginally better than the environmental harm caused by the product's overall existence. For instance, advertising a fuel-efficient sport utility vehicle (SUV) as environmentally friendly when SUVs inherently have higher emissions than smaller vehicles
- *Sin of Fibbing:* This involves outright lying or providing false information about the environmental attributes of a product. An example would be claiming a product is certified by an independent organization when it is not
- *Sin of Worshiping False Labels:* This happens when a product's packaging or marketing prominently displays a certification or eco-label that is either nonexistent, irrelevant, or unverifiable. This misleads consumers into believing the product has been independently certified when it has not

These sins serve as a useful guide for consumers and other stakeholders to critically evaluate environmental claims made by companies. By being aware of these tactics, consumers can make more informed choices and hold companies accountable for their environmental claims. For companies, greenwashing can result in reputational damage, legal repercussions, and loss of consumer loyalty (Montgomery et al. 2023). Moreover, greenwashing impedes genuine progress toward sustainability by diverting attention and resources away from meaningful environmental initiatives (Laufer 2003).

To combat the sins of greenwashing, stakeholders must work together to promote transparency, accountability, and integrity in environmental marketing. As mentioned in Chapter 1, standards for environmental claims are becoming increasingly common, and the European Commission has imposed penalties for false or misleading marketing communications, i.e. greenwashing (European Parliament 2024). Hence, not only do various stakeholders such as NGOs and consumer advocacy groups play a crucial role in exposing greenwashing practices and holding companies accountable for their actions, but also stricter standards contribute.

Through regulatory oversight, consumer activism, and corporate responsibility, we can combat greenwashing and foster a culture of genuine environmental stewardship.

Greenwashing: Disguise of the Environmental Impact of Fast Fashion?

The fashion industry, and in particular companies engaged in fast fashion, has come under scrutiny for its significant environmental impact. Fast fashion is characterized by rapid production cycles, low prices, and disposable clothing trends. However, this model often relies on environmentally harmful practices, such as excessive water usage, chemical pollution, and exploitation of labor. If fast fashion was once something to be proud of, an impressive coming together of great planning, great logistics, and a unique ability to know what the market wants in a month or two, satisfying consumers' need for a continuous flow of consumption opportunities at affordable prices, it is now increasingly criticized by various stakeholders. From resource-intensive production processes over consumer overconsumption to pollution and waste generation, the fast fashion industry faces growing concerns about its sustainability practices. In response, some companies have tried to portray themselves as environmentally conscious to improve their public image and attract environmentally conscious consumers. However, these ambitions often result in companies engaging in greenwashing – making misleading claims about their sustainability efforts (see Figure 6.10).

Figure 6.10 Attractive pieces of clothing that we find in stores are often produced through nonsustainable methods.
Source: Visual Sameer/Adobe Stock.

Synthetics Anonymous, an environmental advocacy group, recently published a report highlighting examples of greenwashing within the textile industry. The report exposes how certain companies use deceptive marketing tactics to portray themselves as environmentally friendly while continuing to contribute to environmental degradation (Trunk et al. 2021).

Examples include, but are not limited to, the following:

- *Misleading sustainability claims*: Several fast fashion brands have been accused of making vague or unsubstantiated claims about their environmental practices. This includes statements about using "eco-friendly" materials or implementing "green" initiatives without providing concrete evidence or transparent information
- *Lack of transparency*: Many companies fail to disclose information about their supply chain practices, making it difficult for consumers to assess the true environmental impact of their clothing. This lack of transparency extends to issues such as sourcing raw materials, manufacturing processes, and labor conditions

(Continued)

(Continued)

- *Greenwashing campaigns*: Some companies invest heavily in marketing campaigns that emphasize their sustainability efforts while downplaying their negative environmental impact. These campaigns often focus on isolated initiatives, such as recycling programs or sustainable collections, while ignoring broader systemic issues within the industry

The prevalence of greenwashing in the fashion industry has several implications for the environment, consumers, and society. First, it undermines efforts to promote genuine sustainability practices by misleading consumers and eroding trust in environmentally friendly brands. Second, it perpetuates the cycle of overconsumption and waste associated with fast fashion, exacerbating environmental degradation and social inequality.

In sum, there is a need for greater transparency, accountability, and regulation to address the environmental impact of fast fashion. Companies must be held accountable for their claims and encouraged to adopt truly sustainable practices that prioritize environmental stewardship and social responsibility. By promoting transparency and consumer awareness, stakeholders can work together to create a more sustainable and ethical fashion industry.

Source: Trunk et al. (2021), Bhardwaj and Fairhurst (2010), and Niinimäki et al. (2020).

The Grassroots Revolution

For many decades, marketers have seen markets as something rather static, but one change that did not occur over one night but nonetheless has been very strong will change the role of marketing in society for many years to come. It's a paradigm shift, a game changer facilitated by the emergence of social media marketing (see Carty 2010).

Grassroots marketing is the principle of purposefully targeting market segments to persuade that group to then propagate your message organically. But you can't be sure they do what you want. Grassroots marketing relies heavily on social media and virality to succeed. Since the idea behind this kind of campaign is to encourage people to share a story, it follows that social media is pivotal in making this happen.

In the past, it was commonly assumed that marketing managers held full sway over marketing communications, although grassroots influences were always present to some degree. However, in today's democratic landscape, it's clear that overlooking the possibility that marketing managers may no longer wield absolute control over marketing communications is shortsighted and unwise. They face challenges not only from grassroots movements but also from burgeoning communications and information departments, which now dictate how a company engages with its diverse stakeholders.

Challenges of Sustainable Marketing Communications in a Grassroots Environment

Understanding sustainability issues and consumer behavior is fundamental for modern marketing practices that aim for sustainable market communication. This foundation guides organizations in targeting specific consumer segments and strategically positioning their offerings with sustainability at the core.

Organizations engage with various stakeholders regularly, including suppliers, customers, shareholders, government bodies, and the European Union. Sustainability considerations should influence how messages are crafted and which channels are utilized for communication. Additionally, there must be a robust strategy for managing communication channels and ensuring transparent dissemination of information without direct influence over the message content, such as through social media, network forums, or editorial articles.

The traditional concept of marketing communication, focused solely on transmitting formulated messages, is outdated in today's dynamic marketing landscape. The rise of grassroots-driven information has compelled companies to prioritize sustainability efforts. Consumers now scrutinize organizations for their ethical practices, resource management, and commitment to fair labor conditions across the entire value chain.

Incidents reported by the media, exposing poor working conditions or exploitation in industries like smartphone manufacturing or fashion, can significantly impact a company's reputation. Companies need a proactive strategy to address such issues, as claims of sustainability and corporate social responsibility (CSR) policies directly affect consumer perceptions. Ethically conscious consumers are quick to boycott companies that engage in unethical practices, while ethical behavior doesn't always guarantee increased customer loyalty.

However, there have been noticeable improvements in practices, with some companies, such as H&M and Walmart, responding to criticism by promising higher wages for workers in developing countries where their products are manufactured. Digitalization and heightened awareness of global inequalities, particularly within fashion supply chains, have empowered not only consumers but also factory workers to demand fair treatment and better working conditions.

To sum up, in a society striving for sustainability, sustainability marketing is likely to grow in importance; however, this might not be easily achieved by all companies. Industry characteristics, management style, organizational culture, and cost structures may impede the realization of sustainable strategies.

Consumers have more control over where, how, and when messages reach them. They are informed about brands, products, and services in the marketplace (e.g. which organization is behind, what should they pay attention to when it comes to production and distribution processes, etc.), and they have obtained influential power about what organizations can do and say when it comes to sustainability. It has become self-evident to consumers that they should gather information from sources not under the control of companies that sell the products and services. It should thus also be self-evident to companies and other organizations that they should stick to this when communicating with various target groups, i.e. an integrated communication marketing strategy across all channels. Genuine measures for increasing sustainability will thus enjoy better conditions for dissemination than previously.

Social media, blogs, and threads on various forums are places where prominent information can be found and discussed (e.g. airbnbhell.com is a website where Airbnb platform users share their dissatisfying experience for others to be aware of some policy issues, common scams, etc.). The ability to find out what other consumers think of a company, its products, and the extent to which it lives up to its commitments has improved considerably. Organizations like for-profit companies can also leverage these opportunities for disseminating information or allowing customers to interact, for instance by not only having a corporate website but also a blog where customers are invited to discuss products or services.

For sustainable communication, what is interesting is the attitude toward what is being communicated rather than which channel is being used. A company aspiring toward sustainable communication should be able to consider using the Internet to create meeting places and forums for discussion. In doing so, they will meet the need for grassroots communication, which will result in consumers, employees, and other target groups becoming more loyal and the brand will thus become more attractive.

Consumers perceive companies that continue to primarily rely on traditional channels, avoiding grassroots-driven channels, are characterized by an objective of control and an outdated marketing approach. Messages will then be slightly general and "boring" – they will lack nerve and will not appeal to consumers' feelings. Despite the methodological issues surrounding websites based on grassroots-driven communication, these have a high level of credibility due to being supposedly independent of the company and the image that the company wants to project – the company can only be hosting an online platform (and setting up guidelines) for discussion of customer issues, not controlling the discussions' content per se. The information should not be tainted by the values of the company.

References

Alden, D. L. (2023). A call for research on climate adaptive products. *Journal of Sustainable Marketing*, 4(1), 1–6.

Bhardwaj, V., & Fairhurst, A. (2010). Fast fashion: response to changes in the fashion industry. *The International Review of Retail, Distribution and Consumer Research*, 20(1), 165–173.

Carty, V. (2010). New information communication technologies and grassroots mobilization. *Information, Communication and Society*, 13(2), 155–173.

Chernev, A., & Blair, S. (2015). Doing well by doing good: the benevolent halo of corporate social responsibility. *Journal of Consumer Research*, 41(6), 1412–1425.

Chouinard, Y. (2006). *Let My People Go Surfing: The Education of a Reluctant Businessman*. Penguin.

Cremer, A. & Lewis, B. (2015). Volkswagen starts telling customers if affected by emissions scandal. *Reuters. Oct.* 2nd, downloaded from: https://www.reuters.com/article/business/environment/volkswagen-starts-telling-customers-if-affected-by-emissions-scandal-idUSKCN0RU15G/.

Delmas, M. A., & Burbano, V. C. (2011). The drivers of greenwashing. *California Management Review*, 54(1), 64–87.

Du, S., Bhattacharya, C. B., & Sen, S. (2010). Maximizing business returns to corporate social responsibility (CSR): the role of CSR communication. *International Journal of Management Reviews*, 12(1), 8–19.

European Parliament (2024). Commission and national consumer protection authorities starts action against 20 airlines for misleading greenwashing practices. *European Commission*. https://ec.europa.eu/commission/presscorner/detail/en/ip_24_2322 (accessed 1 May 2024).

Ewing J. (2015). Volkswagen says 11 million cars worldwide are affected in Diesel Deception. *New York Times*. September 22, 2015. https://www.nytimes.com/2015/09/23/business/international/volkswagen-diesel-car-scandal.html (accessed 15 March 2015).

Ewing, J., & Granville, K. (2019). VW, BMW and Daimler Hindered Clean-Air Technology, European Regulator Says. *New York Times*. April 5, 2019. https://www.nytimes.com/2019/04/05/business/eu-collusion-bmw-vw-daimler-emissions.html (accessed 15 March 2024).

Grant, J. (2007). *The Green Marketing Manifesto*. Chichester: Wiley.

Hart, S. L., & Milstein, M. B. (2003). Creating sustainable value. *Academy of Management Perspectives*, 17(2), 56-67.

Hartmann, P., Apaolaza-Ibáñez, V., & Bigné-Alcañiz, E. (2015). Sustainable fashion consumption and the fast fashion conundrum: fashionable consumers and attitudes towards sustainability in clothing choice. *Journal of Cleaner Production*, 112, 336–346.

Hollender, J. (2010). *The Responsibility Revolution: How the Next Generation of Businesses Will Win*. San Francisco: Jossey-Bass.

de Jong, M. D. T., Huluba, G., & Beldad, A. D. (2020). Different shades of greenwashing: consumers' reactions to environmental lies, half-lies, and organizations taking credit for following legal obligations. *Journal of Business and Technical Communication*, 34(1), 38–76.

Joy, A., Sherry J.F. Jr., Venkatesh, A., Wang, J. & Chan, R. (2012). Fast fashion, sustainability, and the ethical appeal of luxury brands. *Fashion Theory: The Journal of Dress, Body and Culture*, 16(3), 273–296.

Kryger Aggerholm, H., Esmann Andersen, S., & Thomsen, C. (2011). Conceptualizing employer branding in sustainable organizations. *Corporate Communications: An International Journal*, 16(2), 105–123.

Laufer, W. S. (2003). Social accountability and corporate greenwashing. *Journal of Business Ethics*, 43(3), 253–261.

Lee, E. J., Choi, H., Han, J., Kim, D. H., Ko, E., & Kim, K. H. (2020). How to "nudge" your consumers toward sustainable fashion consumption: an fMRI investigation. *Journal of Business Research*, 117, 642–651.

Lu, X, Sheng T, Zhou X, Shen C, Fang B. (2022). How does young consumers' greenwashing perception impact their green purchase intention in the fast fashion industry? An analysis from the perspective of perceived risk theory. *Sustainability*, 14(20), 13473.

Lubin, D. A., & Esty, D. C. (2010). The sustainability imperative. *Harvard Business Review*, 88(5), 42–50.

Luchs, M.G., Naylor, R.W., Irwin, J. R., & Raghunathan, R. (2012). The sustainability liability: potential negative effects of ethicality on product preference. *Journal of Marketing*, 76(1), 68–87.

Luchs, M.G., Kohler, M.J., Smith, R.L. & Naylor, R. (2016). Sustainability through the lens of marketing. *Business Horizons* 59(1), 53–62.

Manning, C. (2023). What are the seven sins of greenwashing? *Impact*. July 11, 2023. https://impactreporting.co.uk/seven-sins-of-greenwashing (accessed 12 May 2024).

Mohr, J. J., Webb, D. J., & Harris, K. E. (2019). Do consumers expect companies to be socially responsible? The impact of corporate social responsibility on buying behavior. *Journal of Consumer Affairs*, 53(3), 673–696.

Montgomery, A. W., Lyon, T. P., & Barg, J. (2023). No end in sight? A greenwash review and research agenda. *Organization and Environment*. https://doi.org/10.1177/10860266231168905

Niinimäki, K., Peters, G., Dahlbo, H., Perry, P., Rissanen, T., & Gwilt, A. (2020). The environmental price of fast fashion. *Nature Reviews Earth and Environment*, 1(4), 189–200.

Parguel, B., Benoît-Moreau, F., & Larceneux, F. (2011). How sustainability ratings might deter 'greenwashing': a closer look at ethical corporate communication. *Journal of Business Ethics*, 102, 15–28.

Patagonia (2024). Environmental + Social Initiatives. *Patagonia*. https://www.patagonia.com/activism (Retrieved May 12, 2024).

Peattie, K. (1999). Trappings versus substance in the greening of marketing planning. *Journal of Strategic Marketing*, 7(2), 131–148.

Polonsky, M. J., Vocino, A., & Landreth Grau, S. (2016). Social media use in sustainable marketing: content analysis of CSR communication within food industry. *Journal of Nonprofit and Public Sector Marketing*, 28(2), 144–165.

Rezaee, Z. (2017). Corporate sustainability: theoretical and integrated strategic imperative and pragmatic approach. *The Journal of Business Inquiry*, 16(1). https://papers.ssrn.com/sol3/papers.cfm?abstract_id=3148705

Santos, C., Coelho, A., & Marques, A. (2023). A systematic literature review on greenwashing and its relationship to stakeholders: state of art and future research agenda. *Management Review Quarterly*, 1–25.

Scandelius, C., & Cohen, G. (2016). Achieving collaboration with diverse stakeholders—the role of strategic ambiguity in CSR communication. *Journal of Business Research*, 69(9), 3487–3499.

Schramm, W. (1954). How communication works. In W. Schramm (Ed.). *The Process and Effects of Mass Communication.* Urbana: University of Illinois Press, pp. 67–78.

Setiawan, B., & Yosephani, A. (2022). The linkage of greenwashing perception and consumers' green purchase intention. *Business and Entrepreneurial Review*, 22(1), 85–96.

Smith, P. R., & Taylor, J. (2004). *Marketing Communications: An Integrated Approach.* London: Kogan Page Publishers.

Sun Y, Shi B., 2022, Impact of greenwashing perception on consumers' green purchasing intentions: a moderated mediation model. *Sustainability*, 14(19), 12119.

The Economist (2022). The cost-plus world of supply chains. https://impact.economist.com/projects/next-gen-supply-chains/images/articles/2022/the-cost-plus-world-of-supply-chains.pdf (accessed 1 April 2024).

Torelli, R., Balluchi, F., & Lazzini, A. (2020). Greenwashing and environmental communication: effects on stakeholders' perceptions. *Business Strategy and the Environment*, 29(2), 407–421.

Trunk, U., Harding-Rolls, G., Banegas, X., Urbancic, N. & Nguyen, A. (2021). Synthetics anonymous fashion brands' addiction to fossil fuels. *Changing Markets.* June 2021. https://changingmarkets.org/report/synthetics-anonymous-fashion-brands-addiction-to-fossil-fuels (accessed 1 March 2024).

Vasilieva, T.; Lieonov, S.; Makarenko, I.; Sirkovska, N., 2017, Sustainability information disclosure as an instrument of marketing communication with stakeholders: markets, social and economic aspects. *Marketing Management Innovation*, 4, 350–357

Veland, S., Scoville-Simonds, M., Gram-Hanssen, I., Schorre, A. K., El Khoury, A., Nordbø, M. J. & Bjørkan, M. (2018). Narrative matters for sustainability: the transformative role of storytelling in realizing 1.5 C futures. *Current Opinion in Environmental Sustainability*, 31, 41–47.

Yasin, R., Huseynova, A., & Atif, M. (2023). Green human resource management, a gateway to employer branding: mediating role of corporate environmental sustainability and corporate social sustainability. *Corporate Social Responsibility and Environmental Management*, 30(1), 369–383.

Chapter 7

Sustainability and Branding

For many decades, companies have worked intensively with their brands to enjoy the benefits of a strong brand. Branding practices have become widespread, and organizations in civil society and the public sectors alike have put forth a lot of effort into strengthening their brands, all in all resulting in a branded world – where brands are everywhere and are used as tools to get through the media clutter. Brands may be very effective, while at the same time bearing lots of responsibilities. Brands make promises to consumers and result in expectations that are linked to the way companies and others communicate. For organizations attempting to have sustainable practices, it is important to understand the methods and mechanisms that shape strong brands and the advantages that come with strong brands.

Learning Objectives

- Understand what makes a brand a sustainable brand
- Explain why brands are crucial in communicating sustainability efforts
- Understand the characteristics of the "branded society"
- Identify key stakeholders for an organization's branding efforts
- Understand the relationship between sustainability claims and sustainable marketing communication

Introduction

In the pursuit of broader corporate social responsibility goals, many companies turn toward sustainability brand strategies. This helps them to both attract customers and uphold ethical values. These sustainability efforts include a broad range of activities such as retailers using more regenerative and renewable energy, mobility providers seeking to reduce emissions from their vehicles, and sustainable clothing brands offering wardrobe staples made from recycled, fairly traded, and environmentally conscious materials.

To meet consumer demand and clear a progressive path to the future, organizations need to embrace sustainable branding. The ones that don't risk rendering themselves irrelevant – even if their practices might be sustainable.

The practice of branding has become more widespread as an increasing range of organizations and industries have started to emphasize and take part in branding efforts. The interest in sustainability is partly interwoven with an increased focus on brands. Hence, sustainable brands are a crucial part of today's society, reflecting companies that succeed with both sustainability and building an attractive brand. Like with all brands, sustainability-oriented brands can't become strong unless the underlying performance is convincing. Accordingly, while truly sustainable companies have a high likeliness of succeeding with building strong sustainable brands, it's unlikely that brands with poor sustainability practices succeed. And that goes back to the basic nature of brands – reflecting various stakeholders' thoughts and associations to a brand.

Sustainable branding is defined as the act of embodying sustainability principles throughout an organization's operations, culture, and communications. This includes environmental and social sustainability (e.g. Czinkota et al. 2014; Kryger Aggerholm et al. 2011).

A sustainable brand is one that has successfully integrated environmental, economic, and social issues into its business operations. However, many companies that consider themselves to be sustainable meet only parts of this definition. Assuming consumers want to make decisions that'll positively impact environmental, social, and economic issues, sustainable branding goes beyond putting forth a certain image, as consumers are sensitive to greenwashing, particularly young and well-educated consumers. Hence, consumers across cultures expect authenticity.

To successfully implement sustainable branding, the organization itself needs to be sustainable to a high extent and should always be working toward advancing its current practices to promote sustainability.

Sustainable branding builds on several pillars (inspired by Bartak 2023) (see Figure 7.1):

Figure 7.1 Pillars of sustainable branding.
Source: Inspired by Bartak (2023).

- It *promotes transparency* in the organization's practices
- There is a strong link to the *communications channels* used – branding and communications are communicating vessels
- *Customer value* must be delivered
- It *promotes transition* toward more sustainable practices
- It *promotes consistency* in what the company stands for – a sustainable brand gives direction and holds things together
- *Environmental sustainability* is as obvious as *social sustainability*

Sustainable branding doesn't only contribute to a healthier planet, it's good for business and could hence contribute to *economic sustainability* (Pätäri et al. 2012;

Kumar and Christodoulopoulou 2014). The social sustainability part is crucial in communicating sustainable branding. Marketing communications has been losing the battle to maintain the sanctity of this concept as authorities, various media outlets, activists, and others throw the word *sustainable* around to refer solely to environmental issues, so the expectations of practices is that they are serious and solid. The environmental side is a good place to start, and it's what most people find being the first association with sustainability. However, a brand can't claim to be sustainable unless its social practices live up to high standards.

Sustainable Brands Avoid Greenwashing

Sustainable branding involves promoting a brand as sustainable, while greenwashing is the deceptive practice of making false or misleading claims about a brand's sustainability. Distinguishing between genuine sustainability efforts and greenwashing is crucial.

Authentic sustainable brands can provide solid evidence to support their claims, such as sustainability certifications, third-party audits, and transparent supply chain tracking. In contrast, brands engaging in greenwashing often use vague language to make their claims sound more impressive than they are. For instance, a brand might say it is "eco-friendly" or "committed to sustainability" without providing specific details.

If a brand claims to be completely carbon neutral or have zero waste, it might be too good to be true. Truly sustainable brands are transparent about their challenges and continuously strive to improve their sustainability performance.

Are Consumers Ready for Sustainable Brands?

In a society emphasizing sustainability, the skill to repair, recycle, and reuse will be valued higher than in a society that has encouraged consumption patterns with an emphasis on "buy and discard" for several decades. We can see that there has been a burgeoning interest in artisans, tailors, shoemakers, and skilled professionals able to repair glass and porcelain. But this is not just due to sustainability concerns – even if we repair some of our possessions, we also consume like never before.

On the one hand, consumers, especially young people like Generation Z (born 1995–2010), clearly favor sustainable brands. These consumers prefer to spend their money on brands that embrace social justice, apply sustainable manufacturing practices, and exercise ethical business standards (Chaturvedi et al. 2020). So, it's clear that some consumers segments prefer sustainable brands. On the other hand, challenges with the state of the economy and significant attitude-behavior gaps reported in various consumption contexts indicate that the question is far from solved. Consumers want sustainable brands – yes – but companies should not take for granted that consumers are willing to pay a higher price unless sustainability efforts are solid and delivered (discussed further in Chapter 10). Moreover, it cannot be taken for granted that the stated willingness to pay that is measured in research studies of consumers in general actually materializes when it comes to real-world purchase situations (e.g. Schäufele and Hamm 2017; Bastounis et al. 2021).

Hence, it is crucial for the success of companies and other organizations alike to build strong brands to reach the desired buyers and show them what the brand is doing. If not, they may end up buying from the company's competitors.

Sustainable Brands Are Based on Reputation

According to Kapferer (2012), brands increasingly want to communicate their ideals to the world. A key sustainability topic that has captured a high level of interest among researchers is the expectation that companies take responsibility for their actions. A number of different standards have been developed to get companies to develop more systematic, progressive, and visible policies for societal responsibility. A company's reputation can be seen as a legitimization process during which experiences are transformed into expectations regarding the future (Pérez-Cornejo et al. 2020; de Quevedo-Puente et al. 2007). Upholding sustainability practices will hence increasingly be expected by consumers and other stakeholders.

It Takes a Lot to Become a Sustainable Brand

Increasingly aware consumers are scrutinizing a company's stance on issues that impact people and the planet, making sustainability a necessity. In numerous industries, sustainability is not an option for companies today – it's an expectation. Accordingly, focusing on sustainability is no longer a niche brand category. As the climate movement moves further to the forefront, consumers are expecting brands to make a difference. Sustainable businesses gain advantages, ranging from the ability to charge higher prices (see Chapter 10) to easier employee recruitment and better retention of their employees as suggested by Bharadwaj and Yameen (2021) who emphasize that employers should embed ethical stances in their policies, practices, and procedures to make sure a skilled workforce is retained.

Building a Sustainable Brand

Building a sustainable brand means pursuing an environmentally and socially conscious course as an organization, including all its policies and practices in an authentic manner. To reach that goal, the organization must work systematically and make smart decisions. Building blocks here include:

- An appealing company culture that transcends sustainability
- Balancing sustainability with other strengths. Sustainable products must be as functional and attractive as nonsustainable products
- Take the entire supply chain into consideration. Many of today's consumers are more likely to prefer a locally sourced, slow-fashion, certified organic brand than buying from the fast-fashion industry or an international low-cost provider with low sustainability performance. Each part of the supply chain must work on sustainable solutions and include sustainability practices in their core operations. If that's not the case, there is a risk that the media, employees, or other stakeholders will find that out and communicate the activities that can hurt the brand
- Co-create value with consumers. This means including and collaborating with consumers to meet their needs. In turn, consumers can help spread the word and talk about which social and environmental issues are important to them
- Avoid greenwashing by keeping marketing communications honest, and be transparent about one's operations
- Treat employees well. From a social sustainability perspective, the fair and just treatment of employees is crucial. They are the ones who both identify sources of sustainable practices and implement them in the organization's everyday practice, and they are also key carriers of the firm's branding message

Keeping Up with Changes in the Marketing Environment – Such as Consumers' Evolved Role in Marketing

A sustainable brand is a brand that succeeds in dealing with the evolution and change demanded by the market and the consumer. It is apparent that this evolution incorporates sustainable development rather than endless and short-term consumption. If a company succeeds in clearly retaining the perceived brand image that it wants its customers to have over time, it will most likely also be able to develop a sustainable brand based on enduring attitudes on products and services.

The level of competition is stiffening in many markets and consumers are becoming increasingly knowledgeable and also becoming more active in social media activities that contribute to shaping brands. The transformation in consumers – like assumed in the past – from passive receivers of marketing messages to actively being involved in marketing through their conversation is called *consumer-generated marketing* and is an important field within social media marketing. It has strong implications for the way brands are built (Dwivedi et al. 2015; Evans et al. 2021; Felix et al. 2017)

Why Did the Body Shop Collapse? A Cautionary Tale of Ethical Branding and Market Adaptation

The Body Shop, once a pioneer in ethical retail, filed for bankruptcy in the United States and Canada in 2024, shortly after its UK-based parent company submitted a comparable filing. The Body Shop was the iconic British company that drew people to the primary shopping areas, offering unique products that allowed customers to purchase desirable products and do good for the environment at the same time. But after almost half a century – the company was founded in 1976 – it became clear that it had failed to properly manage their brand and company and not taken into consideration changes in markets and consumer behavior (see Figure 7.2).

The failure of the Body Shop emphasizes that ethical branding alone is not enough for commercial success. Initially praised for its commitment to sustainable practices and its fight against animal testing, the Body Shop struggled to innovate and adapt to changing market conditions and consumer expectations. Later, economic challenges such as inflation and rising interest rates further contributed to the loss of competitive edge in the marketplace.

Being perceived as an ethical brand for more than half a century is not easy, but that selling point eroded when new competitors emerged and market

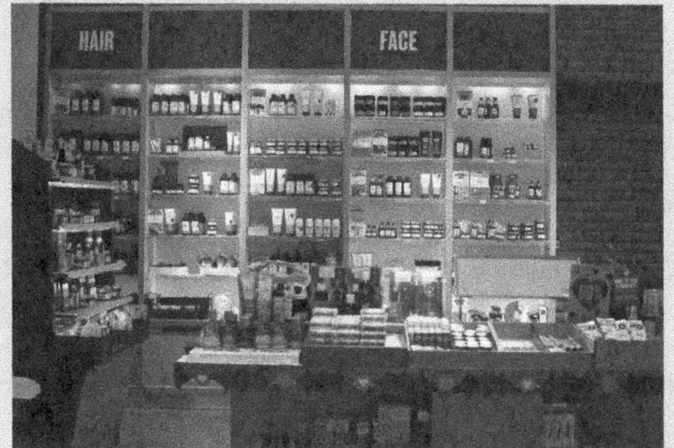

Figure 7.2 Ethical branding alone is not enough for commercial success – sustainable brands must take the three sustainability dimensions into account.
Source: Heorshe/Adobe Stock.

(Continued)

(Continued)

conditions and consumer expectations changed. Despite maintaining its ethical image, the Body Shop failed to keep pace with competitors who introduced new products and initiatives that resonated more with modern consumers. Brands like Lush, Dove, and Boots' No. 7 successfully emphasized social sustainability through community engagement, thereby strengthening their market position and emphasizing their role as sustainable brands that consumers like. Consumers' environmental concerns led to increasing consumers' perceived sense of environmental responsibility and familiarity with eco-products.

The Body Shop's experience demonstrates the consequences of not evolving with the times, even for a brand with a strong ethical foundation. Continuously innovating and being proactive when consumer demands change are crucial for long-term success and emphasize that ethical branding and good intentions alone are insufficient for long-term survival.

It has been suggested that the Body Shop failed to innovate its product range, was not competitive enough in their pricing strategies, and ignored rivals such as Lush and Origins. But competition also grew from the retail side. Supermarkets have proved much more skillful regarding sustainability in recent years, challenging The Body Shop's once unique position. Supermarkets have created ethical initiatives that genuinely help people in need, while also giving shoppers an extra reason to spend money with the shops involved.

Unlike the Body Shop, a few skincare brands have had the foresight in recent years to emphasize caring for people – i.e. social sustainability – in their branding and have been successful in solidifying their ethical image. These include Dove and its "Real Beauty" campaigns and the Boots brand No. 7 with its "Future Renew" product range targeting women aged from 30 to 75. The product promises to restore damaged skin and maintain a natural appearance without resorting to cosmetic procedures. No. 7 also partners with Macmillan Cancer Support to help women with cancer "look and feel like themselves." Similarly, according to Sit (2024, np), Lush's more prominent ethical perspective is centered on its "employees' craftsmanship, well-being, and pride." The company states, "We believe in happy people making happy soap, putting our faces on the products, and making our mums proud" (Lush 2024; Sit 2024).

Consumers who have greater environmental concerns are likely to express a higher level of perceived sense of environmental responsibility. To be considered truly ethical, a company needs to show it cares about social sustainability through treating employees and customers well, and it may also include reaching out to improve the lives of people who never encounter the company's products, such as TOMS, which gave away of a pair of shoes for each pair sold – a practice it ended after almost going bankrupt in 2019 – and the practice of Warby Parker giving away a pair of glasses to someone in need for every pair sold. A combination of factors has led to the Body Shop's downfall, a development seen as unlikely a couple of years ago but that nonetheless emphasizes the necessity of understanding the foundations of sustainable brands.

Sources: Jordan (2024), Sit (2024), Abid et al. (2020), Hessekiel (2021a,b), and Hojnik et al. (2019).

Brands' Role in Sustainability Efforts

A large portion of a company's value is intangible. For many companies, intangible assets such as human capital, patents, and brands are, in principle, their only assets, thus topicalizing issues of reputation, credibility, brand, organizational culture, ethics, social responsibility, and sustainability. All these words and processes revolve around ideals and identity.

Take a Holistic Approach – Brands Do

Sustainability isn't just about the environment. It's also about enacting social justice, treating employees and others involved in the organization's operations well, and establishing a healthy social and economic infrastructure. To be fully sustainable, organizations have to provide an ongoing check on the sustainability implications of what they're doing. In social sustainability, the treatment of employees, business partners, customers, and community is included – but also of people who work with manufacturing, transportation, cleaning, etc.

Brands do take a holistic approach – whether they want to or not. In the minds of consumers, brands reflect the summary of their experiences, what media outlets say about the company, and how their products perform in a narrow, and wide, sense.

Sustainable Brands Are Good for Society

It is clear that sustainable brands are good for society – but for sustainability-focused brands to be truly sustainable over time, they must deliver what consumers want and develop a strong competitive position. In the best case, an organization manages to cover a sweet spot in the market (see Figure 7.3).

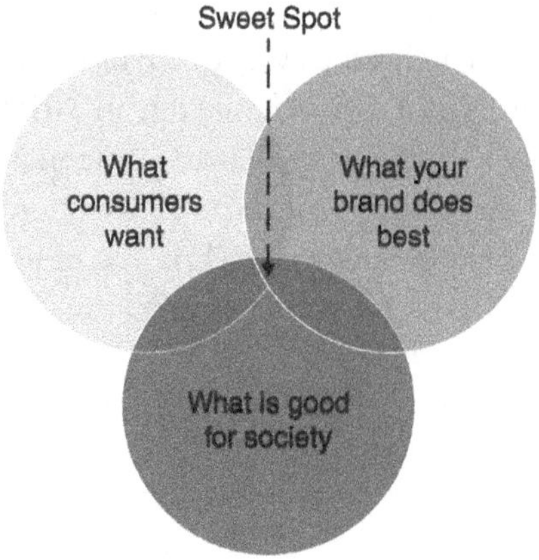

Figure 7.3 The sweet spot of sustainable brands. The diagram identifies the sweet spot that could be very narrow, since it addresses the necessity of doing good for society while also satisfying the needs of customers while doing what the brand does best in relation to its competitors.

The Branded Society

Brands are used just about everywhere, something that makes it increasingly common to talk about a *branded society*. The branded society has brought with it an increasingly complex landscape in which branding takes place. Sustainability claims and desires are part of this complex landscape – and sustainability is reflected in brands. It is clear that brands communicate organizations' practices. The branded society perspective provides crucial insights into the dynamics and interplay between branding and society. Brands are no longer only labels on products; they are also a fundamental concept in society and the way it works. Brands are the meanings people attach to their experience, consuming an organization's products or services, viewing ads about them, and interacting with employees, as well as other consumers (see Figure 7.4).

It is no longer only for-profit companies that sell products to consumer markets that are keen to build strong brands in contemporary society. More and more arenas and industry actors engage in branding. The interest in brand building has reached far into sectors of the economy that traditionally have not taken part in these activities, and domains that are reluctant to adopt branding practices have become fewer. For example, schools, primary healthcare, municipalities and state authorities, civil society organizations such as Greenpeace and the Red Cross, and individuals have become increasingly willing to promote their brands (Kornberger 2010). A clear effect of the increasing use and extended reach of brands is that noncommercial zones have largely disappeared. Whether one

Figure 7.4 In our branded society, brands are around us all the time.
Source: Authors' own.

visits a university campus, a cultural heritage site, a church, a union, or a secondary school, the likelihood of finding commercial messages and signs is higher than ever in history. Enormous amounts of money are spent on branding by nonprofit organizations, and there may be greenwashing involved in some instances – in terms of environmental or social sustainability. Interwoven with this development is that the marketing communications landscape has been filled with an ever-increasing number of commercial messages. Accordingly, the notion of the branded society emerged to understand the consequences of this development (Parment 2011).

In addition, the traditional arena of branding practices (i.e. in consumer markets) has become increasingly complex with regard to branding in the aftermath of contemporary markets experiencing an explosion in terms of available products, services, offers, brands, and – ultimately – consumption choices. On the consumer side of the economy, this has generated buyers with increasingly diverse demands, who are aware of their rights and are less loyal than they used to be. Moreover, there are powerful platforms and other tools at their disposal for getting detailed product information between competitors and price comparisons across many consumer markets but also industrial and governmental markets (Parment 2011, 2024). Sustainability makes this landscape even more complex, as it complicates how organizations work as well as also how consumers make their purchase decisions influenced by the image and value of a particular brand.

The Branded Society – Is It Sustainable?

The branded society refers to societies overcrowded by commercial messages and a never-ending supply of choices and opportunities inspired by the spheres of consumption and popular culture. Successfully navigating through this constantly developing landscape is difficult. Its emergence entails changing attitudes and power patterns offering more power to those who shape the brand images: consumers, who may well be aware of the impact of sustainability.

Branding is more than management efforts and how owners and employees intend to express the brand content. In our transparent world, it is hardly possible to create a brand image different from real experiences by employees and other stakeholders (Parment 2011). This is strongly linked to greenwashing practices.

Corporations and their managers face increasing difficulties running their brands according to their agenda unless stakeholders agree with them. Various stakeholders contribute to the shaping of a brand, and this has become clearer through social media marketing (Dwivedi et al. 2015; Evans et al. 2021; Felix et al. 2017).

Branding also provides interesting stories of management culture, internally powerful groups, jargons, strategies, people's sense of humor, etc. These stories are often shaped by "grassroots" – i.e. the very foundation of a source, group, or collective – and can, in the best case, work as a method to implement a culture that puts more emphasis on effectiveness and striving for a particular culture. In this version, branding – like other internal communications about identity, values, and corporate culture – becomes somewhat manipulative, as it attempts to lead employees toward a specific behavior and result to elicit competencies that management finds necessary (Kärreman and Rylander 2008). Here, we can find methods used by companies to spread the world, primarily to employees and internal stakeholders, regarding sustainability practices with varying coverage in the real practices of the company.

Globalization and internationalization are integral to our branded society. While increased awareness and understanding of other cultures have resulted from more accessible and affordable travel, there has been growing cultural criticism regarding issues such as overconsumption, sustainability challenges, the exploitation of cheap labor in developing countries, and the use of corporate branding to encourage overconsumption among economically disadvantaged people. These practices contribute to environmental and social unsustainability.

When multinational or international corporations take over local businesses, it often has significant sustainability implications. Employees may face harsh treatment, and these larger organizations, driven by controllers focused on cost reduction, often overlook sustainability. However, larger organizations possess greater resources and influence, enabling them to address sustainability in their employer branding and marketing communications. This presents an opportunity for these organizations to implement fair management policies and proactively meet the high expectations of various stakeholders.

Communicating Successful Sustainable Branding Efforts

The goals set by Zara include that all viscose they use will be 100% sustainably produced in 2023. By 2028, 80% of the energy consumption at Zara's headquarters, factories, and stores will come from renewable energy sources. In addition, their facilities should produce zero landfill waste.

"We must be the power of change, not just for the company but for the whole sector," says Pablo Isla, CEO of the Inditex group owning Zara.

Zara is part of the Inditex Group and accounts for 70% of group sales.

"We are the ones who create these goals: the strength and operation of change comes from the commercial team, the people who work with our suppliers, the people who work with fabrics. It's something that happens internally in the company," Isla expresses.

These promises come in conjunction with consumers reviewing sustainability. They demand ethical production methods and responsible retailers, especially in terms of stock surpluses and how unwanted clothes are handled.

The Dow Jones Sustainability Index has ranked Inditex high, often as the most sustainable retailer or in the best two centiles. The FTSE4Good index has given Inditex a score of 4.9 out of 5 several years in a row, and the firm has been acknowledged by Bloomberg in its Gender Equality Index (GEI) among many other prizes. In Inditex, which is the world's third largest clothing company according to Forbes, the brands include Massimo Dutti and Pull & Bear.

Source: Inditex, Annual Report, 2021 and 2023; a variety of sustainability-related indexes.

Storytelling

Research shows that people connect more powerfully with stories than with facts and figures (Kemp et al. 2023; Storr 2020). Accordingly, sharing employee and customer stories can be an effective way to make sustainability a relatable part of the organization's brand. Consumers could also be involved in the storytelling through posting about their experiences with the organization's sustainability efforts. Employees working with sustainability could be involved in the storytelling. However, it should not be perceived as arranged; it must be done in a lively and authentic way (Kemp et al. 2023; Storr 2020).

Storytelling is a powerful tool for communicating sustainability messages in marketing campaigns. By crafting compelling narratives around their sustainability efforts, brands can connect with consumers on an emotional level and inspire them to support their cause.

Outdoor Clothing Brand Patagonia – Sustainability at the Heart of the Company's Brand

Patagonia is well-known for its environmental responsibility. The outdoor apparel brand uses recycled materials in its clothing and donates 1% of its sales to environmental causes. The company also has a number of initiatives in place to reduce its environmental impact, such as a repair program for damaged clothing and a take-back program for old gear. The defining aspect of Patagonia's marketing is transparency – the brand realizes that as part of the problem it's committed to be part of the solution as well.

When the company realized the "pure and natural" cotton it touted actually had major environmental impacts, it was up front about the mistake and how it led to a switch to organic and recycled cotton sources. That has helped it cultivate a deeply loyal following among environmentally conscious consumers.

In 2012, Vincent Stanley was recruited as Patagonia's Chief Storyteller, a role he served for many years before becoming the Director of Philosophy. Patagonia's culture is deeply rooted in storytelling, using it as a primary tool to promote responsible business practices. Stanley, one of the company's leaders, has focused on distinguishing between sustainability and responsibility, favoring the latter to highlight the individual agency each person has.

Initially, Patagonia shared its message with employees during camping trips, fostering a passion for protecting the natural environment. Over time, they expanded their efforts to include written and visual mediums, using stories to address relevant environmental and social issues for both employees and consumers. This approach has helped Patagonia become a leader in sustainability, emphasizing values that go beyond sales and centering on their mission to "save our home planet."

Patagonia's storytelling is both humble and powerful, incorporating the voices of people from diverse backgrounds and cultures. By illustrating the impact of environmental and social issues on those who experience them firsthand, these stories create a sense of community around the brand and inspire action. This approach also promotes inclusivity, drawing support from people across various walks of life who resonate with Patagonia's values.

Stanley emphasized that Patagonia's films, books, and store events are integral to their storytelling efforts. These initiatives create platforms for community-building and advocate for responsible business practices. By leveraging storytelling, Patagonia not only raises awareness about critical issues but also fosters a collective responsibility to make a difference (see Figure 7.5).

Figure 7.5 Patagonia provides an example for others to follow.
Source: МАКСИМ/Adobe Stock.

Patagonia has inspired many other companies. For instance, Patagonia's infamous "Don't buy this jacket" campaign led the way for other brands to consider approaches that leverage sustainably over profit.

Source: Brownwell and Kurtz (2022); Silva (2021).

Tools such as messaging playbooks that guide a brand's communication to ensure uniformity in brand voice, brand tone, and audience perception, can help everyone make the brand's dedication to sustainability an integral part of the brand's identity. IKEA for example, equips its people with a comprehensive "People and Planet" sustainability strategy – and attempts to weave that messaging through every aspect of its communications; however, research and critical investigations of IKEA give an unclear picture of its sustainability performance (cf. Laurin and Fantazy 2017). Investigations that criticize a business who make strong sustainability claims through their storytelling, may discover discrepancies in the story told and actual business practices. When this happens the company storytelling can quickly be undermined and unscrupulous business practices are exposed (e.g. Kerfriden and Deleu 2023) (see Figure 7.6).

Crafting a focused and trustworthy sustainability – a clear and focused narrative – story helps firms to be recognized as truly sustainable brands. Concentrating on the key themes of sustainability messaging – rather than trying to cover everything – helps people understand and engage with the brand's efforts. It also ensures consistent and effective communication within the company. Key elements of a focused sustainability story are that they are in alignment with core

Figure 7.6 Storytelling is often a smart and effective way to promote a brand.
Source: Shutterstock 2284718281.

brand elements to make sure the sustainability messaging is in harmony with the brand's core identity as well as providing concrete proofs to show the impact of sustainability efforts on customers, employees, communities, and other stakeholders. For sustainability stories to be convincing, the firm must be trusted. Transparent communication fosters trust by showing the firm is open and honest. This transparency helps avoid the perception of greenwashing, which can damage trust and harm the reputation.

Logos Matter – How Could They Be Made Sustainable?

Some organizations may want to adopt a new logo. A good sustainable logo should visually communicate a brand's commitment to environmental responsibility and ethical practices. Creating a logo might be a complex endeavor, but keeping key elements in mind that create associations to sustainability may help (e.g. Apollo Technical 2024):

- *Natural elements:* Incorporate elements like leaves, trees, water, or the sun to symbolize nature and sustainability
- *Eco-friendly colors:* Use colors associated with nature and sustainability, such as greens, blues, browns, and earthy tones
- *Circular shapes:* Utilize circular shapes to represent the circular economy and the idea of recycling and renewal

Like with any logo, a clean, simple design makes it more memorable and versatile across various communications channels. In addition, a minimalist logo design approach could support sustainable practices, since it reflects the sustainable practice of avoiding excessive use of resources.

A Good Sustainable Slogan

While a brand may use a slogan for their core products, they may want to include a sustainability-oriented slogan or statement in their brand or company missions or values. By combining a visually appealing and meaningful logo with a strong, inspiring slogan, a brand can effectively communicate its dedication to sustainability and attract like-minded consumers. A sustainable slogan or statement should ideally

- *Be positive:* It should use a positive and inspiring tone to motivate and engage consumers
- *Be concise and memorable:* It should convey the brand's commitment to sustainability and ethical practices and encapsulate the brand's mission and inspire consumers to take action
- *Have a clear message:* It should clearly communicate the brand's focus on sustainability
- *Be action-oriented:* It should encourage consumers to take part in sustainable practices

Slogans such as "Sustainability in Every Step," "For a Greener Tomorrow," "Choose Wisely, Live Sustainably" or "Living Green, Every Day" could be rephrased and recombined in an endless number of ways, but as always when creativity is useful, it's difficult to set up checklists and rules. The information provided here, however, will help in making sure the brand and logo support the company's sustainability approach (see Figure 7.7).

Figure 7.7 Logos can help promote a brand's sustainability efforts.
Source: Shutterstock 1771515470.

Sustainable Brand Personality

Brand personality is a key concept in understanding and applying branding. Jennifer Aaker's 1997 *Journal of Marketing Research* article introduced the theme to a broader research audience; the article is one of the most read and referenced in business and marketing overall.

By merging sustainability with brand personality, a sustainable brand personality is at hand, a concept that refers to the traits and characteristics that a brand projects to signify its commitment to sustainability. This concept extends beyond traditional brand personality by incorporating environmental, social, and economic sustainability dimensions into the brand's identity and consumer perception.

A sustainable brand personality could be useful in the contemporary marketplace as it aligns with the growing consumer demand for environmentally and socially responsible businesses.

Key components of a sustainable brand personality include the three sustainability dimensions:

- *Environmental sustainability*: Brands that are perceived as environmentally responsible often adopt practices such as reducing carbon footprints, utilizing renewable resources, and implementing recycling programs. These brands communicate their environmental efforts transparently to build trust and loyalty among environmentally conscious consumers (Hartmann and Apaolaza Ibáñez 2006)
- *Social sustainability*: This aspect involves the brand's commitment to ethical labor practices, community engagement, and contributions to social causes. Brands like Patagonia and Ben & Jerry's are good at integrating social responsibility into their core values, which enhances their sustainable brand personality (Kotler and Lee 2008)
- *Economic sustainability*: This involves adopting business practices that ensure long-term financial health without compromising ethical standards. It includes fair-trade practices, ethical sourcing, and investments in sustainable technologies (Dyllick and Hockerts 2002)

Research suggests that a strong sustainable brand personality positively influences consumer behavior in the sense that consumers are more likely to purchase from and remain loyal to brands they perceive as responsible and ethical. According to a study by Hwang and Lyu (2018), sustainable brand personality significantly impacts brand trust and loyalty, especially among millennials who prioritize sustainability in their consumption choices.

The benefits of sustainable brand personalities seem to be quite clear – but how do we get there? Authentic and transparent storytelling, as mentioned earlier, is one way. Storytelling, hence, includes sharing the journey, challenges, and successes in achieving sustainability goals (e.g. Parguel et al. 2011). Consumer engagement is another option. Actively engaging consumers in sustainability initiatives, such as recycling programs or social campaigns, can strengthen the brand's sustainable personality and foster a community of like-minded individuals (Grohmann 2009). Consistent actions and communication are a necessity (Delmas and Burbano 2011). An opportunity that might be explored is third-party certifications: obtaining certifications from recognized sustainability standards (e.g. Fair Trade, Leadership in Energy and Environmental Design, and Forest Stewardship Council) can enhance credibility and trust in the brand's sustainability claims (Chen and Chang 2013).

Developing a sustainable brand personality is not without challenges. Brands must navigate the complexities of supply chain transparency, balancing short-term costs with long-term sustainability goals, and avoiding greenwashing. In some industries and for some products, educating consumers about the importance of sustainability and how it aligns with the brand's values requires continuous effort and innovation is a challenge.

By embedding environmental, social, and economic sustainability into their core identity, brands can differentiate themselves, build stronger consumer relationships, and contribute to a more sustainable future. A sustainable brand personality is increasingly becoming a critical factor for brands aiming to thrive in today's socially conscious market. The ongoing commitment to authenticity, transparency, and ethical practices will define the success of brands in cultivating a sustainable brand personality.

In a way similar to that of brand equity, other well-known branding models could also be used to deal with sustainability; e.g. sustainable brand equity, as conceptualized by Aaker and Joachimsthaler (2012), revolves around building a brand that maintains its value over time through consistent and strategic brand management practices. Aaker and Joachimsthaler emphasize the importance of developing brand equity through four key dimensions: brand loyalty, brand awareness, perceived quality, and brand associations. Their framework suggests that sustainable brand equity is not merely about short-term financial gains but about creating long-lasting value that can withstand market fluctuations and competitive pressures. Aaker and Joachimsthaler also stress the need for strategic brand management, which involves continuous monitoring and adaptation to changing market conditions. They advocate for a holistic approach that integrates marketing, corporate strategy, and customer insights. This integration ensures that the brand remains relevant and resonates with its target audience, thereby securing its equity sustainably.

Deceptive Branding Practices

A variety of social criticisms against marketing practices has emerged, largely resulting from firms not thinking beyond immediate consumer needs. Sustainable brands must consider society overall and take the interests of future generations into consideration in attempts to develop their practices – if not, their brands cannot be sustainable in the long run.

Truly sustainable marketing requires a smoothly functioning marketing system in which consumers, companies, public policymakers, and others work together to ensure ethical and socially responsible marketing actions. Accordingly, deceptive practices that lead consumers to believe they will get something they don't get make consumers skeptical – and firms look unsustainable.

Common deceptive practices include but are not limited to the following (see Armstrong and Kotler 2022):

- Poor quality
- Overselling
- Pricing and markups
- Society bears the cost of nonsustainable consumption
- Planned obsolescence

Poor Quality

Poor product quality emerges from products not being well-designed – these products harm the environment and make buyers unhappy. Poor quality takes many forms, including products that deliver little benefit, harmful or unsafe products, poor long-term performance, and high maintenance costs.

Tough competition puts pressure on brands to deliver products of good quality, but there always tends to be a market for products that look good but aren't.

Poor quality products are neither environmentally nor socially or financially sustainable. Unhappy consumers may avoid future purchases and spread the word in various channels, in particular via social media.

Overselling

High-pressure selling results in annoyed and saturated consumers and leads to overconsumption, something that harms the individual customers as well as society overall. When consumers buy products, they had no intention of buying; they may end up having financial problems.

Overselling takes several forms:

- A shopping center salesperson who approaches shoppers and attempts to sell services such as insurance, electricity agreements, and credit cards
- A telemarketing company that calls consumers at odd hours to offer promos with a time limit
- A Hilton hotel customer on the way to a dinner party is recruited to a Hilton Vacation Club sales meeting offering timeshare resorts – and is forced to make a fast purchase decision based on limited offers

- A consumer takes the opportunity to buy two polo shirts for $60, hence enjoying a $30 discount over the regular outlet price of $45 each. At the checkout, after the purchase transaction is completed, the buyer gets a voucher that offers "two polo shirts for $45." As this is 25% cheaper than the price paid, the consumer ends up buying more clothing than needed – although no purchase need exists anymore

Some products are *sold* rather than *bought*, something that reflects the underlying overselling problem. Salespeople – supported by marketing and branding – may inform, help, and support consumers – but when wrongly incentivized, they may also force consumers to buy products and services they do not really need or want. A typical deceptive practice here is when salespeople have strong incentives to sell some products over others not focusing on the need of the consumer or customer and to sell higher volumes than the demand at hand.

Pricing and Markups

There are several rationales for criticizing marketing practices from the perspective of high prices and extensive markups.

While manufacturing has been subject to extensive optimizations to reduce costs and in many cases moved production to low-cost countries, with questionable sustainable practices, the price the consumer pays has often been maintained, a practice that reflects high margins. A common criticism is that channel intermediaries mark up prices beyond the value of their services. With too many inefficient intermediaries, which sometimes provide unnecessary or duplicate services, the criticism is justified, and the result is clear: costs for marketing channels are too high (Kotler et al. 2020).

To an extent, costly marketing communications and packaging have contributed to high prices as well as environmental unsustainability. Here, firms should consider how they work with their marketing to make sure their brands become truly sustainable.

If consumers are asked about the desired level of service, they will say that they prefer long store hours, large assortments, and free returns, even though such practices may be poor from a sustainability perspective. Online stores hardly state the share of their parcels sent that are being returned, but studies show that free returns contribute to higher purchase and more returns (Patel et al. 2021); however, the increasingly common practice of providing customer ratings about product satisfaction has been found to decrease the percentage of returned goods (Sahoo et al. 2018).

Society Bears the Costs of Non-Sustainable Consumption

Contemporary societies are built around an array of consumption arenas. Many arenas contribute to overconsumption, and consumers get used to this practice – partly without reflecting upon how unsustainable it is (see De Graaf et al. 2014).

But who is bearing the cost? In many cases it is the overall society that will bear the costs for pollution, health problems, garbage, and poor mental conditions. Overconsumption and unsustainable marketing practices hence result in societal costs. This is nothing new; take the cost of driving a car as an example. Extensive driving results in traffic congestion, gasoline shortages, and air pollution, which means substantial costs for society. Despite this, many car drivers complain about high taxes, even if they don't cover societal costs. On the other hand, from a social sustainability point of view, car travel may be useful.

With a sustainable perspective, the balance between private and public must be restored to make sure producers and consumers bear a larger or full part of the societal costs incurred by their actions – production and consumption. Many initiatives have been taken, but there is still a long way to go until the balance is restored, and few politicians have the courage to take this argument further than relatively moderate adjustments of the existing system for charging producers and consumers.

Prêt À Manger – One of the First Sustainable Fast-Food Brands?

Sustainability marketing is based on true efforts and described in sufficient detail on the company website. Credible information substantiates the sustainability claims. In addition, social media and grassroots agree on what the company claims and greenwashing hardly exists. A company that has adopted such an approach is UK-based fast food chain Prêt À Manger. Since its inception in London in 1986, the company has grown to around 500 franchises and a revenue of about GBP 1 billion. The entire business model is characterized by sustainability thinking, and it is obvious that it is not just about an extension or restructuring of an existing business model to capture the sustainability aspect. Instead, it is a business model based on the following essential elements:

- Plant milks, tea, coffee, matcha, and hot chocolate powder are all organic, and more than 50% of excess food is donated to charities or food-sharing platforms
- Natural ingredients are used, and preservatives and chemicals are avoided to a high extent

- All food is made with locally sourced ingredients
- All food is prepared in the shop's kitchen
- For chicken and meat, there are clear guidelines regarding their production and associated sustainability considerations
- Packaging is minimized
- The food is distributed by trucks that run on biogas
- Food that has not been used during the day is distributed to the homeless
- All fresh food (obviously not popcorn, drinks, etc.) leaves the store so the customer always gets food that is produced during the day

As Prêt À Manger owns and operates all its stores, the implementation of its business model and associated concept can be ensured. That gives stronger control over the brand and makes sure a consistent sustainable brand experience can be delivered.

Sources: Loth (2024); Pret-a-Manger (2023).

Planned Obsolescence

Some firms plan for obsolescence, meaning that their products become obsolete before they actually need replacement. Obsolescence might have been reached since the general level of product standards and features has been reached – hence, adding value for the buyer – but also because producers are using materials that will break, wear, or rust sooner than buyers should expect. Another instance of obsolescence is so called perceived obsolescence, continually changing styles to encourage more and earlier buying, obvious in the context of clothing fashions or aging smartphones (Abd El Aziz 2022; Hadhazy 2016).

Smartphones – Environmentally Harmful or Planet-Savers?

Apple is selling 200–250 million iPhones every year. It is the dominant product in many countries, but it represents only a fifth of the global smartphone market, which totals more than 1 billion units (see Figure 7.8).

Smartphones have become a necessity in contemporary society, providing unparalleled connectivity, convenience, and functionality. However, their environmental impact is a topic of increasing concern. So, the question is – are

(Continued)

(Continued)

Figure 7.8 Even though we have iPhones around us, Apple sells only a fifth of the smartphones – in 2023 229,1 million out of 1,18 billion units.
Source: Diego Maravilla / Adobe Stock.

smartphones really hurting the environment, or do they contribute to saving the planet?

There are several instances of environmental harm caused by smartphones:

Various types of resource extraction, including mineral mining: Smartphones require rare earth metals such as lithium, cobalt, and tantalum. Mining these minerals is environmentally destructive, often leading to habitat destruction, water pollution, and significant carbon emissions. In addition, labor conditions do not fulfill high standards throughout the supply chain. Mining for these materials often occurs in countries with poor labor regulations, leading to poor social sustainability following exploitative working conditions and human rights abuses.

Manufacturing impact: The manufacturing process of smartphones is energy-intensive, contributing to substantial greenhouse gas emissions. The manufacturing process of a smartphone accounts for about 85% of its carbon footprint, making it the most damaging device to the environment. These emissions mainly come from metal extraction, shipping, and production.

These mini portable computers use as many as 70 elements, equivalent to about 80% of the periodic table. Silicon and plastic take up about half of the materials used in a smartphone, while iron, aluminum, and copper remain the most common metals.

Metal extraction, for one, induces massive solid and liquid waste, according to Dr. Karen Hudson-Edwards, a sustainable mining professor at the University of Exeter in the United Kingdom. In addition, manufacturing involves the use of hazardous chemicals that can lead to pollution if not managed properly.

So called e-waste: The rapid obsolescence of smartphones, driven by technological advancements and consumer trends, leads to vast amounts of electronic waste. Improper disposal of e-waste can release toxic substances into the environment, affecting soil and water quality. In addition, recycling challenges are crucial. Although smartphones contain valuable materials, the recycling rate remains low due to the complexity of the process and the cost of extracting these materials.

While media often report about material such as cobalt – which is mined by hand in developing countries such as the Democratic Republic of Congo – reportedly sometimes by children – or resources in short supply, the end result very much depends on the users but also on companies designing and manufacturing the smartphones.

Although battery efficiency has increased over time, most of the electricity needed for use is generated by burning fossil fuels around the world. One study estimated that a heavy user (e.g. lots of data consumption) can consume as much electricity in a year as in their fridge.

Despite these challenges, it might be argued that smartphones facilitate sustainable practices and hence have a role as planet-savers. Smartphones enable smart home technologies that can reduce energy consumption, such as programmable thermostats, energy-efficient lighting systems, and smart grids. The need for physical goods and services is lower. For example, e-books reduce paper consumption. Smartphones provide access to information and educational resources on environmental issues, promoting greater awareness and advocacy. Apps can help users reduce their carbon footprint, track energy usage, and find sustainable products. Remote work will also be facilitated through smartphones. And a mobile phone in fact replaces video cameras, clock radios, compasses, health tracking equipment, MP3 players, barometers, and GPS devices.

To reduce the environmental impact that smartphones result in, smartphones could be designed to be more durable and easier to repair, resulting in an extended life span. This is a cooperation between designers and users. An increasing practice is the market for secondhand devices and, across countries, the practice of recycling old phones has become more common.

So, despite that a smartphone contributes to global warming and climate change throughout the entirety of its life cycle, starting already before production with the use of gold, cobalt, lithium, and other heavy metals, one could

(Continued)

(Continued)

argue that smartphones help in dematerializing consumption, from owning to accessing goods and services or using apps instead.

Maybe surprisingly, the number of smartphones sold has gone down, despite an increasing world population, which might be a sign that the pace of development has slowed down and the quality has increased, making the mobile phones slightly more sustainable. So, the criticism of the short life span of smartphones has contributed to manufacturers such as Apple and Samsung designing their products to last longer and be more easily repaired so that we throw them away less frequently.

Smartphones embody a paradox of modern technology: they are both environmentally harmful and potential tools for environmental sustainability. The key to harnessing their positive potential lies in addressing the negative impacts through sustainable design, responsible consumption, and improved recycling. By balancing these aspects, smartphones can indeed contribute to a more sustainable future. Or. . .what do you think?

Source: Canalys (2024); Lee (2023); Statista (2024); Hartmann et al. (2020); (McAfee 2019).

Sustainable Brands Don't Engage in Planned Obsolescence

Planned obsolescence refers to the deliberate design and manufacturing of products with a limited life span, ensuring that they will become outdated or nonfunctional after a certain period (Armstrong and Kotler 2022; Kotler et al. 2020; Satyro et al. 2018). Planned obsolescence stands in contrast to sustainability principles and hence poses significant challenges for brands committed to ethical and environmental responsibility. From an ethical perspective, planned obsolescence raises questions about consumer rights and corporate responsibility. This practice, which gained prominence in the early twentieth century, is intended to stimulate continuous consumer demand and sales and stands in contrast with contemporary ethical, environmental, and economic challenges. Sustainable brands committed to promoting long-term environmental stewardship and responsible consumption should be very careful when it comes to planned obsolescence, a practice that promotes a wasteful culture that excessively consumes resources. The concept of planned obsolescence can be traced back to the 1920s and 1930s and spread rapidly across industries.

Planned obsolescence takes two forms (Satyro et al. 2018): *design for fashion or style obsolescence* convinces consumers to replace their products and buy new ones with some design change as with bikes, cars and sports equipment; and *design for functional enhancement* is about adding or upgrading product features, e.g. a computer or smartphone with larger memory or improved camera. The latter strategy is used to make it attractive to replace the existing product.

The environmental impacts of planned obsolescence are profound. The practice contributes to the generation of electronic waste (e-waste), which contains hazardous materials, and the production of new products increases the depletion of natural resources and energy consumption, contributing to environmental degradation and climate change.

What can a consumer do to counteract planned and perceived obsolescence?

- Before buying a new product, ask yourself, "Do I really need this? What benefits will it bring?"
- Investigate the product's life span. Check statistics and reviews to gauge how long a product will last. If a product seems to have a short life span, look for a more durable alternative
- Choose sustainable brands with high ethical standards. If you choose brands that are not transparent about their production processes, materials, and sustainability practices, you may contribute to greenwashing

Physical obsolescence is common (Satyro et al. 2018), e.g. when a smartphone in good condition suddenly stops working or a laptop displays bugs and errors after being used for a couple of years. In addition, while many devices can be repaired, some companies make it impossible for customers to maintain or repair their own devices by, for instance, making spare parts unavailable or overly expensive. Irreplaceable batteries with short lifetimes are another common practice. The fast fashion industry promotes the constant cycle of buying new products through releasing seasonal collections to drive consumption and promoting design fads that last for short periods of time.

References

Aaker, J. L. (1997). Dimensions of brand personality. *Journal of marketing research*, 34(3), 347–356.

Aaker, D. A., & Joachimsthaler, E. (2012). *Brand Leadership*. New York: Simon and Schuster.

Abd El Aziz, M. (2022). How smartphones are contributing to climate change. Infomenio Brainshoring Services. https://infomineo.com/technology-telecommunication/how-smartphones-are-contributing-to-climate-change (accessed 31 May 2024).

Abid, T., Abid-Dupont, M. A., & Moulins, J. L. (2020). What corporate social responsibility brings to brand management? The two pathways from social responsibility to brand commitment. *Corporate Social Responsibility and Environmental Management*, 27(2), 925–936.

Apollo Technical. (2024). Sustainability in Logo Design, Going Green with Your Brand. https://www.apollotechnical.com/sustainability-in-logo-design-going-green-with-your-brand (accessed 23 May 2024).

Armstrong, L. & Kotler, P. (2022). *Marketing. An Introduction.* Fifteenth edition, Global edition, New York: Pearson.

Bartak, V. (2023). What makes a brand sustainable? Bower & Collective. https://bowercollective.com/blogs/news/what-makes-a-brand-sustainable (accessed 23 May 2024).

Bastounis, A., Buckell, J., Hartmann-Boyce, J., Cook, B., King, S., Potter, C., Bianchi, F., Rayner, M. and Jebb, S.A., 2021. The impact of environmental sustainability labels on willingness-to-pay for foods: a systematic review and meta-analysis of discrete choice experiments. *Nutrients*, 13(8), 2677.

Bharadwaj, S., & Yameen, M. (2021). Analyzing the mediating effect of organizational identification on the relationship between CSR employer branding and employee retention. *Management Research Review*, 44(5), 718–737.

Brownwell J. and Kurtz Z. (2022). The Power of Storytelling at Patagonia. University of Vermont. https://blog.uvm.edu/si-mba/2022/05/27/the-power-of-storytelling-at-patagonia (accessed 19 July 2024).

Canalys (2024). Global smartphone market declined just 4% in 2023 amid signs of stabilization. https://www.canalys.com/newsroom/worldwide-smartphone-market-2023 (accessed May 31, 2024).

Chaturvedi, P., Kulshreshtha, K., & Tripathi, V. (2020). Investigating the determinants of behavioral intentions of generation Z for recycled clothing: an evidence from a developing economy. *Young Consumers*, 21(4), 403–417.

Chen, Y. S., & Chang, C. H. (2013). Greenwash and green trust: the mediation effects of green consumer confusion and green perceived risk. *Journal of Business Ethics*, 114, 489–500.

Czinkota, M., Kaufmann, H. R., & Basile, G. (2014). The relationship between legitimacy, reputation, sustainability and branding for companies and their supply chains. *Industrial Marketing Management*, 43(1), 91–101.

De Graaf, J., Wann, D., & Naylor, T. H. (2014). *Affluenza: How Overconsumption Is Killing Us—And How to Fight Back.* Berrett-Koehler Publishers.

Delmas, M. A., & Burbano, V. C. (2011). The drivers of greenwashing. *California Management Review*, 54(1), 64–87.

Dwivedi, Y. K., Kapoor, K. K., & Chen, H. (2015). Social media marketing and advertising. *The Marketing Review*, 15(3), 289–309.

Dyllick, T., & Hockerts, K. (2002). Beyond the business case for corporate sustainability. *Business Strategy and the Environment*, 11(2), 130–141.

Evans, D., Bratton, S., & McKee, J. (2021). *Social Media Marketing.* AG Printing & Publishing.

Felix, R., Rauschnabel, P.A., & Hinsch, C. (2017). Elements of strategic social media marketing: a holistic framework. *Journal of Business Research*, 70, 118–126.

Grohmann, B. (2009). Gender dimensions of brand personality. *Journal of Marketing Research*, 46(1), 105–119.

Hadhazy, A. (2016). Here's the truth about the 'planned obsolescence' of tech. BBC News, https://www.bbc.com/future/article/20160612-heres-the-truth-about-the-planned-obsolescence-of-tech (accessed 5 April 2024).

Hartmann, B. J., Östberg, J., Parment, A., & Solér, C. (2020). *Unboxing marketing: creating value for consumers, firms, and society*, Lund: Studentlitteratur.

Hartmann, P., & Apaolaza Ibáñez,V. (2006). Green value added. *Marketing Intelligence & Planning*, 24(7), 673–680.

Hessekiel, D. (2021a). The rise and fall of the buy-one-give-one model at TOMS. Forbes, https://www.forbes.com/sites/davidhessekiel/2021/04/28/the-rise-and-fall-of-the-buy-one-give-one-model-at-toms/?sh=131264d71c45 (accessed 7 January 2024).

Hessekiel, D. (2021b). Companies Embracing Buy-One-Give-One Strategies: Warby Parker. Forbes. https://www.forbes.com/sites/davidhessekiel/2021/05/06/companies-embracing-buy-one-give-one-strategies-warby-parker/ (accessed 6 April 2024).

Hojnik, J., Ruzzier, M., & Konečnik Ruzzier, M. (2019). Transition towards sustainability: adoption of eco-products among consumers. *Sustainability*, 11(16), 4308.

Hwang, K., & Lee, J. (2018). Antecedents and consequences of ecotourism behavior: Independent and interdependent self-construals, ecological belief, willingness to pay for ecotourism services and satisfaction with life. *Sustainability*, 10(3), 789.

Jordan, D. (2024). The Body Shop: What went wrong for the trailblazing chain? BBC, https://www.bbc.com/news/business-68273425 (accessed 15 February 2024).

Kapferer, J-N. (2012), *The New Strategic Brand Management, Advanced Insights and Strategic Thinking*, 5, London: Kogan Page.

Kemp, A., Gravois, R., Syrdal, H., & McDougal, E. (2023). Storytelling is not just for marketing: cultivating a storytelling culture throughout the organization. *Business Horizons*, 66(3), 313–324.

Kornberger, M. (2010). *Brand Society: How Brands Transform Management and Lifestyle*. Cambridge: Cambridge University Press.

Kotler, P., & Lee, N. (2008). *Corporate Social Responsibility: Doing the Most Good for Your Company and Your Cause*. Chichester: Wiley.

Kotler, P., Armstrong, G., & Parment, A. (2020). *Principles of Marketing*: Scandinavian edition. London: Pearson.

Kryger Aggerholm, H., Esmann Andersen, S., & Thomsen, C. (2011). Conceptualising employer branding in sustainable organisations. *Corporate Communications: An International Journal*, 16(2), 105–123.

Kumar, V., & Christodoulopoulou, A. (2014). Sustainability and branding: an integrated perspective. *Industrial Marketing Management*, 43(1), 6–15.

Kärreman, D., & Rylander, A. (2008). Managing meaning through branding—The case of a consulting firm. *Organization Studies*, 29(1), 103–125.

Laurin, F., & Fantazy, K. (2017). Sustainable supply chain management: a case study at IKEA. *Transnational Corporations Review*, 9(4), 309–318.

Lee, C. (2023). A closer look at smartphone pollution. Fair Planet. https://www.fairplanet.org/story/smartphone-pollution-electronic-waste (accessed 31 May 2024).

Loth, S. (2024). Most sustainable UK restaurant chains revealed, Which? www.which.co.uk/news/article/most-sustainable-uk-restaurant-chains-revealed-aVio22t7pseq (accessed 1 June 2024).

Lush. (2024). The Lush Ethical Charter. https://weare.lush.com/lush-life/our-values/the-lush-ethical-charter (accessed 5 June 2024).

McAfee, A. (2019). *More from less: The surprising story of how we learned to prosper using fewer resources—And what happens next*. New York: Scribner.

Parguel, B., Benoît-Moreau, F., & Larceneux, F. (2011). How sustainability ratings might deter 'greenwashing': a closer look at ethical corporate communication. *Journal of Business Ethics*, 102, 15–28.

Parment, A. (2011). *Generation Y in Consumer and Labour Markets*. London: Routledge.

Parment, A. (2024). *Die Generation Z: Die Hoffnungsträgergeneration in der neuen Arbeitswelt*, Wiesbaden: Springer Fachmedien.

Pätäri, S., Jantunen, A., Kyläheiko, K., & Sandström, J. (2012). Does sustainable development foster value creation? Empirical evidence from the global energy industry. *Corporate Social Responsibility and Environmental Management*, 19(6), 317–326.

Patel, P. C., Baldauf, C., Karlsson, S., & Oghazi, P. (2021). The impact of free returns on online purchase behavior: evidence from an intervention at an online retailer. *Journal of Operations Management*, 67(4), 511–555.

Pérez-Cornejo, C., de Quevedo-Puente, E., & Delgado-García, J. B. (2020). Reporting as a booster of the corporate social performance effect on corporate reputation. *Corporate Social Responsibility and Environmental Management*, 27(3), 1252–1263.

Pret-a-Manger. (2023). Pret revenue rises 20.2% in H1 2023. www.pret.co.uk/en-GB/pr-pret-financial-2023 (accessed 1 June 2024).

de Quevedo-Puente, E., De La Fuente-Sabaté, J. M., & Delgado-García, J. B. (2007). Corporate social performance and corporate reputation: two interwoven perspectives. *Corporate Reputation Review*, 10, 60–72.

Sahoo, N., Dellarocas, C., & Srinivasan, S. (2018). The impact of online product reviews on product returns. *Information Systems Research*, 29(3), 723–738.

Satyro, W. C., Sacomano, J. B., Contador, J. C., & Telles, R. (2018). Planned obsolescence or planned resource depletion? A sustainable approach. *Journal of Cleaner Production*, 195, 744–752.

Schäufele, I., & Hamm, U. (2017). Consumers' perceptions, preferences and willingness-to-pay for wine with sustainability characteristics: a review. *Journal of Cleaner Production*, 147, 379–394.

Silva, C. (2021). Patagonia's Storytelling Strategy, Medium. https://cesilvam.medium.com/patagonias-storytelling-strategy-a2fdf4570404 (accessed 5 May 2024).

Sit, K. J. (2024). The collapse of The Body Shop shows that 'ethical' branding is not a free pass to commercial success. *The Conversation*. https://theconversation.com/the-collapse-of-the-body-shop-shows-that-ethical-branding-is-not-a-free-pass-to-commercial-success-218733 (accessed 5 May 2024).

Statista (2024). iPhone unit shipments as share of global smartphone shipments, downloaded May 17th 2024 from: https://www.statista.com/statistics/216459/global-market-share-of-apple-iphone/

Storr, W. (2020). *The Science of Storytelling: Why Stories Make us Human and How to Tell Them Better*. London: Abrams.

Chapter 8

Sustainable and Circular Business Models

Business models represent the starting points and end results of all business activities. They start with a thorough understanding of how consumers think, act, and behave while taking market characteristics into consideration, and if successful, they will provide consumers, employees, and other stakeholders with great value. Regarding sustainability and circularity, the things that evolve around business models look different. This chapter discusses what sustainable and circular business models are and how they differ from traditional business models without sustainability concerns.

Learning Objectives

- Understand the role of business models in sustainable development
- Describe key characteristics of circular business models
- Explain product-service systems
- Describe key characteristics of social enterprises
- Explain peer-to-peer platform business models

Introduction

A company's operations are largely governed by activities, measurements, checks, and analyses of revenues and costs using calculations, budgets, and impact analyses. Companies' time perspectives, however, are often short-term; this applies to limited liability companies (LLCs) publicly listed on the stock market, which report to shareholders quarterly. For many years, there has been much talk of "quarterly capitalism" when describing the short-term orientation that seems to govern many listed LLCs – the price of stock shares can drop sharply following a quarterly report that would indicate lower profits than expected for investors despite that it is difficult to make conclusions about long-term future earnings from such quarterly results. This massive focus on the short-term naturally entails problems from a sustainability perspective.

There are at least three overarching problems affecting companies from a sustainability perspective. First, it is not likely that companies will accept unnecessary costs just to be able to act like "good social citizens" (cf. Esty and Porter 1998). On the other hand, companies can be motivated to make such investments if they see potential revenue increases or value creation by means of an augmented brand. Reduced waste management costs are one example of a measure that can be presented to customers as an increased level of responsibility. In parts of the corporate social responsibility (CSR) literature, there has been a naive belief that companies will go from prioritizing self-interest to becoming altruistic – eventually, there needs to be some profits from integrating sustainability in their business model (Velte 2022). A more sober understanding of companies' reasons for having an increased focus on sustainability thus becomes necessary. At the same time, it is obvious that over time, companies have increased their level of responsibility. Several decades ago, scandals about dumping waste in unsuitable places or using dangerous chemicals in products were common. The question concerns the driving forces of companies in taking such measures and how sustainability efforts can be followed through.

Second, in the contemporary economic system there is an overarching problem that overusing resources is not being priced correctly in relation to the potential damage it may create on the planet and communities. Polluting or ignoring ethical issues is relatively cheap for companies, sometimes even free. To solve this problem, natural resources should be priced in a way that reflects socio-environmental long-term consequences. The most effective way is to impose taxes on harmful chemicals and emissions to soil, air, and water, and waste. In this way, companies that do not minimize these problems will incur higher costs than competitors who choose to have effective emission and waste management (Porter and van der Linde 1995). Additionally, authorities receive revenues that cover at least parts of the costs incurred in managing emissions and waste in public waterways and contaminated land.

Third, there is a need to improve and further develop companies' methodology and practice, not least with regard to cost accounting and economic decision-making data. A typical example of this is so-called *additional benefits*, meaning benefits (over and above direct cost reductions) resulting from energy-efficiency investments in companies. Examples of measurable benefits may include improved working environments and increased staff health, but in the calculations of the business sector, the primary focus is on investment costs. This entails benefits not being taken into consideration or priced reasonably, which, in turn, disappears from the decision-making data. Using a benefit perspective, a much broader set of effects would be taken into consideration during decision-making.

Even though factors such as quality, cost, and delivery times are important, sustainability issues (which are external to the company) are becoming increasingly essential to customers. Externalities (i.e. consequences from a commercial activity that affect third parties, without these costs or benefits being reflected in the prices paid by customers) such as inadequate ethics thus need to become internalized within companies' economic decision-making data. These tendencies exist even today, such as when manufacturing companies choose to use sustainable materials despite these being more expensive, or when they compensate for the CO_2 emissions created during production – this can be voluntary or imposed by taxes. However, it is far from self-evident that public companies will focus on anybody else other than their shareholders and their profit-seeking motives. Such traditional focus is covered in the classic business model literature, which we will discuss more thoroughly later in this chapter.

The Role of Business Models in Sustainable Development

As discussed by Tushman and Nadler (1980) a company buys and uses input and processes and transforms this input to deliver its output. Business models are conceptual visualizations or tools used to show the input versus output process, or in other terms a company's structure, logic, or architecture (Zott et al. 2011; Wirtz et al. 2016). A business model can be said to describe how a company creates, captures, and delivers different types of value (Baden-Fuller and Morgan 2010). In a business model, a number of activities interact, and the relationships between these different activities are clarified in the business model. A business model is not static; the dynamic nature of its elements has to be explained as these are what make a company unique. The business model of a company should explain which actors are involved, which transactions take place, and how and what type of value the organization is aspiring to *create* (e.g. shareholder value, customer value, value to other stakeholders, such as employees), *capture* (revenues), and *deliver* (products, service, solutions). Here, the term *competitive advantage* also enters the picture: what are we doing better than our competitors, and what makes our customers, or employees, turn to us specifically? The business model explains how competitive advantages arise; however, this must also be communicated to the groups concerned – targeted customer segments.

Business model conceptualizations became popular during the 2000s, and literature reviews emphasize the extensive attention this area has received in research and from practitioners (cf. Massa et al. 2017). One of the most famous visualizations of a business model is the canvas introduced by Alexander Osterwalder and Yves Pigneur (see Figure 8.1).

Business Model Canvas – The World's Most Famous Visualization of a Business Model

The business model canvas is perhaps the most famous visualization of the business model concept in the world today (Osterwalder and Pigneur 2010). The canvas covers all the essential parts of the business model and consists of three overall areas – the front stage, the backstage, and the value proposition. The front stage of the business model covers all customer-facing elements of the canvas – value proposition, customer relationships, customer segments, channels, and revenues. The backstage of the canvas covers all internal processes – key partners, key activities, key resources, and costs. The value proposition finally combines the company's backstage activities with its front-stage activities. To succeed in the market, the company must be able to transform its activities and resources into a value offering that can be delivered to customers.

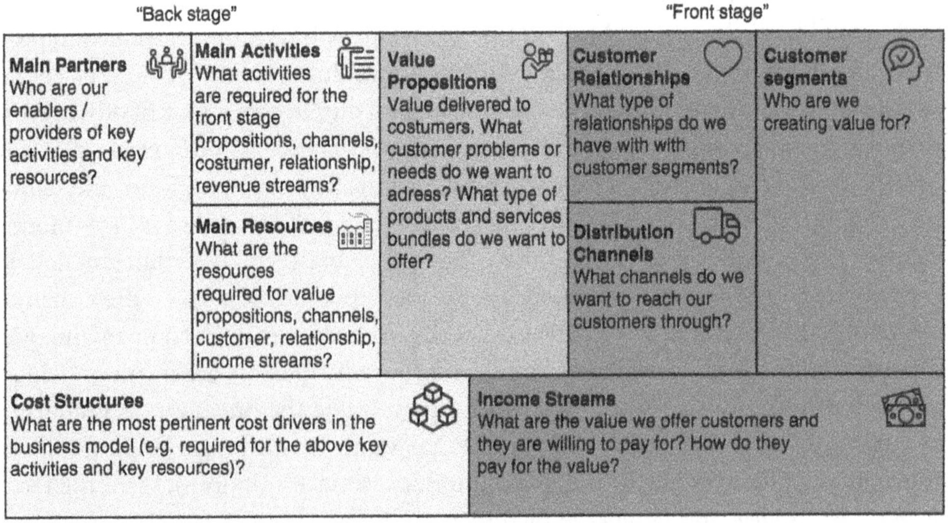

Figure 8.1 The business model canvas.
Source: Adapted from Osterwalder and Pigneur (2010).

Sustainable Business Models

At present, we find ourselves in a situation with a global consumption level that is more resource-demanding than the planet is capable of re-creating. The economic system that created this situation must be changed and reformed to meet the long-term demands of coming generations and not just the short-term needs of the current generation. Companies wanting to be part of this transition must re-define their business models with a sustainability orientation. To realize a transformation toward a more sustainable economic system, companies are pivotal through their unique possession of resources and capabilities (Porter and Kramer 2011).

While traditional business models are set within the traditional linear economy, a sustainable business model lays the foundations for an organization's actions in relation to the sustainability dimensions (i.e. economically, environmentally, and socially). The academic interest in sustainable business models has grown significantly in recent years and in relation with the increase in sustainability considerations of business activities. Examples of different concepts and frameworks that integrate business models with sustainability are sustainability business models (Stubbs and Cocklin 2008), business models for sustainability (Schaltegger et al. 2012), and sustainable business model archetypes (Bocken et al. 2014).

Sustainable business models as described by Evans et al. (2017, p. 5) are based on five propositions:

1. Sustainable value incorporates economic, social, and environmental benefits conceptualized as value forms.
2. Sustainable business models require a system of sustainable value flows among multiple stakeholders, including the natural environment and society as primary stakeholders.
3. Sustainable business models require a value network with a new purpose, design, and governance.
4. Sustainable business models require a systemic consideration of stakeholder interests and responsibilities for mutual value creation.
5. Internalizing externalities through product-service systems (PSSs) enables innovation toward sustainable business models.

Outsourcing – A Challenge for Sustainable Business Models

An important part of a business model is whether a company will do everything on their own or outsource activities to other companies, something that has been claimed to result in the company losing control over those who

(Continued)

(Continued)

provide the services (see, for instance, Baitheiemy 2003). In particular, it is difficult to keep track of process-based control, such as over production (Tiwana and Keil 2007).

Trust is crucial in outsourcing (Langfield-Smith and Smith 2003), and this is particularly important when key functions are outsourced. The business world is characterized by strong cost pressure, and to stay competitive, companies must buy key products and services from third-party suppliers. This reduces costs and makes the business model slimmer but at the same time contributes to problems related to a lack of control over suppliers' practices. They may, in turn, buy products and services from their suppliers, and there is a risk that their suppliers and subcontractors will do things that are difficult to combine with sustainability claims.

Companies today sometimes use code of conducts for suppliers such as that the supplier should provide a workplace free of harassment or discrimination based on age, gender, language, religion, political or other opinion, ethnic origin, nationality, and union affiliation. However, it is trickier to regulate the suppliers' suppliers or even the suppliers' suppliers' suppliers. The risk is thus that companies that claim to have a sustainable business model still might get negative publicity due to unsustainable business practices from certain outsourced activities in the business model.

According to Abdelkafi and Täuscher (2016), sustainable business models incorporate sustainability as an integral part of the company's logic for value creation. Upward and Jones (2016) also emphasize the multifaceted character of sustainable business models "by which an enterprise determines the appropriate inputs, resource flows, and value decisions and its role in ecosystems, [in a way that] sustainability measures [which] are those indicators that assess the outputs and effects of business model decisions [. . .] might be claimed as successfully sustainable" (p. 98). Geissdoerfer et al. (2017a) further stress that a sustainable business model creates, delivers, captures, and exchanges sustainable value with a broad range of stakeholders, relying upon collaboration with these. The sustainable business model canvas in Figure 8.1 summarizes this discussion and visualizes how a sustainable business model must incorporate a wider perspective on all parts of the canvas. Rather than having a solely company-centric view, it also incorporates the wider value chain (e.g. suppliers, partners, etc.), the system level, the planet, and the people and society.

How Can Sustainable Food Producers Survive on the Market?

Sustainable food producers (SFPs), such as ecological or climate neutral producers, often face significant challenges to their profitability. The challenges for these companies' business models are several. First, the trend has been for many years that even though many consumers view sustainability as important, they often choose to buy cheaper traditional nonsustainable products instead. This is an example of the attitude-behavior gap discussed in Chapter 3. Second, for small premium producers of sustainable food, it is hard to stay profitable if selling directly to power retailers such as Walmart, Carrefour, and Tesco that primarily focus on low prices. The production of sustainable food is often much costlier due to increased space or land for animals, and locally grown feed grains without GMOs and antibiotics.

However, there are some well-known solutions related to business model choices that might make SFPs long-term competitive:

- SFPs should avoid selling through the power retailers since these actors will focus on cutting prices rather than paying more for a premium product. Rather, SFPs should focus on targeting specialized stores for premium meat or premium vegetables
- SFPs should consider selling directly to end consumers or use different forms of platforms that offer end consumers a chance to buy food from local producers (Figure 8.2)
- It is also important to charge a premium price in segments with higher environmental concerns. If prices are set too low, they do not correspond to either the higher production costs or consumers' expectations
- Keep quality at the highest possible level and always be transparent with how the food is being produced
- Become certified with third-party certifications. Such certifications have the highest credibility among end consumers

Source: Herin (2024).

(Continued)

Figure 8.2 Vegetable box from sustainable farming.
Source: Shutterstock 2346232379.

Sustainable Business Model Innovations

Business model innovations are said to yield higher returns than product or process innovations (Loorback and Wijsman 2013), but many business model innovations can also fail (Patel 2015), which would contribute to delays in the adoption of sustainable solutions (Geissdoerfer et al. 2017a,b). Sustainable business model innovation combines business model innovation with sustainability considerations. It requires the following:

1. Sustainable development or positive (or reduced negative) impact on the environment, society, and the long-term prosperity of the organization and its stakeholders
2. Adopting solutions or characteristics that foster sustainability in its value proposition and creation and captures elements or its value-network (Geissdoerfer et al. 2018a)

According to Geissdoerfer et al. (2018a), there are four types of sustainable business model innovations:

- *Sustainable start-ups:* A new organization with a sustainable business model is created
- *Sustainable business model transformation:* The current business model is changed, resulting in a sustainable business model

- *Sustainable business model diversification:* Without major changes in the existing business models of the organization, an additional sustainable business model is established
- *Sustainable business model acquisition:* An additional sustainable business model is identified, acquired, and integrated into the organization

When it comes to practice and implementation, a sustainable business model must, first, be commercially successful. Hence, consumers must find the proposition valuable and be willing to pay. Second, which is maybe needless to say, it must also contribute toward a sustainable society. Third, it must have future potential. Ideas that may soon be threatened by substitute products may soon lose their potential and should thus be avoided.

Bocken et al. (2016) identified archetypes of sustainable business models, which were updated by Ritala et al. (2018):

- To maximize material and energy efficiency
- To close resource loops
- To substitute with renewables and natural processes
- To deliver functionality rather than ownership
- To adopt a stewardship role
- To encourage sufficiency
- To repurpose for society or the environment
- Inclusive value creation
- To develop sustainable scale-up solutions

Circular Business Models (CBMs)

Climate change, growing urbanization, and other sustainability challenges underline the need for a radical transition in economies from a linear model to an increasingly circular model. The concept of a circular economy (CE) is based on the notion to decouple economic growth from resource consumption and create growth by utilizing the value in what is usually considered as waste (Stahel 2019). The transition toward a CE depends on the development of CBMs that incorporate CE principles (Kirchherr et al. 2017). Instead of a traditional business model based on the linear model that needs virgin resources for value creation, CBMs utilize the residual value embedded in products after use to create additional monetary and nonmonetary values (Geissdoerfer et al. 2018a,b). (See Figure 8.3. See also Chapters 4 and 5).

Companies' development of CBMs is a challenging process as it forces companies to question their business-as-usual paradigm (Bocken et al. 2019). The transition from a traditional linear business model to CBMs must be based on business

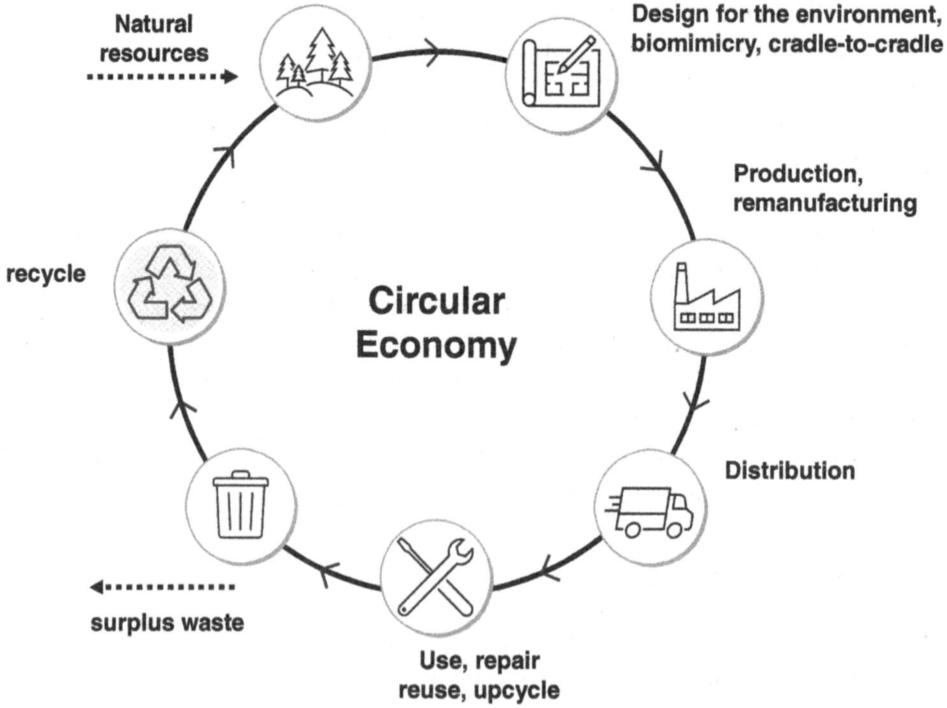

Figure 8.3 CBMs are based on the notion to decouple economic growth from resource consumption and create growth by utilizing the value in what is usually considered as waste. The effect is to reduce the use of natural resources.
Source: Authors' own.

model innovations (Geissdoerfer et al. 2018a,b, 2020; Guldmann et al. 2019). Either companies innovate their traditional linear business models by implementing circular activities or they create a new CBM (Geissdoerfer et al. 2018a,b). For most companies, it is no longer enough to assume that their traditional business models can remain stable or fixed. Instead, companies must continuously change and renew their business models. This means that many companies must be able to manage multiple business models to be able to handle new customer requirements and changing markets (Kindström and Ottosson 2016). Chesbrough (2010) even emphasizes that a company has at least as much to gain from developing the business model as in developing new technology.

Barriers to Circular Business Models

Even though circularity is high on the political agenda and, the European Union and the United Nations all have goals and political ambitions to increase the circular economy, only 7% of all material inputs into the global economy are materials that are cycled back after the end of their useful life, otherwise known as *secondary materials* (Circularity gap 2023). This means that more than 90% of materials end up in landfills, lost, or remain unavailable for reuse. The reasons for the low adoption rate of CBMs have been studied by many researchers. Different types of financial barriers have been identified (Werning and Spinler 2020). Lack of profitability is a major concern (Guldmann and Huulgaard 2020), and it has been shown to be difficult to forecast the profitability for CBMs (Kazancoglu et al. 2020). And yet, it is crucial for a successful implementation (Svensson and Funck 2019; Werning and Spinler 2020). Many companies that investigate the implementation of different forms of CBMs find that such might reduce their profit generated through the sales of products. Hence, for product manufacturers keeping products in use for longer becomes an unprofitable endeavor.

Outdated laws in certain areas that forbid waste as resources are also a major barrier. For example, both nitrogen and phosphorus are found in waste or byproducts from industries. Lime and fibers – which can be used to improve soil structure and soil fertility – are found in large quantities in residual sludge from the paper and pulp industry. Greater use of sludge and fibers in agriculture would reduce the need for fertilizer produced by fossil gas, but a prerequisite for this to happen is that legislation is changed. There is thus a significant, largely untapped potential in the form of waste and residual products, which are today excessively incinerated, placed in various landfills, or used as filling material. Recycling these is the easiest, cheapest, and above all fastest way to reduce dependence on mineral fertilizers and thus make the food system more robust. In the United States, as well as in many other countries, the laws are also a patchwork consisting of multiple agencies that lack a comprehensive approach to circularity (American bar 2024).

Examples of Circular Business Models

Business Model #1: Product as Service

Benefits: Products are used by one or many customers through lease or pay-for-use arrangements. Rather than a one-time sale, the product or asset is transitioned as a service where value is based on outcomes and performance rather than the physical asset.

Examples: Tool rentals, energy as a service, and clothing rentals (see Figure 8.4).

(Continued)

(Continued)

Figure 8.4 Milk cows produces manure that can be converted into biogas, an example of resource recovery.
Source: bilanol/Adobe Stock.

Business Model #2: Sharing Platforms

Benefits: Stimulating increased use of underutilized resources. Collaboration among individuals, organizations, or a combination of both, to acquire the greatest productivity or value from a product that could otherwise be underutilized.

Examples: Home sharing, car sharing.

Business Model #3: Product Life Extension

Benefits: Extend the current life cycle of a product: repairability, upgrading, reselling

Examples: Secondhand stores, repair, remanufacturing

Business Model #4: Resource Recovery

Benefits: Eliminate material leakage and maximize economic value of product flows

Examples: Biogas systems, collection of used beverage containers in vending machines.

Business Model #5: Circular Supplies

Benefits: Supply fully renewable, recyclable, or biodegradable resource inputs to support circular production.
Examples: Biodegradable packaging solutions, multi-use products.

Source: https://circularprocurement.ca/business-models.

Product-Service Systems (PSSs)

PSSs are business models that provide a cohesive delivery of products and services, often used to enable increased sustainability through more efficient resource use. The ambition of PSSs is to reduce material consumption; hence, they serve both consumers' desire for sustainable products and companies' aims to be more sustainable. According to Oksana Mont's definition of a PSS, it is as

> "a system of products, services, supporting networks, and infrastructure that is designed to be competitive, satisfy customers' needs, and have a lower environmental impact than traditional business models" (Mont 2001, p. 9) (See Figure 8.5).

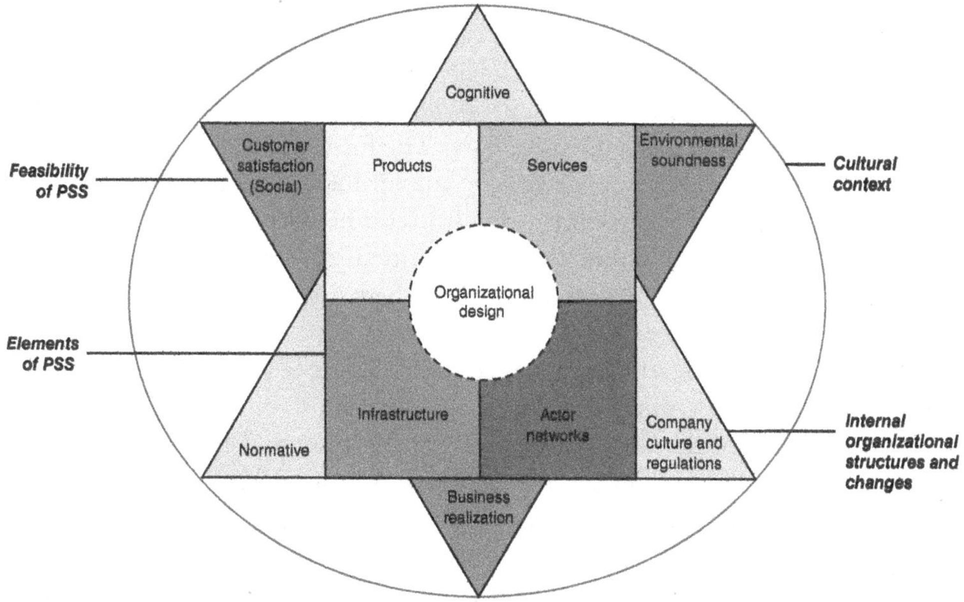

Figure 8.5 The Product-Service Systems (PSSs)
Source: Based on Mont (2001).

The focus of a PSS is on user needs, and it came about from changes in the larger business environment, changing market forces, and the recognition that services in combination with goods could provide higher profits than goods alone. In business-to-business (B2B) marketing, and to an extent in business-to-consumer (B2C) marketing, this is called *solution selling*. Increased competition and more demanding consumers with more choices mean that companies must compete – and PSS with sustainability claims could work as a framework for standing out in the competition.

A PSS takes a broad perspective on businesses and, according to recent research published by Brambila-Macias et al. (2018), includes seven areas: business orientation, collaboration, cost aspects, flexibility, performance indicators, requirement, and services. Hence, it has a strong link to business models that, likewise, focus on the variety of aspects that, when combined, constitute a well-functioning company.

Moreover, a PSS seeks to accomplish continuous improvement, preferably by being receptive and self-learning. Digitization and big data offer many such opportunities. Typically, there are three types of PSS business models:

- *Function-based PSS:* Companies add new functions to increase product value and gain competitive advantages over competitors
- *Value-added PSS:* Companies add new features to increase the value of a product to expand its value to consumers, thus gaining a competitive advantage
- *Evidence-based service:* Providers present actual savings based on evidence and past performance from various implementation projects

In all three types, a PSS could learn from accumulating data and experiences. For instance, when it comes to running a carpool, a train transport system, a health-promoting system for employees, or a climate system for a resort, a PSS could optimize resources and maximize user value. By integrating PSS design with big data analytics, optimization could take place faster. The focus of a PSS is thus to provide access to goods, rather than ownership; examples include carpools, toy libraries, firms lending manufacturing tools to other firms through leasing contracts, or firms renting out household tools and cumbersome items to customers. Most of these practices are based on a rental business model, where the customer pays a price per use and/or membership fees.

Van Ostaeyen et al. (2013) emphasize the complexity of PSSs and propose a categorization of PSS types according to two distinguishing features: the performance orientation of the dominant revenue mechanism and the degree of integration between product and service elements. According to the former, a PSS can be designated as *input-based*, *availability-based*, *usage-based*, or *performance-based*. According to the latter, a PSS can be designated as segregated, semi-integrated, and integrated, depending on the extent to which the product and service elements are combined into a single offering. The more there are, the better the purpose of a PSS is achieved.

Van Ostaeyen et al. (2013) also further subdivide the performance-based PSS types into the following:

- *Solution-oriented PSS:* i.e. selling a promised level of fuel savings or reduction of carbon emissions
- *Effect-oriented (EO) PSS:* i.e. selling a certain level of functionality or reliability, or guaranteeing indoor climate ranging from 19° to 22° all year round
- *Performance-based effect-oriented (PB-EO) PSS:* e.g. selling a promised temperature level in a building instead of selling radiators
- *Demand-fulfillment-oriented (PB-DO) PSS:* e.g. selling a promised level of thermal comfort for building occupants instead of selling radiators

A challenge of PSS thinking is to make sure that all three sustainability dimensions are properly addressed. Yang and Evans (2019) show that various types of PSS affect sustainability performance differently. For example, results-oriented PSS are shown to have great potential to deliver economic and environmental benefits through enhanced resource efficiency in production as well as consumption. At the same time, however, social sustainability effects are limited. Yang and Evans conclude that PSS business models do not have significant effects on social sustainability. We also discussed these paradoxical tensions within the triple-bottom line in Chapter 1.

Famous examples of PSS are Rolls-Royce's Power-by-the-Hour service package for aircraft engines (maintenance, repair, and overhaul services are charged per hour) or Atlas Copco's Contract Air service (air compressors are sold per m^3 of compressed air delivered). These have advantages for the buyer as well as the seller:

- The buyer will get a solution that minimizes risks and concerns that important parts of the operating business might not work properly. Hence, it minimizes management time as well as financial and operating risks
- The seller finds a way of presenting the solution provided in an attractive way and can charge a higher price if problems are solved for the buyer while a superior product is delivered

For an airline, for instance, pay per hour is a solution that makes it easier to calculate operating costs. Similarly, the owner of a fleet of cars would prefer costs that are possible to forecast instead of taking risks on their own, as in Michelin's fleet management solution whereby cars are charged per kilometer driven based on vehicle configuration. Michelin takes responsibility for the qualities of their products in everyday life.

As a matter of fact, manufacturers often believe a bit more in their products than their users, which is why the risk perception is different between the parties. The seller will normally have a lower risk perception regarding products sold and delivered than the buyer, who must often be convinced through various means such as warranties, guarantees, free repair, rebates, and other promotional tools.

Social Enterprises

Social enterprises are organizations that pursue a social mission through market-based strategies (e.g. Pearce 2003). Social enterprises have business models that integrate the social mission with financial self-sufficiency (Austin et al. 2006). Many of these enterprises aim to solve some of the challenges facing our planet, so-called wicked problems (e.g. Rittel and Webber 1973; Huff and Barnhart 2022).

Social enterprises are often started by social entrepreneurs whose initiatives often start out small scale with a nonprofit focus but with a vision of doing business with a social purpose, which is doing something good for society. For example, social entrepreneurs who opened up clothing libraries in Sweden discuss their purpose of prolonging the life of clothes, reducing textile waste, and also democratizing clothes to those who may not be able to afford new clothes (Albinsson and Perera 2018). However, larger for-profit or hybrid versions of social enterprise business models exist as well. The overall mission for a social enterprise is "creating social value for the public good" (Austin et al. 2006, p. 3). There is often a continuum for companies' business models, which ranges from purely profit driven to creating social value. The social value proposition (SVP) is at the core of a social enterprise. This lies in the intersection between people, capital, and opportunity in the marketplace but is also dependent on the context or environment it operates within. The well-being of current and future generations is at the core of many of these enterprises' business models (Bonfanti et al. 2024).

One type of social enterprise is the certified benefit corporation, or B-Corporation, or B Corp for short. These corporations have to legally create sustainable value over time to get the designation as a B Corp (Mion et al. 2021). According to B Lab US & Canada, B Corps are

> "for-profit companies that meet high standards of social and environmental performance, transparency, and accountability."

B Lab U.S. & Canada is a nonprofit that assists in assessing corporations to become B Corps certified by creating "standards, policies, tools, and programs that shifts the behavior, culture, and structural underpinnings of capitalism" (B Lab). They aim to mobilize their business community to address some of society's wicked problems. According to B Lag, currently there are more than 6300 B Corps in 85+ countries and 160 industries.

It is important to note that even the B Corp certification has been recently critiqued to be a glorified greenwashing technique by some critics as large brands such as Nespresso have become certified (Bennett 2024; Raval 2023). However, discussions from business leaders state that the certification "holds businesses accountable for their actions and statements" (Buchholz 2023); however, have certifications like this become yet another burden for consumers to decipher? What do you think?

Is this why peer-to-peer platforms have become so popular? We will discuss these next (see also Chapter 5).

Peer-to-Peer Platform Business Models

Most of the peer-to-peer (P2P) exchanges and services of the sharing economy (discussed in Chapter 5) are platform-based (or network-based) business models. P2P platforms have been analyzed as multisided or two-sided markets to better understand the phenomenon (de Oliveira and Cortimiglia 2017; Dreyer et al. 2017; Guyader and Piscicelli 2019). For instance, Constantiou et al. (2017) developed four business models of platforms based on different value propositions and strategic intents:

- "Franchiser" platforms with a high competition between peer-providers, which have a tight control over participation (e.g. Uber)
- "Chaperone" platforms with a high competition between participants as well, but a looser control (e.g. Airbnb)
- "Principal" platforms with a lower rivalry and charging standard price but who exercise a tight control over peer-providers to propose a standardized supply of services to consumers (e.g. TaskRabbit, an online platform that connects consumers with peer-service providers called "Taskers" who can help with various tasks and errands, like assembling an IKEA furniture, doing household chores, designing a website)
- "Gardeners" platforms with lower rivalry, letting participants price their offer as they want, and less governance control as they use social norms and community values instead of strict rules (e.g. BlaBlaCar, a platform that connects drivers with empty seats in their vehicles with passengers traveling in the same direction; or CouchSurfing, social networking platform that allows travelers called "surfers" to stay as guests at a host's home, aka their couch, for free)

Field et al. (2018) argue that peer-to-peer platforms have the competitive advantage (i.e. operational strategy) of being asset-light and able to efficiently close competitive market gaps (i.e. unmet needs) by developing service offering bundles. Moreover, the value of network-based P2P platforms is the connectivity and co-creation, meaning "not in creating the nodes (whether people, things, or data) but in fostering the connections between the nodes" (Bonchek and Libert 2017).

Regarding platform business models, economists Rochet and Tirole (2006) argue it is all about two-sided markets. A market is two-sided

> "if the platform can affect the volume of transactions by charging more to one side of the market and reducing the price paid by the other side by an equal amount; in other words, the price structure matters, and platforms must design it so as to bring both sides on board"

(p. 665). Most platforms charge one side of the market comparatively more than the other side; in other words, making money on one side (whichever can bear it) and having costs on the other side (whichever needs to increase in size). Either way, the more users, the greater the network effects and both sides of the platform benefit from externalities (Evans and Schmalensee 2010; Muzellec et al. 2015; Rochet and Tirole 2006).

Van Alstyne et al. (2016) argue that information technology facilitates platform development, but what is key for platform strategies is understanding network effects (i.e. value increasing proportionally to the number of participants in platform exchanges). For instance, online platforms such as Airbnb or Booking.com are attracting so many travelers that hotels and other accommodation providers have little choice but to use them if they want to make themselves available to these masses. Moreover, Muzellec et al. (2015) argue that online platforms have two types of participants ("sides"):

> "a business side (B2B), which very often is the business customer (they pay for a service), and an end-user side (B2C) who is the consumer of the service, and who may or may not pay for the service" (p. 140).

Many sharing economy platforms have aggressively marketed their operations and thus gained a lot of media attention (e.g. Uber, Airbnb). But there are many efficient collaborative models – often run by nonprofit organizations – that operate locally and offline (e.g. public tool libraries set up by cities, neighbors sharing cars), and they also influence how people understand and carry out collaborative consumption. Söderholm (2016) has studied a tool library in Berkeley, through interviews with borrowers, and he found that their motives were availability of the tool library, low need for the tools, and low costs. The fact that many tools are used only rarely makes a tool library a great solution for many people. People who start borrowing tools or renting clothes from a "fashion library" might also sign up to a car-sharing service and rent out their home to travelers. People learn how P2P services are exchanged, and they apply their understanding of the sharing norms (i.e. institutional logics) and adapt their expectations when moving on to the next new "Uber for X."

"Uber for X"

The "Uberization" phenomenon refers to Internet entrepreneurs establishing new platforms and associated mobile apps striving to replicate the success of Uber (e.g. Carney 2014). The ride-hailing company has inspired a flood of startups similar to Uber but for X: Uber for laundry (Washio), Uber for grocery shopping (Instacart), Uber for dog sitting (DogVacay), etc (See Figure 8.6). These all provide on-demand services through mobile phone apps.

Figure 8.6 Dog walkers.
Source: Shutterstock 2051387972.

Mobility-as-a-Service (MaaS) Business Models

One contemporary and innovative business model in the shared mobility sector, which is based on multi-actor collaboration, has experienced significant interest: mobility as a service (MaaS) (see Figure 8.7). This business model aims to provide an integrated mobility solution by combining a variety of mobility services from multiple actors from the transportation sector (e.g. public transportation, ride hailing, bike sharing, car rental, etc.) into a single digital platform to address the transportation needs of customers in a user-friendly manner (Guyader et al. 2021a). In the tech industry, a MaaS is envisioned as the "Spotify of mobility" (MaaS Alliance 2021). Ideally, this business model would reduce car usage and hence bring down greenhouse gas emissions, congestion in city centers and suburbs, traffic accidents, and the need for parking spaces.

By 2030, such integrated mobility solutions are forecasted to produce societal benefits such as improved safety and connectivity for urban residents, equivalent to $600 billion annually per city (McKerracher et al. 2016). Due to these potential sustainable benefits and to face issues related to increasing urbanization, a growing number of regional governments have, or are planning to develop, MaaS in Europe (e.g. Whim in cities in the United Kingdom, Austria, and the Nordic countries), in the United States (e.g. MOVE PGH in Pittsburgh, Pennsylvania; Vamos in San Joaquin Valley, California), and elsewhere (e.g. Australia, Japan) – we have entered the "MaaS Gold Rush" (Hazan et al. 2019).

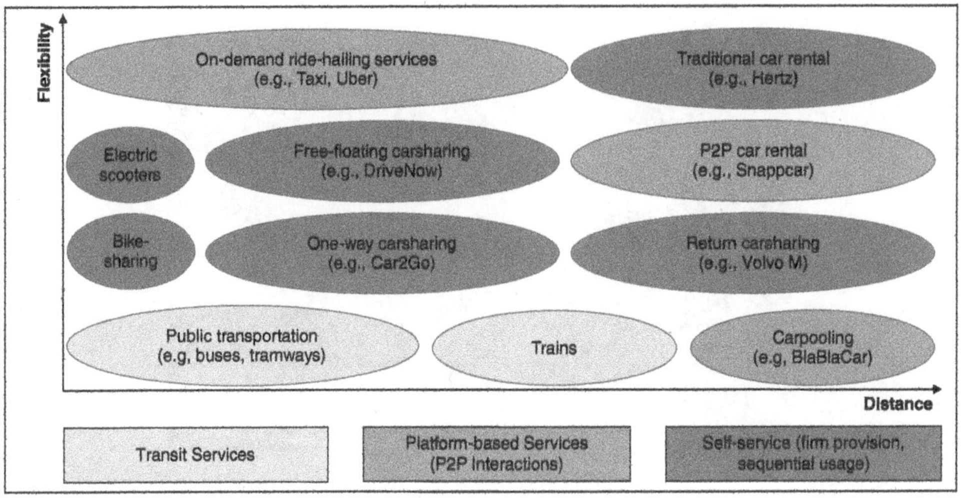

Figure 8.7 The diversity of transportation modes in the shared mobility sector. Note that this representation excludes basic car ownership, leasing (which resembles permanent ownership), MaaS or mobility-as-network (MasN) systems and other "all-in-one" integrated solutions (as they combine different shared mobility modes into one single app), e-scooters (which can be considered a form of bike sharing for shorter distances), and walking.
Source: Guyader et al. (2021a) with permission.

However, despite the initial enthusiasm, many MaaS business models have failed to emerge (Guyader et al. 2021b). Thus, considering the promising potential that MaaS possesses to generate transformative value and address societal and environmental challenges, we deem it necessary to improve our understanding of the underlying factors that inhibit its successful widespread.

Consultancy reports and other forms of research indicate that a shared car may replace between 13 (Martin et al. 2010) and 15 cars (Transport and Environment 2017). However, data from car-sharing companies indicates that utilization is between 9% and 12%. People's willingness to pay is also limited, with an expanding range of services such as Uber and platforms that connect providers and buyers of taxi services both putting downward pressure on prices and might be questioned from a social sustainability point of view. At the end of the day, there is a risk that platform owners earn a lot of money while buyers pay a low price, and providers work under very tough conditions. In cities such as Vienna, where shared cars get subsidies, it is a lot easier to make this profitable.

References

Abdelkafi, N., & Täuscher, K. (2016). Business models for sustainability from a system dynamics perspective. *Organization and Environment*, 29(1), 74–96. https://doi.org/10.1177/1086026615592930.

Albinsson, P.A., & Perera, Y.P. (2018), Access-based consumption: from ownership to non-ownership of clothing, in *The Rise of the Sharing Economy: Exploring the Challenges and Opportunities of Collaborative Consumption.* (Albinsson, P.A., & Perera, B.Y. eds.) Praeger: Santa Barbara, CA, pp. 183–212.

American bar, 2024. Adoption of a circular economy in the United States. https://www.americanbar.org/groups/environment_energy_resources/publications/ed/adoption-of-a-circular-economy-in-the-us (accessed 2 May 2024).

Austin, J., Stevenson, H., & Wei-Skillern, J. (2006). Social and commercial entrepreneurship: same, different, or both? *Entrepreneurship Theory and Practice*, 1, 1–22.

Baden-Fuller, C. & Morgan, M. (2010). Business models as models. *Long Range Planning*, 43, 156–171.

Baitheiemy, J. (2003). The seven deadly sins of outsourcing. *Academy of Management Executive*, 17(2), 87–98.

Bennett, E. (2024). As greenwashing soars, some people are questioning B Corp certification. BBC.com. https://www.bbc.com/worklife/article/20240202-has-b-corp-certification-turned-into-corporate-greenwashing (accessed 28 May 2024).

Bocken, N.M.P., et al., 2014. A literature and practice review to develop sustainable business model archetypes. *Journal of Cleaner Production,* 65, 42–56.

Bocken, N.M.P., de Pauw, I., Bakker, C., & van der Grinten, B. (2016). Product design and business model strategies for a circular economy. *Journal of Industrial and Production Engineering*, 33(5), 308–320. https://doi.org/10.1080/21681015.2016.1172124.

Bocken , N.M.P., Strupeit, L., Whalen, K. & Nußholz, J. 2019. A review and evaluation of circular business model innovation tools. *Sustainability,* 11(8), 2210.

Bonchek, M. & Libert, B. (2017). You don't need to be a Silicon Valley startup to have a network-based strategy. *Harvard Business Review*, 14. https://hbr.org/2017/07/you-dont-need-to-be-a-silicon-valley-startup-to-have-a-network-based-strategy.

Bonfanti, A., De Crescenzo, V., Simeoni, F., & Loza Adaui, C. R. (2024). Convergences and divergencies in sustainable entrepreneurship and social entrepreneurship research: a systematic review and research agenda. *Journal of Business Research,* 170, 1–19.

Brambila-Macias, S.A., Sakao, T. & Kowalkowski, C. (2018). Bridging the gap between engineering design and marketing: insights for research and practice in product/service system design. *Design Science*, 4, 1–61.

Buchholz, L. (2023). B Corp: Are they really the gold standard of sustainability? Sustainability Magazine. https://sustainabilitymag.com/esg/b-corp-are-they-really-the-gold-standard-of-sustainability (accessed 28 May 2024).

Carney B.M. (2014). Let's Uberize the Entire Economy. Forbes. https://www.forbes.com/sites/realspin/2014/10/27/lets-uberize-the-entire-economy/#4c600e154c60. (accessed 15 May 2023).

Chesbrough, H. (2010). Business model innovation: opportunities and barriers. Long Range Planning, 43(2–3), 354–363.

Circularity gap. (2023). The Circularity gap report 2023. https://www.circularity-gap.world/2023.(accessed 2 May 2024).

Constantiou, I., Marton, A. & Tuunainen, V.K. (2017). Four models of sharing economy platforms. *MIS Quarterly Executive*, 16(4), 231–251.

Dreyer, B., Lüdeke-Freund, F., Hamann, R. & Faccer, K. (2017). Upsides and downsides of the sharing economy: collaborative consumption business models' stakeholder value impacts and their relationship to context. *Technological Forecasting and Social Change*, 125, 87–104.

Esty, D.C. and Porter, M.E. (1998), Industrial ecology and competitiveness. *Journal of Industrial Ecology*, 2, 35–43. https://doi.org/10.1162/jiec.1998.2.1.35.

Evans, D.S. & Schmalensee, R. (2010). Failure to launch: critical mass in platform businesses. *Review of Network Economics*, 9(4).

Evans S., Vladimirova D., Holgado, M. Van Fossen K., Yang M., Silva E.A., & Barlow C.Y. (2017). Business Model Innovation for Sustainability: Towards a Unified Perspective for Creation of Sustainable Business Models. *Business Strategy and the Environment*, 26, 597–608.

Field, J.M., Victorino, L., Buell, R.W., Dixon, M.J., Meyer Goldstein, S., Menor, L.J., Pullman, M.E., Roth, A.V., Secchi, E. and Zhang, J.J., 2018. Service operations: what's next? *Journal of Service Management*, 29(1), 55–97.

Geissdoerfer, M., Savaget, P. & Evans, S. (2017a). The Cambridge business model innovation process. *Procedia Manufacturing*, 8, 262–269.

Geissdoerfer, M., Savaget, P., Bocken, N.M.P. & Hultink, E.J. (2017b). The circular economy – a new sustainability paradigm? *Journal of Cleaner Production*, 143, 757–778.

Geissdoerfer, M., Vladimirova, D. & Evans, S. (2018a). Sustainable business model innovation: A review. *Journal of Cleaner Production*, 198(10), 401–416.

Geissdoerfer, M., Moriaka, S.N., de Carvalho, M.M. & Evans, S. (2018b). Business models and supply chains for the circular economy. *Journal of Cleaner Production*, 190, 712–721.

Geissdoerfer, M., Pieroni, M., Pigosso, D. C. & Soufani, K. (2020). Circular business models: a review. *Journal of Cleaner Production*, 277, 123741.

Guldmann, E., Bocken, N. & Brezet, H. (2019). A design thinking framework for circular business model innovation. *Journal of Business Models*, 7, 39–70.

Guldmann, E., & Huulgaard, R. D. (2020). Barriers to circular business model innovation: A multiple-case study. *Journal of Cleaner Production*, Volume 243, 118160.

Guyader, H. & Piscicelli, L. (2019). Business model diversification in the sharing economy: the case of GoMore. *Journal of Cleaner Production*, 215C (April), 1059–1069.

Guyader, H., Friman, M. and Olsson, L.E., (2021a). Shared mobility: evolving practices for sustainability. Sustainability, 13(21), 12148.

Guyader H, Nansubuga B, Skill K. (2021b). Institutional logics at play in a mobility-as-a-service ecosystem. *Sustainability* 13(15), 8285.

Hazan, J. l., N. Lang, and H. E. A. Chraibi. (2019). Seeking perpetual motion with mobility as a service. https://www.bcg.com/publications/2019/seeking-perpetual-motion-mobility-as-service.(accessed 15 May 2024).

Herin, P. (2024). Tuffare för ekomat – men Bjärefågel trotsar trenden. [Tougher for organic food – but Bjärefågel defies the trend.] Dagens Industri. https://www.di.se/nyheter/tuffare-for-ekomat-men-bjarefagel-trotsar-trenden (accessed 4 June 2024).

Huff, A.D. & Barnhart, M., 2022. UNRAVEL-ing gnarly knots: a path for researching market-entangled wicked social problems. *Journal of Business Research*, 144, 717–727.

Kazancoglu, I., Kazancoglu, Y., Yarimoglu, E., & Kahraman, A. (2020). A conceptual framework for barriers of circular supply chains for sustainability in the textile industry. *Sustainable Development*, 28(5), 1477–1492. https://doi.org/10.1002/sd.2100.

Kindström, D. & Ottosson, M. (2016) Local and regional energy companies offering energy services: key activities and implications for the business model. *Applied Energy*, 171, 491–500.

Kirchherr, J., Reike, D. & Hekkert, M. (2017). Conceptualizing the circular economy: an analysis of 114 definitions. *Resources, Conservation and Recycling*, 127, 221–232.

Langfield-Smith, K. & Smith, D. (2003). Management control systems and trust in outsourcing relationships. *Management Accounting Research*, 14(3), 281–307.

Loorback, D.A. & Wijsman, K. (2013). Business transition management: exploring a new role for business in sustainable transitions. *Journal of Cleaner Production*, 45, 20–28.

MaaS Alliance (2021). Interoperability for Mobility, Data Models, and API: Building a Common, Connected, and Interoperable Ground for the Future of Mobility. https://maas-alliance.eu/wp-content/uploads/2021/11/20211120-Def-Version-Interoperaability-for-Mobility.-Data-Models-and-API-_-FINAL.pdf.(accessed 13 March 2023).

Martin, E., Shaheen, S., & Lidicker, J. (2010). The impact of carsharing on household vehicle ownership. *Transport Research Record: Journal of the Transportation Research Board*, 2143, 150–158.

Massa, L., Tucci, C. & Afuah, A. (2017). A critical assessment of business model research. *Academy of Management Annals*, 11, 73–104.

McKerracher, C., Orlandi, I., Wilshire, M., Tryggestad, C., Mohr, D., Hannon, E., Morden, E., Nijssen, J.T., Bouton, S., Knupfer, S., Ramkumar, S., Ramanathan, S. and Moeller, T. (2016). An Integrated Perspective on the Future of Mobility: Bloomberg: New Energy Finance; McKinsey & Company: Center for Business & Environment. https://assets.bbhub.io/professional/sites/24/2016/10/BNEF_McKinsey_The-Future-of-Mobility_11-10-16.pdf. (accessed 1 November 2023).

Mion, G, Loza Adaui, C. R. & Bonfanti, A. (2021). Characterizing the mission statements of benefit corporations: Empirical evidence from Italy. *Business Strategy and the Environment*, 30, 2160–2172.

Mont, O. (2001). Introducing and developing a product-service system (PSS) concept in Sweden. IIIEE Reports, 6. https://www.researchgate.net/publication/228863029_Introducing_and_Developing_a_Product-Service_System_PSS_Concept_in_Sweden#fullTextFileContent (accessed 5 May 2024).

Muzellec, L., Ronteau, S. & Lambkin, M. (2015). Two-sided internet platforms: a business model lifecycle perspective. *Industrial Marketing Management*, 45(February), 139–150.

de Oliveira, D.T. & Cortimiglia, M.N. (2017). Value co-creation in web-based multisided platforms: a conceptual framework and implications for business model design. *Business Horizons*, 60(6), 474–758.

Osterwalder, A, and Pigneur, Y., 2010, *Business Model Generation: A Handbook for Visionaries; Game Changers; and Challengers*. Chichester: Wiley.

Patel, N. (2015). 90% of Startups Fail: Here's What You Need to Know about the 10%. *Forbes*. https://www.forbes.com/sites/neilpatel/2015/01/16/90-of-startups-will-fail-heres-what-you-need-to-know-about-the-10/?sh=38b0ecb66792 (accessed 15 May 2024).

Pearce J. (2003). *Social Enterprise in Anytown*, Calouste Gulbenkian Foundation, London, UK.

Porter, M.E. & Kramer, M.R. (2011). Creating shared value. *Harvard Business Review*, 89(1/2), 62–77.

Porter, M.E. & van der Linde, C. (1995). Toward a new conception of the environment competitiveness relationship. *Journal of Economic Perspectives*, 9, 97–118.

Raval, A. (2023). The struggle of the soul of the B Corp movement. *The Financial Times*. https://www.ft.com/content/0b632709-afda-4bdc-a6f3-bb0b02eb5a62 (accessed 28 May 2024).

Ritala, P., Huotari, P., Bocken, N., Albareda, L. and Puumalainen, K., (2018). Sustainable business model adoption among S&P 500 firms: a longitudinal content analysis study. *Journal of Cleaner Production*, 170, 216–226.

Rittel, H.W.J., & Webber, M.M. (1973). Dilemmas in a general theory of planning. *Policy Sciences* 4, 155–169.

Rochet, J.C. & Tirole, J. (2006). Two-sided markets: a progress report. RAND *Journal of Economics*, 37(3), 645–667.

Schaltegger, S., Lüdeke-Freund, F., and Hansen, E.G., 2012. Business cases for sustainability: the role of business model innovation for corporate sustainability. *International Journal of Innovation and Sustainable Development*, 6 (2), 95.

Svensson, N., & Funck, E.K. (2019). Management control in circular economy. Exploring and theorizing the adaptation of management control to circular business models *Journal of Cleaner Production*, 233, 390–398.

Söderholm, J. (2016). Borrowing tools from the public library, *Journal of Documentation*, 72(1), 140–155.

Stahel, W. R. (2019). *Circular Economy – A User's Guide*. London: Routledge

Stubbs, W. & Cocklin, C., 2008. Conceptualising a sustainability business model. *Organization and Environment*, 21(2), 103–127.

Tiwana, A. & Keil, M. (2007). Does peripheral knowledge complement control? An empirical test in technology outsourcing alliances. *Strategic Management Journal*, 28, 623–634.

Transport & Environment. (2017). Does sharing cars really reduce car use? https://te-cdn.ams3.digitaloceanspaces.com/files/Does-sharing-cars-really-reduce-car-use-June202017.pdf (accessed 15 May 2024).

Tushman, M. & Nadler, D., 1980. A model for diagnosing organisational behavior. *Organizational Dynamics*, 9(2), 35–51.

Upward, A., & Jones, P. (2016). An ontology for strongly sustainable business models: defining an enterprise framework compatible with natural and social science. *Organization and Environment*, 29(1), 97–123. https://doi.org/10.1177/1086026615592933

Van Alstyne, M. W., Parker, G. G. and S. P. Choudary. (2016). Pipelines, platforms, and the new rules of strategy: Scale now trumps differentiation. *Harvard Business Review*, (April): 54–62.

Van Ostaeyen, J., Van Horenbeek, A., Pintelon, L. and Duflou, J.R. (2013). A refined typology of product–service systems based on functional hierarchy modeling. *Journal of Cleaner Production*, 51, 261–276.

Velte, P. (2022). Meta-analyses on corporate social responsibility (CSR): a literature review. *Management Review Quarterly*, 72, 627–675. https://doi.org/10.1007/s11301-021-00211-2.

Werning, J. P., & Spinler, S. (2020). Transition to circular economy on firm level: barrier identification and prioritization along the value chain. *Journal of Cleaner Production*, 245. 10.1016/j.jclepro.2019.118609.

Wirtz, B.W., Pistoia, A., Ulrich, S., Göttel, V. (2016). Business models: origin, development and future research perspectives. *Long Range Planning*, 49(1), 36–54.

Yang, M. & Evans, S. (2019). Product-service system business model archetypes and sustainability. *Journal of Cleaner Production*, 220, 1156–1166.

Zott, C., Amit, R., and Massa, L., 2011. The business model: recent developments and future research. *Journal of Management*, 37 (4), 1019–1042.

Chapter 9

Sustainable Value Chains and Marketing Channels

For a very long time, a century or so, marketing channels have had the key function of physically distributing goods from manufacturers to buyers via intermediaries such as wholesalers and retailers, e.g. channels. An increasing service share in the economy, more competition, and stronger consumer rights have put lots of demands on marketing channels to evolve. Moreover, the advent of sustainability concerns is a key factor that is fundamentally reshaping marketing channels. In this chapter, we discuss sustainable marketing channels and the challenges that value chain management brings.

Learning Objectives

- Explain and understand sustainable supply chains
- Explain and understand sustainable marketing channels
- Explain and understand the challenges in making marketing channel practices more sustainable
- Understand profitability and sustainability challenges in relation to marketing channels

Introduction

Transports account for one-fifth of global carbon dioxide (CO_2) emissions. Besides transporting passengers, transports of goods by trucks, ships, aviation, and rail produce emissions of CO_2 (Our world in data 2024). All the steps including identifying key suppliers, procuring materials from them, sourcing components, transporting goods and delivering products and services to end users affect the climate. Hence, an important part of a sustainability strategy, although not often discussed, is marketing channels, which must be dedicated to sustainability. Neither research on marketing and sustainability nor recent developments of marketing channels research addresses the issue of sustainability in marketing channels sufficiently. Using sustainable channels not only allows organizations to reach their target audiences but also shows to what extent they are committed to sustainability (Baldassarre and Campo 2016; Melović et al. 2020) (See Figure 9.1.)

Marketing channels include a set of activities that transfer the product from the producer to the end user – and that's exactly where, in many instances, sustainability-oriented companies fail. Not even using green carriers for home delivery may solve the sustainability challenge, since the green carriers are sometimes compromising with what they promise. We see this happening across the world. Shipping companies that use liquefied natural gas (LNG) instead of traditional fossil fuels want the public and policymakers to believe that it's the best option. LNG is natural gas that has been cooled down to a liquified state. Despite being advertised as "a fuel for the future," as a "transitional fuel," or as "paving the

Figure 9.1 In times of transitioning to e-commerce, it is crucial for both companies and consumers to rethink sustainability of the marketing channels.
Source: Shutterstock.

way for the uptake of sustainable nonfossil fuels," these claims are not consistent with scientific knowledge. While LNG can have some positive impact when it comes to air quality, it might make climate change worse because of methane slips and leakages associated with the production and use of this fuel (Transport and Environment 2023a). Supply chains have a crucial role in making marketing channels sustainable, and there are lots of deceptive practices that firms with sustainability ambitions should avoid.

Sustainable Value Chains

This is a book on marketing; accordingly, much focus will be on the downstream value chain activities. However, upstream value chain activities are also crucial, for two reasons. First, they are necessary to make the downstream activities come about. Second, with sustainability claims, one cannot offer a sustainable value chain by focusing only on the downstream side. Genuine sustainability starts early, in the very first steps of product design and manufacturing.

Just like supply chain and value chain may be used interchangeably, sustainable supply chains and sustainable value chains are concepts that appear to be similar. However, regardless of which is chosen, the upstream supply chain includes all activities related to the organization's suppliers: those parties that source raw material inputs to send to the manufacturer. The downstream supply chain (e.g. marketing channels or distribution) refers to the activities post-manufacturing, namely, distributing the product to the final customer. With a sustainability perspective, the entire chain has to be committed to sustainability (e.g. Vurro et al. 2009).

Value chains for our most purchased goods extend globally, exemplified by something as ubiquitous as a frozen lasagna. Picture tonight's dinner: even if it's produced in Mexico, it's likely the minced meat hails from Brazil or Argentina, the tomato sauce and pasta originate from Italy, the milk and cheese for the sauce come from Canada, and the garlic arrives from China. Perhaps the onion is sourced in California. How does such a simple dish become a mosaic of ingredients from around the world? The answer lies in the movement of goods facilitated by various trade agreements globally, fostering specialization and large-scale farming of food. Globalization has fostered competition among countries supplying similar products, leading to the formation of global value chains that standardize production and farming methods. In the case of our lasagna, the brand owner can cherry-pick ingredients from countries offering the best combination of price, quantity, and quality.

While global value chains optimize production efficiency, they present challenges in controlling sustainability performance.

Fast Fashion Retail: Sustainable Certifications or Regulations

The fashion industry's impact on the environment is staggering, accounting for 2–8% of global carbon emissions due to its reliance on raw material extraction, lengthy supply chains, and energy-intensive production processes. To put this in perspective, it surpasses the combined emissions of the shipping and aviation industries, which make up about 5% of global emissions.

Efforts to mitigate the fashion industry's pollution are underway, including initiatives like the United Nations (UN)–backed Fashion Charter. However, despite these efforts, greenwashing remains a significant challenge. A recent study revealed that 60% of sustainability claims made by major European fashion brands are unsubstantiated and misleading. This has led to confusion among consumers and eroded trust in sustainable practices.

Nevertheless, the fashion industry possesses immense marketing power and has the potential to drive positive change toward sustainability. The Sustainable Fashion Communication Playbook serves as a guide for fashion communicators, including marketers, brand managers, influencers, and media, to combat greenwashing and promote progress aligned with the Paris Agreement and Sustainable Development Goals.

Companies like H&M, Uniqlo, and Zara are striving to embrace sustainability within the fast fashion realm. However, their reliance on unsustainable practices, particularly in cotton production, poses significant challenges. Cotton farming, laden with pesticides, not only threatens the health of farmers but also contributes to water shortages. Moreover, garment factories in countries like Bangladesh, Cambodia, and Myanmar often pay wages insufficient to support a decent standard of living for workers.

To address these issues, retailers utilize sustainable certifications and labeling to convey the idea of guilt-free consumption. Slogans like "sustainable choice" or "the good choice" are emblazoned on products to signal their environmental and social benefits. Yet, the proliferation of different certifications, including Organic (e.g. GOTS), Fairtrade, and the Better Cotton Initiative, add to consumer confusion.

The fundamental challenge lies in reconciling the fast fashion business model, built on mass-producing inexpensive garments, with sustainability imperatives. H&M, for instance, is transparent about its efforts to negotiate with the Bangladeshi government to raise minimum wages for textile workers. Higher wages would not only improve workers' living standards but also enable the sourcing of sustainable garments from Bangladesh on equal footing with other suppliers.

H&M and Zara have recently been linked to environmental degradation through harmful environmental practices such as excessive water consumption, greenhouse gas emissions, and pollution from chemical usage in their supply chains. According to an investigation by NGO Earthsight, Better Cotton–certified producers linked to environmental and human rights abuses in a sensitive ecoregion in Brazil are regularly selling tainted cotton into H&M and Zara's supply chains. The findings raise questions both about the credibility of Better Cotton, one of the industry's most widely used sustainability certifiers, and about Zara's and H&Ms' control of their supply chains and their sustainability performance. The investigation comes as toughening supply-chain regulations are increasing the pressure on brands to get a better handle on exactly where their materials come from. Sourcing transparency has become a crucial aspect of sustainable marketing channels.

Numerous reports call for greater transparency and accountability from these brands to address their environmental impact and urge consumers to consider more sustainable fashion choices. In essence, the fashion industry faces a critical juncture where sustainability must be integrated into its core practices to ensure a viable future while meeting consumer demand for ethical and environmentally conscious products.

Source: Earth Sights (2024); Hoskins (2017); Kent (2024).

Re-thinking Global and Local in Designing Value Chains to Promote Sustainability

Marketing has always struggled with the tricky balance of global efficiencies and local responsiveness. Traditional approaches often prioritize either global efficiency or local responsiveness (Roth and Morrison 1990), but sustainability goals mean a new pathway to reach complex goals while not compromising on sustainability (cf. Vurro et al. 2009).

At its core, sustainability demands a holistic view that transcends geographical boundaries. Global value chains have revolutionized production, allowing for cost-effective manufacturing and wider market reach. However, this globalization often comes at the expense of environmental degradation and social inequality. To address these challenges, a paradigm shift is imperative. Rather than viewing global and local as opposing forces, embracing their symbiotic relationship can unlock innovative solutions. Designing value chains with sustainability as the focal point requires a delicate balance between global integration and local adaptation.

One approach is to foster collaboration across the entire value chain, from multinational corporations to local suppliers and communities. By incorporating local knowledge and resources into global strategies, companies can enhance efficiency while simultaneously promoting local development and resilience. This collaborative model empowers local stakeholders, fosters inclusive growth, and reduces the ecological footprint of production processes.

Moreover, re-thinking value chains through a sustainability lens involves redefining success metrics. Beyond mere profitability, success should encompass environmental stewardship, social equity, and long-term resilience. Implementing circular economy principles, such as waste reduction, resource efficiency, and product longevity, can transform value chains into regenerative systems that benefit both the planet and its inhabitants.

Furthermore, digital technologies offer unprecedented opportunities to optimize value chains for sustainability. Advanced data analytics, blockchain, and artificial intelligence enable real-time monitoring, traceability, and transparency throughout the supply chain. By leveraging these technologies, companies can identify inefficiencies, mitigate risks, and ensure compliance with sustainability standards at both the global and local levels.

In essence, re-thinking global and local in designing value chains requires a shift from a linear, extractive model to a circular, inclusive one. It entails embracing diversity, fostering collaboration, and prioritizing sustainability at every stage of the value chain. By transcending traditional boundaries and embracing interconnectedness, we can pave the way for a more sustainable and equitable future for all.

Re-thinking the Value Chain to Make it Sustainable

Marketing channels demand a new approach to align with sustainable practices. Within the broader context of society, culture, and the environment, every aspect of creating customer value must contribute positively to sustainability, thereby benefiting not only consumers but also society overall. But also, consumers are increasingly supporting what is good for society. Products, services, or brands perceived by consumers as making a meaningful sustainability difference are likely to outperform those that neglect or trivialize sustainability concerns.

Consider brands like IKEA, Wayfair, BestBuy, or Uniqlo, which have historically succeeded by offering meaningful benefits to consumers in the fast fashion and fast furniture industries, respectively. While previously, consumers may have only assessed personal benefits from such products, the inclusion of various sustainability and social justice considerations now adds complexity for both consumers and companies.

Fast Furniture

In a consumption-oriented world, where convenience and cost often guide consumer buying decisions, the significance of fast furniture is beyond doubt. Although media focus a lot on fast fashion, also fast furniture is worth investigating to improve sustainability. Fast furniture, characterized by its low cost, trendy designs, and high availability, has become increasingly popular, but the significant sustainability challenges fast furniture comes with cannot be ignored. Challenges such as resource depletion and increased waste, alongside labor rights concerns entangled in intricate supply chains, underscore the hidden costs behind the allure of inexpensive and fashionable furniture. Thus, as we progress, we are presented with a chance to redefine not only our living environments but also our global footprint.

One of the primary concerns with fast furniture is its environmental impact. Fast furniture production often involves cheap materials and manufacturing processes that contribute to resource depletion and environmental degradation. This includes the overuse of wood from forests, the emission of greenhouse gases during production and transportation, and the generation of large amounts of waste at the end of the product life cycle.

In addition, fast furniture is notorious for its short life span. Many fast furniture products use low-quality materials and construction that lead to rapid wear and tear, something that encourages constant consumption and disposal, further exacerbating the environmental footprint of the furniture industry.

Furthermore, the production of fast furniture is often associated with unethical labor practices. To keep costs low, manufacturers may exploit workers by paying low wages, providing poor working conditions, and disregarding labor rights. This exploitation can occur at various stages of the supply chain, from the extraction of raw materials to the manufacturing process and distribution.

Addressing the sustainability challenges posed by fast furniture requires a multifaceted approach. Consumers can play a significant role by making more conscious purchasing decisions, opting for durable, high-quality furniture that is ethically produced and environmentally friendly. Policymakers can implement regulations to promote sustainable practices within the furniture industry, such as certification standards for sustainable materials and fair labor practices.

The awareness of these issues has grown, and a 2023 documentary by ARTE, a European culture TV channel, on how IKEA plunders the planet, has gained increased traction toward the theme. The documentary explores

(Continued)

(Continued)

the environmental impact of IKEAs operations including the use of materials, production processes, and supply chain practices, and their implications for sustainability. The documentary may also scrutinize IKEA's efforts toward sustainability, including initiatives such as renewable energy use and sustainable sourcing. It could highlight criticisms or controversies surrounding IKEA's sustainability practices, offering perspectives from experts, activists, and stakeholders. Ultimately, by raising awareness of the sustainability challenges associated with fast furniture and advocating for change, we can work together toward creating a more sustainable and ethical furniture industry for the future.

Source: Connybear (2022); FAO (2020); Kamin (2022); Perry (2022).

Greenwashing in Supply Chains

Supply chain greenwashing is an immoral practice employed by companies in various industries. A common way of engaging in this type of greenwashing is to selectively disclose information regarding upstream suppliers – occasionally after exaggerating the environmental benefits of their own products. One example is car manufacturers, on the one hand addressing their important role in climate change, on the other hand not disclosing information about sustainability issues in their global value chains.

Even with transparency and regulation, a lot of information may go unnoticed for consumers and other stakeholders. A study investigated the conditions under which a retailer who engages in greenwashing will disclose information of an unethical foreign supplier under pressure from enhanced scrutiny by a nongovernmental organization (NGO) (Chen and Duan 2023). This situation is rather similar to the car manufacturers investigated by Human Rights Watch (HRW) (see box below). earlier. Chen and Duan's study suggest that when the increase in the NGO's utility from targeting the unrevealed upstream supplier is sufficiently large, the greenwashing retailer prefers to disclose the unethical foreign supplier's information – hence turning the focus away from the retailer's poor sustainability practices – whereas when the increased utility is low, the greenwashing retailer prefers to hide the unethical foreign supplier. In other words, the retailer calculates the risk that the poor sustainability practices will be identified and acted upon by consumers and other stakeholders. This is a typical instance of unethical behavior. Different from the common belief that increased information transparency may be beneficial, the study finds that it does not necessarily lead to reduced social damage. On the contrary, when the unethical foreign supplier has a low capacity for compliance, the supply chain's transparency advantage will lead to more fake green goods being sold, thus causing greater social damage (Chen and Duan 2023).

These mentioned shady practices, however, will become more difficult since various stakeholders' attention toward poor sustainability practices has increased. Increasingly aware consumers are raising these issues as are the media and politicians. In the European Union, for instance, a new law that bans greenwashing and misleading product information was introduced in 2024 (European Parliament 2024).

The transition toward more sustainable logistics might also be forced through pressure by stakeholders, who demand better sustainability performance. For instance, there has been significant pressure on the vehicle leasing subsidiary of BNP Paris – ALD to stop leasing fossil fuel cars by 2028 (Transport and Environment 2023b).

It should help – and does help – when not only lawmakers and policymakers stand behind an agenda to improve sustainability practices in marketing channels. In a 2016 study, multinational corporations (MNCs) who are members of the Fortune Global 250 (FG250) and their sustainability reporting efforts, with focus on supply chain impacts, were investigated. To determine whether greenwashing was occurring or whether MNCs had committed to operating a truly sustainable/green supply chain, a quantitative analysis of 25 MNC corporate social responsibility (CSR)/sustainability reports as well as a qualitative analysis using content analysis were conducted. Twenty percent of the MNCs did not report on their supply chain activities at all, 48% reported on their supply chain impacts at the value and goal level, while the rest (32%) reported at the management approach level. Due to the lack of detailed quantitative information, the conclusion was established that most sampled MNCs could be accused of greenwashing due to the poorly specified environmental impacts of their supply chains (Lewis 2016). With regulations that demand companies to report on their sustainability efforts, accompanied by a true willingness among consumers, companies, public authorities, civil society, and others that use the products and services, practices will obviously improve.

Challenges in Supply Chain Transparency

In general, firms have more control over their marketing channels, where their goods and services meet the end users, than in their supply chains. It is more difficult to control upstream external suppliers and their practices, especially if they are located far away and adhere to different regulations and laws. Moreover, suppliers in foreign countries may have subsuppliers with poor sustainability performance. The increasing demand by several stakeholders for increased transparency on supply chain sustainability is fundamentally a positive thing – but may not be an unequivocal advantage. As the value chain becomes more globalized over time, with some disruptions such as the COVID-19 pandemic and wars, there is a higher likeliness that retailers will outsource the manufacturing of their products to foreign suppliers rather than sourcing domestically.

Social Sustainability Issues in Automotive Value Chains

Social sustainability in automotive value chains has gained increasing attention due to concerns regarding human rights violations and labor exploitation. This vignette delves into two reports published by HRW in 2021 and 2024, highlighting critical issues within the aluminum and automotive industries.

In 2021, HRW addressed the human rights abuses and environmental damage associated with aluminum production, a vital component of automotive manufacturing. Unsustainable practices include instances of forced labor in the bauxite mines of Guinea, a significant aluminum ore-producing region. Workers, including children, endure hazardous conditions and exploitation. In addition, environmental degradation is the unavoidable consequence of aluminum production processes that contribute to deforestation, water pollution, and high greenhouse gas emissions. Despite awareness of these issues and their impact on local communities, car manufacturers have failed to address human rights and environmental concerns within their aluminum supply chains, demonstrating a lack of corporate accountability.

In 2024, HRW revealed extensive use of forced labor in China's automotive supply chains. Car parts manufactured in Xinjiang involve the exploitation of Uyghur Muslim minorities subjected to forced labor in factories and detention camps. There is a lack of supply chain transparency: Despite growing evidence of forced labor in Xinjiang, car companies have failed to ensure transparency and accountability in their supply chains, neglecting to conduct adequate due diligence to prevent human rights abuses. Accordingly, the sustainability and ethical statements that car companies communicate fail to deliver on their promises; hence, numerous car companies could be accused of greenwashing.

China's role in car production is very strong. In 2023, 30.2 out of the world's 93.5 million vehicles were produced in China – more than the second-place United States (10.6), third-place Japan (9), fourth-place India (5.9), and fifth-place South Korea (4.2) combined. Chinese companies also produce and export large quantities of parts used in car manufacturing, ranging from electric vehicle batteries to alloy wheels. Many of the industry's largest brands, such as BYD, General Motors, Tesla, Toyota, and Volkswagen, utilize China for both production and development, while it remains an important market for sales.

One significant development in recent years is the emergence of brands like XPeng, NIO, BYD, and Zeekr with highly attractive car models. So far, they have not sold particularly well outside China. However, if the trend continues, they will pose a threat to car brands from all nations traditionally seen as leaders. The old notion that China excels in components but never catches up in complete vehicle production no longer holds (see Figure 9.2).

An important issue concerns sustainability matters such as human rights and responsible procurement policies – many car manufacturers claim to implement strict sustainability policies in their operations. Nearly a tenth of the world's aluminum, a crucial material for car manufacturing, is produced in the Xinjiang Uyghur Autonomous Region, where the Chinese government conducts oppression against Uighurs and Muslim communities. This includes arbitrary detentions of hundreds of thousands of people with elements of torture, mass surveillance, cultural and religious persecution, family separation, sexual violence, and violations, as well as subjecting Uighurs and others to forced labor in the Xinjiang region.

Several car manufacturers have succumbed to government pressure to apply lower standards for human rights and responsible procurement in Chinese joint ventures than in their global operations generally. Other manufacturers have been careless in identifying possible links to Xinjiang. Meanwhile, car manufacturers often remain unaware of the extent of exposure to forced labor in their operations.

Aluminum is used in many car parts, from engine blocks and chassis to wheels. Car manufacturers account for 18% of aluminum production in 2021,

Figure 9.2 In car factories, practices are not always as good as they may seem at first glance.
Source: Nataliya Hora/Adobe Stock.

(Continued)

(Continued)

according to the International Aluminum Institute (IAI), and aluminum is particularly crucial for electric vehicles, as lightweight materials significantly impact range. The automotive industry's demand for aluminum is also expected to double by 2050, and here, of course, China, which produces almost 60% of the global demand, will remain a leading player. Chinese producers emit 23% more carbon dioxide equivalents per unit volume than the global average, with coal being heavily used in production.

All of this is significant from both an ideological and commercial perspective. Increasingly sustainability-conscious consumers may become more informed and hesitant to buy vehicles with poor sustainability performance. This will also pressure manufacturers to improve.

Car companies have a responsibility for human rights under the UN Guiding Principles. This involves identifying, preventing, and mitigating the occurrence of forced labor and other human rights violations in the company's supply chains. The current extent of repression and surveillance in Xinjiang, including threats to workers and auditors tasked with examining the work, makes it impossible for companies to credibly investigate allegations of forced labor.

In July 2023, HRW wrote to BYD (China), General Motors (USA), Tesla (USA), Toyota (Japan), and Volkswagen (Germany) to obtain information on how they are working to map their aluminum supply chains and eliminate forced labor in Xinjiang. Volkswagen met with HRW to discuss the matter and responded to questions. General Motors and Tesla provided written responses to HRW. Toyota and BYD did not respond at all. HRW also reviewed the five companies' responsible procurement policies and public statements on efforts to eliminate links to forced labor. Three of the car companies contacted by HRW – General Motors, Toyota, and Volkswagen – operate in China through joint ventures, with stakes of up to 50%. This applies to cars sold under the companies' global brands. Volkswagen and other car manufacturers have stated that they have limited control over their joint ventures' operations and supply chains. Volkswagen told HRW that the company is not legally liable under German human rights legislation concerning Chinese joint ventures because the law only covers subsidiaries where companies have decisive influence. Volkswagen claims to have delegated operational control to its Chinese partner SAIC. Similarly, General Motors stated in its 2022 annual report that it has limited control over its joint ventures, especially when it has a minority interest. They admit that they cannot prevent violations of applicable laws within the framework of the joint venture cooperation with certainty. Tesla, which builds cars for both China's domestic market and export at its Gigafactory in Shanghai, provided the most detailed information to HRW about the company's aluminum procurement. The company stated that it has intensified the mapping of its aluminum supply chain, partly driven by global trade rules to combat forced labor. Tesla has mapped parts of its supply chain and has not found evidence of forced labor.

With China poised to become an even more dominant player in the global automotive industry, governments and the EU need to ensure that companies building cars in China or purchasing parts from Chinese suppliers identify and eliminate links to repression and other human rights violations. It is likely that attention to these issues will increase and pressure companies to improve practices – buyers will become more diligent about these types of issues.

By prioritizing human rights, ensuring supply chain transparency, and implementing robust due diligence, car manufacturers can mitigate the risks of labor exploitation and environmental harm, fostering a more socially responsible automotive industry. Failure to act not only leads to human suffering but also jeopardizes the long-term viability and reputation of automotive brands in a world where buyers are increasingly aware of sustainability.

Source: HRW (2021, 2024).

Child Labor in Supply Chains

Another instance of unsustainable marketing channel practices is child labor. From a normative perspective, it's easy to agree on the unsustainable characteristics of child labor; hence, it should be banned. However, as with transparency, regulation has its limits. Studies certainly provide support for banning child labor, e.g. Dessy and Knowles (2007).

In 2019, the United Nations General Assembly unanimously adopted a resolution declaring 2021 the International Year for the Elimination of Child Labor. Member states should take immediate and effective measures to end child labor in all its forms by 2025, as stipulated by Target 8.7 of the Sustainable Development Goals. The International Labor Organization is responsible for leading the charge. However, although such a goal is easy to agree on, it's removed from the daily social, political, and economic dynamics of poor countries where child labor is common, in some cases even resulting in a downward spiral. Through the UN decision, countries and agencies commit to development goals that are impossible to meet, and there is a lot of evidence from various research programs.

The main problem here is that setting unreachable targets at the global level may be counterproductive. Eliminating all forms of child labor sounds good but could be gravely detrimental to the well-being of children, while the project as a whole grossly ignores the rights and needs of millions of children around the world (Ratna 2021). A child labor ban may portray children as criminals instead of survivors in an inequitable society and force working children to become invisible, something that puts them at even higher risk of exploitation. Working children and their parents usually belong to marginalized communities. These families must do all they can to stay afloat, including taking on exploitative, underpaid, and incompatible work with school. A child labor ban may make this survival strategy more difficult and put these children's lives at risk.

Policies aimed at eradicating child labor will need to address the broad range of underlying factors that contribute to the incidence of child labor, such as poverty, market imperfections, and access to education. A study from India examines the consequences of India's landmark legislation against child labor, the Child Labor (Prohibition and Regulation) Act, showing that child wages decreased and child labor increased after the ban (Bharadwaj et al. 2020). These results are consistent with a theoretical model building on the seminal work of Basu and Van (1999) and Basu and Zarghamee (2005), where families use child labor to reach subsistence constraints and where child wages decrease in response to bans, leading poor families to utilize even more child labor.

Bans may also contribute to increasing social divides. According to a recent study, banning child labor is likely to increase schooling if the adult wage exceeds the sum of schooling cost and subsistence consumption expenditure. Once the economy reaches the advanced stage, banning child labor is desirable to take the stable equilibrium to full schooling equilibrium, but before that stage is being reached, some research points to that banning child labor has primarily negative effects in some cases (Chakraborty et al. 2024).

Challenges in Achieving Sustainability in Marketing Channels

To reach sustainability in marketing channels, several criteria not present in every company must be fulfilled. First, without sustainability being a top priority for management, an organization is unlikely to succeed in establishing sustainable marketing channels. A genuine interest lays the foundation for success. Second, it's imperative that all parties involved in marketing channels are treated fairly and ethically. Therefore, collaborating with companies that exploit suppliers, partners, or gig workers should be avoided at all costs. Here, companies must be careful selecting suppliers and partners. It requires a delicate balance, but prioritizing sustainability concerns is paramount. Whether it's collaborating on co-branded events with local businesses or selecting financial institutions, sustainability should be a guiding principle in every partnership decision (see Garcia et al. 2016). Third, considering the impact of transportation on CO_2 emissions, it's essential to explore nudging strategies, such as offering buyers the option of slower, more environmentally friendly delivery methods. Fourth, the entire business model should be revised to minimize the environmental footprint. For instance, in traditional brick-and-mortar stores, significant resources can be conserved by implementing measures such as optimizing climatization, reducing plastic and cardboard usage, implementing efficient lighting, and adopting energy-saving equipment. Stores should operate heating and cooling systems only during opening hours to conserve energy. Lastly, addressing the environmental impact of shipping entails developing sustainable physical distribution channels. Many online retailers, in their pursuit of customer satisfaction, overuse packaging materials and prioritize fast delivery. Emulating the practices of Vietnamese and Thai supermarkets, who utilize banana leaves instead of plastic for packaging, not only pleases customers but also benefits the environment. Why encase bananas in unnecessary plastic?

REKO Products – Direct Sustainable Marketing Channels

The REKO (meaning "fair consumption") sustainable marketing channel business model offers consumers a way of ordering products directly from the producer, without the need for middlemen. REKO rings, operating primarily on Facebook as closed groups, facilitate orders and deliveries without monetary compensation for administrators. Consumers in urban areas can connect with local food producers, sometimes even visiting production sites like farms.

For producers, REKO presents an avenue for increased revenue through direct consumer sales, adhering to principles of nonresale, proximity of production to consumers, and ethical, preferably organic, practices. In Finland, there are roughly 180 REKO rings, with approximately 20 in the Helsinki area, contributing to food tourism and local food integration. Challenges include profitability, logistics in a sprawling urban landscape, and integrating REKO into tourism efforts. The operation relies on digital platforms like Facebook, fostering grassroots connections without formal administration. While REKO promotes quality over quantity in a market dominated by large retailers, challenges include sporadic ring continuity and decentralized logistics affecting sustainability goals. Despite its benefits, reliance on private car transportation for product delivery remains a concern.

(Continued)

(Continued)

Future sustainable marketing channels must align with eco-rationality across all dimensions of sustainable development, including moral, environmental, technological, legal, economic, social, and political aspects. This echoes the ethos of the REKO system. Originating in Finland, the REKO system has gained traction in other Scandinavian countries, the Netherlands, and Italy. Its core values warrant consideration for adoption in numerous other nations, albeit potentially encountering hurdles in doing so. Finland stands out for its high educational standards, extensive social digitalization, and commitment to legality. Implementing the REKO system necessitates widespread Internet access and proficiency in social networking, alongside producer integrity in fostering appealing local businesses, and consumer environmental consciousness and local pride.

Source: Mulu (2018); REKO (2021); Szymoniuk and Valtari (2018).

Attempts to Make Marketing Channels Sustainable: Greenwashing or Real Change?

Many companies have implemented measures to mitigate criticism against nonsustainable practices. IKEA has introduced a furniture rental service in select markets, aiming to serve multiple purposes. First, it offers consumers the opportunity to refresh their interior decor without the need for significant up-front investments in new furniture. Second, it promotes sustainability by discouraging the disposal of furniture due to style changes or evolving needs. However, the true impact of these initiatives remains uncertain. While they may enhance IKEA's eco-friendly image and alleviate consumer guilt, their long-term environmental effects are yet to be determined. An intriguing question arises regarding consumer acceptance of renting pre-owned furniture with visible wear and tear.

Similarly, other companies have launched recycling programs, fostering the impression of progress toward a circular economy. Yet, these efforts may ultimately yield a negative net effect, as they primarily cater to maintaining existing consumption patterns rather than fostering genuine environmental improvement.

The extent to which market offerings contribute meaningfully to our world varies across industries. In sectors like aviation, inherent challenges exist, as air travel poses significant environmental concerns. While it may offer short-term conveniences, its global and long-term impact on the planet raises questions about the true meaningful difference it makes and whether such issues can be mitigated solely through increased financial resources.

Online Channels Might be More or Less Sustainable

Purchasing goods online has the potential to be more environmentally friendly than traditional in-store shopping due to the consolidation of deliveries, where a single truck or van can replace numerous individual car trips to stores. However, this advantage hinges on the mode of transportation used for delivery. An inherent issue with online shopping is that vehicles are often not fully utilized, leading to inefficiencies in terms of greenhouse gas emissions.

Research indicates that if delivery vehicles were fully loaded, online shopping could be up to 87% more efficient in terms of CO_2 emissions and vehicle-miles traveled compared to in-store shopping (Miguel Jaller, US Davies). However, this potential efficiency is counterbalanced by consumers' demand for fast delivery. Same-day or next-day delivery options, such as Amazon Prime, alter the efficiency equation, often resulting in vehicles being underutilized, with occupancy dropping from 80% to as low as 10% or 20%, negating the emissions benefits of online shopping.

The desire for rapid delivery may not solely originate from consumers but also from the convenience-focused options provided by many e-commerce companies. This leads to vehicles being dispatched before they are optimally filled, contributing to unnecessary emissions. One strategy that can be used is nudging, i.e. guiding consumers toward more environmentally friendly transportation options. Studies indicate a willingness among consumers to make more informed decisions if provided with clearer information and nudged toward sustainable choices (Axelsson and Gärdin 2018).

Moreover, it's not merely a binary choice between e-commerce and physical stores. Optimizing which purchases are made online and which are conducted in physical stores can offer a subtler yet effective approach. Many consumers prioritize knowing when an item will arrive over the immediacy of same-day delivery, indicating a potential disconnect between consumer preferences and industry assumptions (cf. van Loon 2015).

A study on the environmental impact of shopping online versus brick-and-mortar found that mall shopping can be up to 60% more environmentally sustainable than online shopping. The study, conducted by Deloitte on behalf of Simon Property Group (Simon 2016), found that several factors, including increased returns and additional packaging, contributed to e-commerce's negative environmental impact. The lower emissions associated with brick-and-mortar shopping locations were driven by shoppers making more purchases per trip and combining their mall visits with other activities as part of their trip chain (Simon 2019).

Reusing Clothes May be a Viable Business Opportunity

There is obviously a market opportunity for reusing clothes (see Chapter 8). Fashion varies by country, culture, and context, and consumers have different preferences.

It has been estimated that about 30 kg of clothes and textile per capita and year are thrown away in the United States (Claudio 2007) as well as in the United Kingdom (Allwood et al. 2006). Many pieces of clothes are thrown away because people are tired of them or just want something new. Meanwhile, fashion companies also throw away clothes – because they have not been sold in season and have thus become more cumbersome to stock and costly to sell than to be thrown out.

What really happens to old clothes dropped in in-store recycling bins is also an important question. They somehow compete with charities for unwanted clothes – it is more sustainable to reuse clothes as such, rather than recycling them or using them as burning fuel (Guyader et al. 2019). Numerous fashion companies have launched take-back programs with messages about recycling unwanted textiles, thereby claiming to make fashion sustainable. Customers are urged to donate any clothes or home textiles that are no longer wanted or needed so they can be given a new purpose. Frequently, however, this material is not transformed into a new piece of clothing but rather resold for industrial usage thousands of kilometers away from the point of sale or point of collect. Recycling clothes into new clothes is costly and difficult.

Author and environmentalist Elizabeth Cline says that less than 1% of clothing is recycled to make new clothing. Many of the apparel sold in stores is made of blended fibers, which means they do not break down easily. Recycling cotton and wool diminishes the quality of the material, she says. H&M's own sustainability reports acknowledge this challenge. Of all the material used to make its estimated half a billion garments a year, only 0.7% is recycled material (Matteis and Agro 2018).

Best Practices in Sustainable Marketing Channels

In developing sustainable marketing channel practices, there is a great deal of inspiration to collect from good examples, such as TOMS shoes. Since 2006, TOMS has been ensuring that for every pair of shoes sold, a person in need receives a pair as well, creating a sustainable and impactful model. This not only aids those without shoes but also offers benefits such as low manufacturing costs and marketing advantages for the company. Employees and stakeholders also benefit from being associated with a socially responsible organization. With more than 100 million pairs donated by 2020, TOMS has made a significant impact (see Figure 9.3). While TOMS moved away from their original business model in 2021, they are still committed to "doing good" by donating a third of their profits to grassroots organizations (TOMS 2024).

Roma Boots, established in 2010 by a Romanian refugee in Dallas, follows a similar model. For every pair of rain boots sold, the company donates a pair to those in need in Romania and 26 other countries. Additionally, 10% of profits support

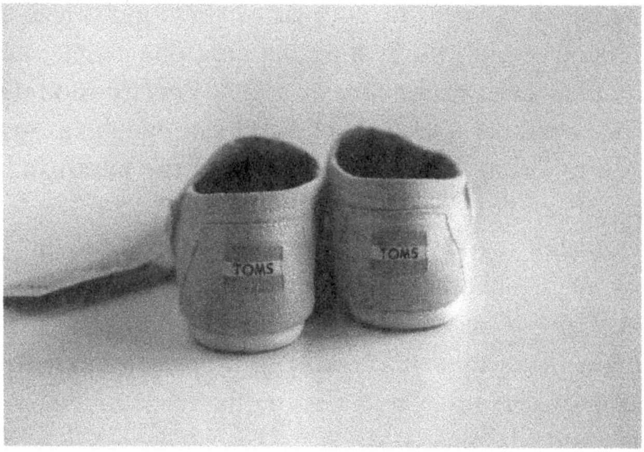

Figure 9.3 TOMS shoes – is that a sustainable marketing practice?
Source: theartofpics/Adobe Stock.

educational resources. Roozt, an online marketplace founded in 2009, hosts various "buy one, give one" products, primarily accessories and jewelry. This model allows customers to express their style while sharing the story of giving back. Roozt was acquired by NOVICA in 2014, aiming to empower artisans worldwide by offering fair prices and unique handmade products.

Critics argue that TOMS' model fails to address root causes of poverty and may harm local businesses. To address this, TOMS has launched initiatives like a local factory in Haiti. Similarly, Mealshare in Canada tackles hunger by partnering with restaurants, where a portion of each meal sold goes toward feeding someone in need. This not only helps combat hunger but also enhances the restaurants' image and attracts socially conscious customers.

Warby Parker and SoapBox are examples of companies integrating social impact into their business models. Warby Parker donates glasses to those in need for every pair sold, while SoapBox donates soap products and partners with Sundara to recycle hotel soap. Despite their positive impacts, sustainable marketing practices often face challenges in balancing economic, social, and environmental sustainability dimension

Social Sustainability in Marketing Channels

A crucial part of sustainability is how people are treated. Labor market polarization, as defined by Acemoglu and Autor (2011), describes the trend of increased employment in both high-skill and low-skill occupations, relative to medium-skilled occupations.

This polarization often leads to a scenario where individuals in strong labor market positions benefit, while those in weaker positions are relegated to low-wage jobs. Particularly, urban areas experience heightened polarization due to the rising demand for service-oriented roles. This phenomenon highlights social sustainability challenges, as it results in compromises regarding the health and safety of individuals across the labor value chain.

The impact of labor market polarization on marketing channels is significant, as it poses a risk of involving poorly treated individuals in business operations and marketing strategies. One consequence is the exacerbation of inequality, with consumers of higher education levels benefiting from increased disparity while low-wage service providers struggle to sustain themselves in high-cost urban environments (Lindley and Machin 2014).

This polarization trend is prevalent across many Western countries and poses a critical question for marketers: how do consumer attitudes toward sustainability influence marketing strategies? If consumers are willing to pay a premium for sustainable products, marketing channels can be tailored accordingly. However, if consumers are not inclined toward sustainability, balancing the various dimensions of sustainability becomes challenging.

Research by Nielsen (2019) indicates that most global consumers (73%) are willing to change their consumption habits to reduce environmental impact. Furthermore, 81% believe that companies should actively contribute to environmental improvement (Nielsen 2018). These findings underscore the growing consumer demand for sustainable practices across demographics and geographic regions.

Ultimately, achieving lasting sustainability requires collaborative efforts from consumers, companies, policymakers, regulators, and other stakeholders. Only through collective action can meaningfully progress toward sustainability be attained.

References

Allwood, J. M., Laursen, S. E., de Rodriguez, C. M., & Bocken, N. M. (2015). Well dressed?: The present and future sustainability of clothing and textiles in the United Kingdom. *Journal of the Home Economics Institute of Australia*, 22(1), 42.

Acemoglu, D., & Autor, D. (2011). Skills, tasks and technologies: Implications for employment and earnings. In *Handbook of Labor Economics* (Vol. 4, pp. 1043–1171). Amsterdam: Elsevier.

Axelsson, M. & Gärdin, H. (2018). Nudging in e-Commerce: A useful tool to promote more environmentally friendly transportation? Master thesis. Linköping University.

Baldassarre, F., & Campo, R. (2016). Sustainability as a marketing tool: to be or to appear to be? *Business Horizons*, 59(4), 421–429.

Basu, K. and Van, P.H. 1999. The economics of child labor: reply. *American Economic Review*, 89(5), 1386–1388.

Basu, K. and Zarghamee, H., 2005. Is product boycott a good idea for controlling child labor? *Unpublished paper* (Cornell University, Ithaca NY).

Bharadwaj, P., Lakdawala, L.K. & Li, N. (2020). Perverse consequences of well-intentioned regulation: evidence from India's child labor ban, *Journal of the European Economic Association*, 8(3), 1158–1195.

Chakraborty, P., Singh, R., & Soundararajan, V. (2024). Import competition, formalization, and the role of contract labor. *The World Bank Economic Review*, lhae007.

Chen, Q., & Duan, Y. (2023). Impact of information disclosure on global supply chain greenwashing: is more information transparency always better? *Transportation Research Part E: Logistics and Transportation Review*, 178, pp. 103288.

Claudio, L. (2007). Waste couture: Environmental impact of the clothing industry, *Environmental Health Perspectives*, 115(9), A449-A454.

Connybear, C. (2022). The dark side of fast furniture. *The Merionite*. https://themerionite.org/3645/opinions/the-dark-side-of-fast-furniture (accessed 15 March 2024).

Dessy, S. & Knowles, J. (2007). Why is child labor illegal? IZA Discussion Paper No. 2901, PIER Working Paper No. 01-043. https://ssrn.com/abstract=290085 or http://dx.doi.org/10.2139/ssrn.290085 (accessed 19 July 2024).

Earthsight. (2024). Press release: European retail giants linked to dirty Brazilian cotton, April 11th, https://www.earthsight.org.uk/news/fashioncrimes-pressrelease (accessed 20 July 2024).

European Parliament. (2024). MEPs adopt new law banning greenwashing and misleading product information. https://www.europarl.europa.eu/news/en/press-room/20240112IPR16772/meps-adopt-new-law-banning-greenwashing-and-misleading-product- (accessed 2 February 2024).

Food and Agriculture Organization (FAO) of the United Nations. (2020). *The State of the World's Forests 2020. Forests, Biodiversity and People*. https://www.unep.org/resources/state-worlds-forests-forests-biodiversity-and-people (accessed 19 July 2024).

Garcia, S., Cintra, Y., Rita de Cássia, S. R., & Lima, F. G. (2016). Corporate sustainability management: a proposed multi-criteria model to support balanced decision-making. *Journal of Cleaner Production*, 136, 181–196.

Guyader, H. (2019). *The Heart & Wallet Paradox of Collaborative Consumption*. Linköping University.

Hoskins, T. (2017), H&M, Zara and Marks & Spencer linked to polluting viscose factories in Asia. *The Guardian*, Guardian sustainable business, June 13th, https://www.theguardian.com/sustainable-business/2017/jun/13/hm-zara-marks-spencer-linked-polluting-viscose-factories-asia-fashion (accessed 20 July 2024)

HRW. (2021). Aluminum: the car industry's blind spot. Why car companies should address the human rights impact of aluminum production. *Human Rights Watch & Inclusive Development*. https://www.hrw.org/sites/default/files/media_2021/10/global_bauxite0721_web.pdf (accessed 15 May 2024).

HRW. (2024). Asleep at the wheel. car companies' complicity in forced labor in China. *Human Rights Watch*. https://www.hrw.org/sites/default/files/media_2024/01/china0224web_1.pdf (accessed 15 May 2024).

Kamin, D. (2022). Fast Furniture is cheap and Americans are throwing it in the trash. *International New York Times*, Oct, 31st. https://www.nytimes.com/2022/10/31/realestate/fast-furniture-clogged-landfills.html (accessed February 2, 2024).

Kent, S. (2024), Sustainability: Are H&M and Zara Harming Forests in Brazil? *Business of Fashion*, April 11th. https://www.businessoffashion.com/articles/sustainability/zara-h-and-m-brazil-cerrado-better-cotton-deforestation-human-rights-earthsight-investigation (Retrieved March 3, 2024).

Lewis, J.K. (2016). Corporate social responsibility/sustainability reporting among the fortune global 250: greenwashing or green supply chain? In: Bilgin, M., Danis, H. (eds) *Entrepreneurship, Business and Economics – 1. Eurasian Studies in Business and Economics*. Springer, Cham, pp. 347–362.

Lindley, J. & Machin, S. (2014). Spatial changes in labour market inequality. *Journal of Urban Economics*, 79 (January), 121–138.

Matteis, S., & Agro, C. (2018). *What really happens to old clothes dropped in those in-store recycling bins*. Canadian Broadcasting Company.

Melović, B., Cirović, D., Backovic-Vulić, T., Dudić, B., & Gubiniova, K. (2020). Attracting green consumers as a basis for creating sustainable marketing strategy on the organic market—relevance for sustainable agriculture business development. *Foods*, 9(11), 1552.

Mulu. (2018). Rural-urban governance agreements and planning instruments. REKO (Rejäl Konsumtion – Fair consumption) ring. https://rural-urban.eu/sites/default/files/G-HEL3%20REKO%20Fair%20Consumption%20Network.pdf (accessed 3 January 2024).

Nielsen. (2018). Global consumers seek companies that care about environmental issues. https://nielseniq.com/global/en/insights/analysis/2018/global-consumers-seek-companies-that-care-about-environmental-issues (accessed 5 June 2024).

Nielsen. (2019). A 'natural' rise in sustainability around the world. https://nielseniq.com/global/en/insights/analysis/2019/a-natural-rise-in-sustainability-around-the-world (accessed 5 June 2024).

Our world in data. (2024). Cars, planes, trains: where do CO_2 emissions from transport come from? https://ourworldindata.org/co2-emissions-from-transport (accessed 15 May 2024).

Perry, F. (2022). Like fast fashion, fast furniture is a problem for our planet. CNN. https://www.cnn.com/style/article/fast-furniture-problem-for-our-planet/index.html (accessed 8 March 2024).

Ratna, K. (2021). Banning child labour jeopardises working children's right to survive. Open Democracy. https://www.opendemocracy.net/en/beyond-trafficking-and-slavery/banning-child-labour-jeopardises-working-childrens-right-to-survive/ (accessed 18 October 2021)

REKO. (2021). REKO. Rejäl konsumtion sedan 2013. https://www.pedersore.fi/assets/Dokumentarkiv/Om-Pedersoere/REKO/Reko_svenska.pdf (accessed 19 July 2024).

Roth, K., & Morrison, A. J. (1990). An empirical analysis of the integration-responsiveness framework in global industries. *Journal of International Business Studies*, 21, 541–564.

Simon. (2016). Does shopping behavior impact sustainability? Sustainability White Paper. https://simon-malls.cld.bz/Simon-2016-Sustainability-White-Paper/2 (accessed 15 March 2024).

Simon. (2019). *New Study Reveals In-Store Shopping is up to 60 Percent More Favorable for the Environment than Online Shopping*, Dec. 19th, https://investors.simon.com/news-releases/news-release-details/new-study-reveals-store-shopping-60-percent-more-favorable (accessed 20 July 2024)

Szymoniuk, B., & Valtari, H. (2018). The REKO system in Finland: a new model of sustainable marketing channel. *Problems of Sustainable Development*, 13(2), 103–111.

TOMS (2024). TOMS Our Story. https://www.toms.com/us/about-toms.html (accessed 21 July 2024).

Transport & Environment (2023a). https://www.transportenvironment.org/articles/fossil-gas-the-greenwashing-pill-shipping-wants-you-to-swallow (accessed 9 March 2024).

Transport & Environment (2023b). Leasing giants called out for weak climate leadership and low ambition on electric cars in the EU – new investigation. https://www.transportenvironment.org/articles/leasing-giants-called-out-for-greenwashing-and-low-ambition-on-electric-cars-in-new-investigation (accessed 9 March 2024).

Van Loon, P., Deketele, L., Dewaele, J., McKinnon, A., & Rutherford, C. (2015). A comparative analysis of carbon emissions from online retailing of fast moving consumer goods. *Journal of Cleaner Production*, 106, 478–486.

Vurro, C., Russo, A., & Perrini, F. (2009). Shaping sustainable value chains: Network determinants of supply chain governance models. *Journal of Business Ethics*, 90, 607–621.

Chapter 10

Prices of Sustainable Products and Pricing Strategies

Sustainable business practices often lead to higher costs that may be passed on to consumers or assumed by companies. In this chapter, we discuss prices of sustainable products and pricing strategies. Many studies show that sustainable products often come with a green premium that some consumers are willing to pay extra for. However, because of the attitude-behavior gap (previously discussed in Chapter 3), consumers' stated willingness to pay does not always materialize in all purchase decisions. Companies may need to re-think their pricing strategies to balance the difficulty of being competitive in the marketplace, selling more sustainable products, and reaching profitability.

Learning Objectives

- Understand willingness to pay and explain its influential factors
- Define green premium
- Understand different sustainable pricing strategies
- Describe smart pricing with examples
- Comprehend the interplay between pricing and sustainability, and between value and pricing

Introduction

Sustainable prices include the social and environmental costs of production and sale: waste, carbon footprint, ethical welfare etc. These factors might increase the price. Fair and responsible labor and sustainable sourcing of materials improve the social and ecological impact but might increase the final price of products. The transition toward a sustainable economy is a huge challenge, and consumers will have to pay higher prices for sustainable products (DiPerna 2023). Fashion, beauty, and health are the most affected sectors, since obtaining raw materials can increase the cost by up to 200%. Moreover, obtaining sustainable product certificates and limited production volume both increase the retail price for the consumer. Promoting sustainability also incurs costs attributed to branding and marketing.

This is a good example of a trade-off between sustainability dimensions. Environmental sustainability conflicts with economic sustainability. Sustainable products may be up to double the price of less responsible versions. This directly conflicts with the users' wish to be more sustainable and their preference to consume this type of product since the price is a key factor in its achievement.

Sustainable pricing is a multidimensional approach, linking economic objectives with environmental considerations. It's about realizing that pricing isn't a dry, mathematical routine but rather a powerful lever for driving sustainable change – and a shared responsibility among stakeholders.

Three Cs of Pricing

In all firms, pricing strategies are essential components that are linked to, and influence, positioning, branding, consumer behavior, etc. As opposed to other marketing mix components and sustainability, pricing is the only measure that directly contributes to the firm's revenues. To promote sustainability, the overall profitability of the company is of key concern. Hence, an important starting point here is to introduce the established framework of the three Cs of pricing – cost, competition, and customer (see Figure 10.1). It provides a fundamental approach for setting prices (Kotler et al. 2024).

One might think that cost is the price ceiling whereas the customer's value perception is the price roof, but that might not always be the case. A firm may produce a product or service more expensively than its competitors, and the customer may have a lower price perception than for competitors' prices for one or another reason – or even lower than the production costs.

The increasing emphasis on sustainability requires a reevaluation of these elements through an environmental and social lens. Integrating sustainability into the three Cs of pricing ensures that businesses not only remain economically viable – but also contribute positively to the environment and society in various ways.

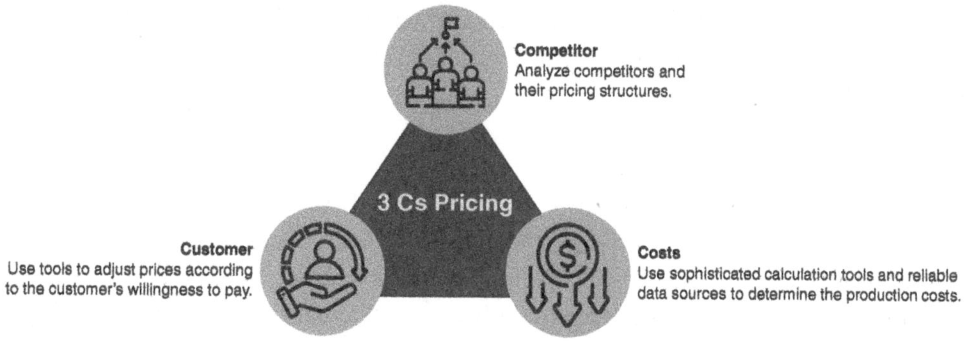

Figure 10.1 Three Cs of pricing.
Source: Adapted from Kotler et al. (2024).

Integrating sustainability into the three Cs of pricing – cost, competition, and customer – requires a holistic approach that considers environmental and social impacts alongside economic factors. By adopting sustainable cost management practices, benchmarking and innovating within competitive markets, and aligning pricing strategies with consumer values, businesses can achieve long-term success while contributing to a more sustainable future. This comprehensive approach not only meets the growing demand for responsible business practices but also ensures resilience and profitability in an evolving market landscape (Liozu and Cros 2023).

Cost

Traditionally, cost-based pricing involves determining the cost of production and, at least in the case of profit-making entities, adding a markup to ensure profitability. From a sustainability perspective, this approach could also include the full life-cycle costs of a product, including environmental and social externalities. This includes the cost of raw materials, energy consumption, emissions, waste management, and labor practices, etc. (Liozu and Cros 2023; Kotler et al. 2024).

The following are examples of methods that include sustainability in the cost calculation:

Life-cycle assessment (LCA): As briefly introduced in Chapter 3, implementing LCA allows businesses to evaluate the environmental impacts associated with all stages of a product's life, from raw material extraction through use to disposal. LCA promotes transparency and ensures that prices reflect the true cost of a product.

Internalizing externalities: Incorporating the costs of environmental degradation and social impacts into pricing strategies contributes to internalizing externalities. For instance, companies can include the cost of carbon emissions or fair wages in their pricing models. This approach encourages sustainable production practices and reduces negative impacts on the environment and society.

Competition

Competition-based pricing involves setting prices based on competitors' pricing strategies. From a sustainability perspective, this should involve considering how competitors address sustainability challenges and leveraging these insights to create a competitive edge. A true competitive advantage in a market where sustainability is important includes sustainability performance in the analysis (Liozu and Cros 2023; Kotler et al. 2024).

The following are examples of methods that include sustainability in the analysis of competitors' prices:

Collaborative competition: Companies can engage in collaborative efforts with competitors to enhance industry-wide sustainability standards. For example, participating in industry coalitions to set common sustainability goals can lead to collective benefits and drive positive change in an industry.

Benchmarking sustainability: Analyzing competitors' sustainability efforts helps identify industry standards and best practices. By adopting and exceeding these practices, companies can differentiate themselves and appeal to environmentally and socially conscious consumers – and charge a higher price to cover the costs, which might be higher.

Innovating: Investing in sustainable innovation can provide a competitive advantage. Companies that lead in sustainable products or processes can position themselves as market leaders, justifying premium pricing based on superior sustainability performance.

Customer

Customer-based pricing focuses on the perceived value of a product to the consumer. In the context of sustainability, this involves understanding consumers' growing preference for environmentally and socially responsible products and aligning pricing strategies accordingly (Liozu and Cros 2023; Kotler et al. 2024).

The following are examples of methods that include sustainability in the judgment of customers' perceived value:

Value-based pricing: Developing pricing models that reflect the added value of sustainability features can attract conscious consumers. For example, products with lower carbon footprints, organic ingredients, or ethical sourcing can be priced to reflect their positive impact, appealing to consumers who prioritize these factors.

Segmenting consumers: Identifying and targeting segments of the market that prioritize sustainability can help identify consumers who are willing to pay a premium for products that align with their values, allowing businesses to set higher prices based on sustainability attributes.

Consumer awareness and education: Educating consumers about the sustainability attributes of products can enhance perceived value. Transparent communication about sustainable practices, certifications, and the benefits of eco-friendly products and brands can justify higher prices, as seen in Chapters 6 and 7 (Liozu and Cros 2023; Kotler et al. 2024).

Pricing and Sustainability Interplay

In the traditional sense, pricing has been a matter of profit margins and bottom lines, while sustainability has been linked with ecological conservation and responsible resource use. Sustainable pricing challenges this old-school division.

Pricing and sustainability, hence, interplay. Where it all ends up has to do with the tricky balance between shareholder value (i.e. the traditional capitalist perspective of businesses primarily seeking profit) and stakeholder value (i.e. a contemporary understanding of sustainable commerce, which isn't merely about acknowledging the intersection of pricing and sustainability). It's about fully embracing their interplay.

What is the True Cost of Sustainable Pricing?

Traditional pricing models, while straightforward and seemingly fair, often turn a blind eye to the underlying societal and environmental costs of our consumption. These costs are hidden, wrapped in the shadows of production and distribution processes, and range from the energy consumed during manufacture to the carbon emissions released in transport and delivery. It's a price paid in the quality of our environment and the health of our planet but not reflected in the final price tag consumers pay for the product. Sustainable pricing brings these hidden costs into the spotlight. The goal is to not only include these costs in the final price but to give a clear, comprehensive representation of a product's environmental footprint, an approach that might entail a total makeover of our existing pricing structures.

The path to reflecting the true cost in our pricing involves examining a product's life-cycle, looking at each stage of production with an environmental lens. It's about developing the willingness to quantify these often-overlooked environmental impacts and challenge existing industry standards.

Reshaping Price Perceptions

Price perceptions must be reshaped when we put the sustainability lens on. This involves overhauling business practices and educating consumers. At the end, it's a thorough, comprehensive understanding of the value related to the environmental and social costs over the life-cycle of using the products. To make it happen, transparency and trust are crucial.

Sustainability Comes at a Price – Who's Paying?

Businesses and nonprofit organizations alike are increasingly recognizing their responsibility to limit their impact on the environment and society at large. Many organizations put a lot of effort into actively improving environmental, social, and economic sustainability.

A sustainable pricing strategy involves setting prices that cover a company's social and environmental costs for each sale. It aims to contribute to a sustainable economy and to reduce the impact on the planet and its people, thus meeting the United Nations, Sustainable Development Goals. Given its importance for the future and its weight for many users, it is vital for businesses to know how to integrate sustainable prices into their pricing strategy and to know the pros and cons of doing so.

Yet, while many organizations may be committed to providing better and more equitable access to sustainable products, managers are also ultimately responsible for the financial viability of their organizations. Hence, consumers and other buyers will have to pay for the higher costs that sustainable products incur, or there may be other, smarter solutions.

The obvious solution is that the higher costs are being passed on to consumers; hence, the higher sustainability performance is assumed to materialize in a price premium in the marketplace. However, buyers may decide to choose cheaper alternatives or not to purchase at all – even if they state in surveys and other marketing research instruments that they are willing to pay a significant price premium for sustainable products. One possibility is, of course, that the company selling the products absorbs the costs, but this may result in a hit on profits or may result in serious sacrifices in terms of quality delivered.

The Price of Sustainable Products

It has been long established that many consumers perceive sustainable products as expensive and have a low willingness to pay a higher price for them compared with the regular/traditional product alternative (Gleim et al. 2013; Ha-Brookshire and

Norum 2011; Litvine and Wüstenhagen 2011; Meise et al. 2014; Olson 2013). For example, a recent consumer survey showed that 40% of 1 021 Swedish consumers ranked price as the number one barrier for purchasing organic food (Krav 2011). We've already mentioned the attitude-behavior gap for sustainable products (in Chapter 3), which is mostly based on this high-price perception.

The thing is, studies show that "green consumers" making a purchase choice will give greater importance to information related to the sustainability attributes of the supply chain rather than price (Laroche et al. 2001; Meise et al. 2014) (See Figure 10.2) for an illustration. But when such information is unavailable or not provided, consumers base their choice solely on the price tags (Meise et al. 2014; Zeithaml 1988). So, it is important for marketers to inform consumers of their sustainability initiatives or fair-trade products or whatever the information is to increase their willingness to pay a price premium for sustainable products; e.g. the taste of green food is not enough (Barber et al. 2012; Didier and Lucie 2008; De Pelsmacker et al. 2005).

Why are sustainable products more expensive, though?

Green Premium

A survey shows that a great majority of consumers, 76%, choose organic product alternatives if the price, product attributes, and brand are the same as nonorganic foods (Swedish Consumer Agency 2021). Great! Well, the problem is that the price is never the same between organic and nonorganic products or between sustainable and traditional products. The good thing is that some consumers are

Figure 10.2 A man carefully reads information on a package of frozen beans while shopping in a grocery store. How much more will he be willing to pay if those beans are certified organic, non-GMO, or from this local region 20% more, or 200%?
Source: shutterstock 1045336438.

willing to pay more. This (niche) segment of consumers, those who are sustainable, are ready to pay a 10% price premium for "greener" products compared with their traditional counterparts (Brouwer et al. 2008; Cotte et al. 2009). However, the sustainable market share index (NYU 2023) indicates that the price premium for eco-friendly products is about 28% (in the United States), which is much higher than the 10% most consumers are willing to pay!

Consumers are also willing to pay a premium for "clean energy," but it depends on where they are: McKinsey reported that 37% of German customers and 46% of UK customers said they would pay *up to 10% extra* for clean energy; and 25% of German customers and 9% of UK customers would pay *more* than 10% (Bloomers et al. 2001). However, there are also consumers who are very price-sensitive and who cannot afford sustainable products (Gleim et al. 2013).

Kotler (2011) argues that sustainable manufacturers can integrate some of their negative externalities (e.g. pollution, social welfare) into their pricing because "environmentally involved customers may be willing to pay more" (p. 133). For instance, marketers of coffee labeled with third-party brand Fairtrade take social externalities into account and pay farmers a higher wage, which makes the final price of coffee higher. Thus, consumers must pay a *green premium* to cover such costs (Killian et al 2006; Simms 1992). The *green premium* is the price difference between purchasing a so-called green product versus an alternative, nongreen product (Chen et al. 2024). The term was coined by Joly (1990) in a research paper on the "greening" imperative for businesses. However, previous research in retailing shows that marketers can use premium pricing on some products as they have added value due to their environmentally friendly characteristics, i.e. being sustainable and not just because of added manufacturing costs (Simms 1992). For instance, the green premium paid by consumers of sustainable coffee results from the sustainable production of coffee beans, which brings additional costs to the farmers (Killian et al. 2006); e.g. due to organic production that yields 22% less than conventional production (Lyngbæk et al. 2001), costly fair-trade certifications (Valkila and Nygren 2010), and organic certifications (Lohr 1998). Thus, the green premium is necessary for the final consumer who wants to consume responsibly (Li et al. 2022). Without this green premium to compensate sustainable farmers for reducing socio-environmental externalities, organic or fair-trade coffee would not even be produced (Killian et al. 2006; Archer et al. 2007; Valkila and Nygren 2010). It's important to note that price premium such as the green premium is not the same as premium pricing. While price premium is set based on the increased manufacturing costs (Cao and Xu 2023), *premium pricing* is when marketers set a high price relative to the competition and a high price relative to customer value (Hinterhuber and Liozu 2018).

In 2015, some of the authors of this textbook collected data for a marketing experiment. We asked consumers to choose an option among several alternatives for four products (Guyader et al. 2017). When purchasing coffee beans, 33% chose to pay 8% more for organic coffee, 21% chose to pay 20% more for organic coffee, and 11% chose to pay 50% more for fair-trade coffee. For laundry softener, 42% chose to pay a 32% premium for an eco-friendly version. For a can of tomatoes, 53% chose to pay 4% more for organic tomatoes, 12% chose to pay 28% more for fair-trade tomatoes, and 5% chose to pay 46% more for organic tomatoes. For a can of beans, 50% chose to pay a 26% premium for organic beans, and 14% chose to pay a 51% premium for fair-trade beans. We then asked 130 other consumers to answer the following questions: how much you are willing to pay extra for (i) ecological coffee (ii) and fair-trade coffee? On average, they responded (i) 16.73% more and (ii) 17.87% more. This is still less than the 28% price premium for eco-friendly products (NYU 2023).

Interestingly, Murphy and Jenner-Leuthart (2011) find that consumers' taste expectations of coffee are hindered by the fair-trade certification. They expect fair-trade coffee to taste worse than regular coffee. Similarly, various studies show that consumers must be informed to be willing to pay a green premium for organic or fair-trade products; a flavorful taste is not enough (Barber et al. 2012; Delate et al 2003; De Pelsmacker et al. 2005; Didier and Lucie 2008). For instance, providing information about fair-trade practices increases the green premium shoppers are willing to pay (Murphy and Jenner-Leuthart 2011). Gifford and Bernard (2011) find that 46.4% of their sample of US consumers are willing to pay a higher green premium for natural and/or organic chicken *after* information has been provided.

Porter and van der Linde (1995) argued that not only the cost side but also the revenue side could be improved by being proactive in relation to increased environmental requirements, instead of being defensive or reactive. According to the authors, empirical research has shown that it is a necessity to put a premium price on "green" goods and services. It will thus be possible to charge more for a sustainable product than for a nonsustainable equivalent. Based on their studies, Porter and van der Linde thus argue that companies that adapt their operations to integrate sustainability concerns will be able to establish a direct competitive advantage on both the cost and revenue sides by enhancing their resource and energy efficiency. Moreover, these companies would also attract new consumers (i.e. the "green consumer") and be able to enter new markets.

Sustainable Products – No Longer for a Niche Market Segment

A recent Deloitte Insights report posits that sustainable products are no longer for a niche market segment. As the purchase of eco-friendly products becomes more common, consumer expectations for sustainability are advancing across a broader range of product categories. Besides, consumers are indicating their intention to support innovative brands that fulfill their sustainability commitments, showing a readiness to pay an average price premium of 27%.

When asked about their most recent sustainable purchase, approximately 40% of consumers reported paying more than for a comparable alternative. On average, those who paid extra estimated the premium at 27%. The willingness to pay a premium, however, varies by category. Consumers are more inclined to pay extra in lower-cost, frequently purchased categories like groceries, household goods, and personal care, where the trade-offs are better understood and the risk of trying is relatively low. However, the premiums in these categories are generally smaller. Conversely, fewer consumers reported paying a green premium for less frequent, higher-cost items such as home furnishings, appliances, and vehicles, but the premiums tend to be higher. Companies that offer higher-priced items face a challenge: while the market for consumers willing to pay premiums for expensive goods is smaller, those consumers are likely to pay more.

Source: Pleters et al. (2023).

Drivers of Willingness to Pay a "Green Premium"

This section is dedicated to the reasons why some sustainable consumers are willing to pay a green premium (i.e. the price premium for sustainable products or services). The consumers' willingness to pay (WTP) varies across product categories (Essoussi and Linton 2010; McDonald et al. 2009) and depends on the sustainable attributes that a product exhibits (Bask et al. 2013; Krystallis et al. 2006).

Retailers can influence green purchase decisions by informing consumers inside the store with point-of-purchase (PoP) information displays and other components in the physical store environment (e.g. using price tags; Yang et al. 2009) and signage in the actual servicescape (Chen et al. 2024). In addition, marketers can display and highlight green information on the product packaging (such as method and origin of production, quality cues, and third-party eco-certifications and labels) that increase consumers' knowledge (Chen et al. 2024; Li et al. 2022; Gleim et al. 2013). As mentioned in Chapter 2, knowledge about the environment plays a

Figure 10.3 Despite the higher up-front cost a significant number of consumers are willing to pay a premium for Tesla's electric vehicles due to their sustainability credentials. Tesla's Model 3, for instance, attracts consumers who value its environmental benefits, innovative technology, and commitment to reducing carbon emissions. This willingness to pay a premium is indicative of a broader shift in consumer behavior toward supporting sustainable and eco-friendly automotive options, even at a higher cost.
Source: Shutterstock 2183882519.

multifaceted role in influencing behavior (Laroche et al. 2001; White et al. 2019). Thus, providing information to consumers enables them to understand the green premium, which can increase the willingness to pay for these products.

A lack of knowledge or understanding hinders consumers from making green purchase decisions (Gleim et al. 2013; Grunert et al. 2014). Consumers seem to express a willingness to pay more for eco-friendly products (see Figure 10.3), but they still need to be convinced. The problem is that in the absence of green-related information, consumers evaluate products based on the price difference between competing products (Meise et al. 2014; Zeithaml 1988). Consequently, retailers can bridge consumers intentions and actions by providing information to help consumers to "walk the talk" from pro-environmental intentions to behavior (Chen et al. 2024; Gleim et al. 2013). In addition, the more information that is provided, the higher consumers' perceived expertise on eco-friendly products (Chen et al. 2024; Gleim et al. 2013).

Paying a Green Premium for Organic Food

From an in-store survey of US consumers, Loureiro et al. (2002) found a price premium of 5% for eco-labeled apples compared to regular apples; and they further suggest that organic apples may yield an even higher price premium than eco-labeled apples. Krystallis et al. (2006) measured a much higher premium in Greece where consumers are on average willing to pay a 31.5% premium for organic-labeled food (i.e. olive oil, raisins, bread, oranges, and wine). A more conservative but interesting result comes from a Spanish study: it was found that on average consumers are willing to pay a 10% premium for organic food, whereas regular consumers would pay a 15% premium (Ureña et al. 2008). It seems that sustainable consumers believe that the high prices of sustainable food are not justified, and thus, they are willing to pay a lower premium than more traditional consumers (c.f. Krystallis et al. 2006). The same goes for US consumers of sustainable apparel: "[. . .] the stronger attitudes the consumers have toward the environment, the less likely they were willing to pay a premium for organic and sustainable cotton shirts" (Ha-Brookshire and Norum 2011, p. 349).

The following are a few more examples on the green premium for diverse sustainable food:

- 24.2% for eco-labeled seafood (Johnston et al. 2001)
- 15% for organic products on average (Ureña et al. 2008)
- 30% for environmentally certified pork chops (Ubilava et al. 2010)
- 15% for organic and animal welfare-labeled salmon (Olesen et al. 2010)
- 35% for general organic-labeled chicken breasts, 104% for USDA organic-labeled chicken breasts (Van Loo et al. 2011)

Regarding organic chicken, Gifford and Bernard (2011) found that US consumers informed about what organic farming is are willing to pay a 14.8% premium (reduced to a 12.8% premium without information). Alphonce and Alfnes (2012) found that urban Tanzanians are willing to pay a premium for local and organic tomatoes, as a food safety insurance against pesticides. From a sample of US wine consumers, a study reveals a 15.9% premium for environmentally friendly wine (Barber et al. 2012). Eventually, Stanton et al. (2012) found that "locavores," consumers of locally grown produce, are on average willing to pay 23.5% more for organic food than regular consumers. However, it is interesting to note that the green premium significantly decreases when there are "cosmetic imperfections" in the product appearance (Yue et al. 2009; Zhang et al. 2010). In a nutshell, sustainable consumers are willing to pay more for organic food products, such as the average green premium ranges from 10% to 20%.

Green Premium for Fair-Trade Food

Here are a few examples of the green premium for diverse sustainable food with the fair-trade attribute:

- 3% for coffee labeled as fair-trade, shade-grown, or organic (Loureiro and Lotade 2005)

- 10% for fair-trade bananas, 20% for fair-trade chocolate (Rousu and Corrigan 2008)
- 27% for organic and fair-trade labeled chocolate (Didier and Lucie 2008)

There are far fewer studies on the economic added value of fair-trade product attributes. De Pelsmacker et al. (2005) found that at least 35% of Belgian consumers are willing to pay a mean price premium of at least 10% for fair-trade labeled coffee in a supermarket. The premium is higher when the coffee is directly consumed, as Murphy and Jenner-Leuthart (2011) found that Australian consumers are willing to pay 12.7% more for fair-trade coffee in a café. Eventually, Taylor and Boasson (2014) stated that 37.6% of their American sample is willing to pay a 22% premium on average for fair-trade products. In other words, sustainable consumers are willing to pay more for fair-trade food products, such as the average green premium ranges from 10% to 20%.

The following Table 10.1 summarizes the previously mentioned study findings about the green premium for sustainable food. No clear difference can be highlighted between ecological (i.e. organic) and social (i.e. fair-trade) product attributes. Moreover, in Central America, price premiums for organic certified coffee can be much higher than for fair-trade certified coffee (Killian et al. 2006, p. 325). But in France, Didier and Lucie (2008) find that consumers' WTP for organic and fair-trade chocolate is on average 27% higher than conventional chocolate; however, consumers are willing to pay slightly more for chocolate labeled as fair-trade than organic. Thus, there is a need to further research the difference in the green premium that sustainable shoppers are willing to pay, depending on the organic and fair-trade product attributes.

We have seen that the actual market price premium of sustainable food is much higher than what consumers are willing to pay (Loureiro et al. 2002; De Pelsmacker et al. 2005; Didier and Lucie 2008; Murphy and Jenner-Leuthart 2011). This is also true for other product categories: Olson (2013) states that Norwegian consumers expect to pay a 13% price premium for a hybrid car, whereas it actually is 25% at the dealership and a 17% price premium for a LED TV, whereas it actually is 42%

Table 10.1 Estimated green premium consumers would pay for sustainable food products.

Organic food:	**Fair-trade food:**
5% for eco-labeled apples (US)	10% for fair-trade coffee (Belgium)
10% for organic food (Spain)	10% for fair-trade bananas (US)
14.8% for organic chicken (US)	12.7% for fair-trade coffee (New Zealand)
15.9% for eco-friendly wine (US)	10% for fair-trade chocolate (US)
23.5% for fresh organic food (US)	22% for fair-trade products (US)
35% for organic-chicken breasts (US)	27% for fair-trade chocolate (France)
104% for USDA organic chicken breasts (US)	

in retail. Controversially, the stated WTP is often higher than the actual price paid, e.g. 23.7% higher for eco-friendly labeled wine (Barber et al. 2012). Even though stated intentions are behavioral predictors (Ajzen and Fishbein 1980), the attitude-behavior gap is particularly impudent to sustainable consumption.

Certifications, Labels, and Country of Origin

One of the first sustainability marketing studies was by Henion (1972) who showed that the display of information about a product's ecological attributes positively influences consumer behavior toward a more sustainable consumption. As such, products providing relevant information about sustainable consumption would positively influence the consumers' shopping behavior of these specific particular products. Many research studies have confirmed this since then. For example, Hustvedt and Bernard's (2008) study on sustainable apparel shows that consumers are willing to pay more for socks that are locally produced, organic, and made of non-genetically modified materials; but only labeling the socks as such is able to capture the premium associated with each of these sustainable attributes. A key finding of this study is that consumers' value information about the local origin of fibers; without the information provided by the label, consumers would not be willing to pay a green premium. In addition, Bauer et al. (2013) find that the display of an organic label on cereals positively affects the willingness to pay and the price premium – and this effect holds regardless of whether the brand is global (e.g. Kellogs), local (e.g. Seitenbacher in Germany, General Mills in the United States, Nissin Cisco in Japan) or private (retailers such as Aldi in Germany, Costco in the United States, Aeon in Japan).

McDonald et al. (2009) pinpoint that the relevant information needed by the consumer to differentiate products and to make a sustainable purchase depends on the product category, e.g. labels for fast-moving consumer goods (FMCG) such as gum, milk, fruit and vegetables, and toilet paper; travel guides for tourism that explain ethical and environmentally friendly behavior while traveling (Holmes et al. 2021); and point-of-purchase information for white goods, i.e. appliances.

Another driver of willingness to pay a green premium is the origin of the product (Hustvedt and Bernard 2008). Comparing local versus organic food product attributes, Stanton et al. (2012) find that "locavore" households (those who regularly eat local food produce) are willing to pay more than "nonlocavore" households for certified organic fruits and vegetables. As discussed, only certification transforms this preference into positive willingness to pay, i.e. certifications reassure consumers about the product's origin. Koschate-Fischer et al. (2012) find that country of origin (COO) certification positively influences consumers' willingness to pay, when

Figure 10.4 Wheels of Parmesan cheese in Italy.
Source: shutterstock 2108587961.

the country where the product comes from has a positive image. Aprile et al. (2012) has similar findings for Italian consumers of olive oil: they are willing to pay for the EU appellation system of Protected Designation of Origin (PDO), for which the price premium is actually 17% higher than for the organic label. These studies show that consumers' willingness to pay is influenced by information on a product's origin and that the green premium is even higher for certified-local products compared to non-certified-local products.

Take Parmesan for example, known as Parmigiano-Reggiano, a cheese that comes only from specific regions in Italy (see Figure 10.4). The PDO status guarantees that the cheese is made with specific methods and ingredients, which results in consistent quality that consumers can trust. The PDO certification ensures that the cheese is authentic and not an imitation. The PDO status supports the local economy by protecting the jobs and livelihoods of those involved in its production. It ensures that profits remain within the designated regions, benefiting local farmers, cheesemakers, and related businesses. The PDO also encourages the preservation of local landscapes and biodiversity, contributing to environmental sustainability.

Perceived Product Quality and Security

One of the general motives for sustainable consumption is the higher perceived quality of sustainable products, which positively influences consumers' willingness to pay a higher price for them. In other words, a higher-priced product (e.g. eco-friendly coffee) can be perceived as of higher quality when compared to a lower-priced alternative (e.g. regular coffee). Similarly, Kriwy and Mecking (2012) show that some consumers perceive organic food consumption as an investment in individual health; and the concern for health prevails over the concern for environment preservation. For instance, Krystallis et al. (2006) explain that consumers are willing to pay for organic produce in Greece, because they perceive the quality, taste, and healthiness to be superior to conventional food.

When evaluating a product, consumers do not want to feel uncertain about the performance of an unknown sustainable product when they know that the conventional product is reliable. The same uncertainty is experienced when evaluating some recycled versus newly produced products (Essoussi and Linton 2010). For example, consumers' willingness to pay is negatively correlated to the perceived functional risk associated with a product, which varies along different product categories: e.g. the perceived risk is higher for recycled tires than for recycled paper. Besides, consumers tend to trust popular brands more compared to lesser-known brands, due to their lower perceived risk. Nevertheless, many consumers are not willing to sacrifice quality, meaning that the product must perform just as effectively as its non-sustainable counterparts (Pickett-Baker and Ozaki 2008).

Smarter Pricing

The quality-price dilemma is well-known. Sustainable business practices lead to higher costs, which can either be passed on to consumers, with the risk that they may decide to choose cheaper alternatives or not purchase at all, or be absorbed by the company. Marco Bertini, an expert in monetization and revenue growth, calls the dilemma a "taboo trade-off," (Wathieu and Bertini 2007) however, he also believes that there is a way to mitigate – and perhaps even eliminate green premiums by using smarter pricing (Bertini and Koenigsberg 2014). The method is to involve all market actors to minimize externalities and their associated costs produced along the value chain of a product. Instead of adding up costs that will become a burden at the end of the process, we can tackle the problem beforehand.

Bertini, with colleagues from Boston Consulting Group, developed a strategy for rethinking price mechanisms based on three self-reflective questions for organizations: What are customers paying for? Who is going to pay? When and how do we transact? Bertini and Koenigsberg (2021) argue that the responses to critical questions will help leaders strike a better balance between sustainability and financial viability. They also offer six recommendations to guide leaders through the process of rethinking prices to find solutions that are profitable, scalable, and attractive to consumers.

Six Steps to Smarter Prices

Bertini has developed six recommendations to help business leaders develop new solutions to the three fundamental pricing questions. Using this framework, they suggest, will help to strike a balance between sustainability goals and financial obligations (Bertini and Koenigsberg 2021).

- *Make the "green premium" transparent and actionable:* Providing clarity and visibility around the reasons for the higher costs of sustainable products allows people to make informed purchasing decisions
- *Focus on outcomes, not products:* Encourage a mind shift from "selling clothes" to "clothing people" or "selling cars" to "providing mobility"
- *Align payments and benefits:* Up-front payments are often misaligned with the benefits achieved. Alternatives such as subscriptions, leasing, or pay-as-you-go shift payments to coincide with benefits, while also making products and services more affordable
- *Serve populations, not segments:* When a solution has broad applicability, focus on providing benefits for the entire population rather than delivering to individuals depending on their ability to pay
- *Activate the ecosystem*: Creative approaches to pricing often involve multiple partners, from financing structures to final delivery, that are outside the core remit of the producer
- *Create a shareholder tailwind:* Significant changes to price mechanisms require effective communication and engagement to illustrate and emphasize their long-term value creation

This broader way of thinking about prices, according to Bertini and Koenigsberg (2021), may not be the ultimate answer to global challenges. But what it does offer is an alternative to the taboo trade-off between easing the burden of business on society and finding someone to foot the bill.

Best Practices of Smart Pricing

There are many pricing strategies in place that range from traditional make and sell price modeling to subscriptions, memberships, and pay-as-you-go models. The business-to-business (B2B) sector has contributed with revenue-sharing agreements and performance-based contracting while some other practices have been inspired by the sharing economy and collaborative consumption.

Innovative pricing models are useful for reaching the goal, as indicated at the outset of the chapter, of contributing toward the transition toward a sustainable economy while reaching profitability. Every company has to seek an answer to the "what," "who," "when and how" questions on pricing.

In the solar energy sector, companies have asked what customers are actually paying for. The cost of installing solar energy panels is still very high for many households. After the initial investment, it may take many years before homeowners can enjoy savings on their energy bills. By assuming that savings is what buyers are looking for, solar energy companies end up having problems convincing buyers of the investment – in particular as there is a fast development of solar panel performance in relation to costs.

When solar energy suppliers re-examined the rationales of purchasing solar energy panels, they realized that consumers want cleaner energy rather than the equipment (solar panels) necessary to produce it – or a low price (see also Figure 10.5). Through smart price-setting, consumers could enjoy clean energy and pay a green premium on the rates while not having to invest in equipment. Meanwhile, the solar energy company enjoys high margins that cover the investment costs at a fast pace.

Figure 10.5 Solar energy companies have shifted their approach by offering clean energy directly to consumers at a premium rate, eliminating the need for high initial investments in installing solar panels at home, thereby aligning with consumer desires for sustainable energy while ensuring profitable margins.
Source: Shutterstock 2004938228.

Not Everything Can Be Solved with Money, Like the Pink Tax

Improving social justice issues, for instance, gender equality, cannot be solved solely with money. Firms operate within legal frameworks and codes of conduct for marketing and advertisement that forbids, for example, sexist advertisements; but to what degree are firms actively seeking to create meaningful differences for gender equality with their offerings? What springs immediately to mind is the gender price gap, called the pink tax in the United Kingdom. The pink tax is not actually a tax, but a label given to the phenomenon that some beauty and care brands charge a higher price for female beauty and care products (shower gels, deodorants, razors, skincare, toiletries) than for male-oriented products. Should such products marketed to women cost more than those for men?

Before we lose ourselves in a functional debate arguing that women's products need more research and development and better ingredients, this itself is a sexist argument. If the brands that are engaging in these practices were to leave their profit-calculation-Excel sheets for just a moment, and instead begin asking themselves how they are creating meaningful differences toward gender equality, the answer would be quite clear. In addition, this type of product comes with substantial profit margins – it would perhaps be different if margins were wafer-thin. Companies with sustainability ambitions should take responsibility to create meaningful differences when it comes to society, and that includes price-setting.

Source: BBC 2019.

References

Ajzen, I. & Fishbein, M. (1980). *Understanding Attitudes and Predicting Social Behavior*. Englewood Cliffs, NJ, Prentice-Hall.

Alphonce, R. & Alfnes, F. (2012). Consumer willingness to pay for food safety in Tanzania: an incentive-aligned conjoint analysis. *International Journal of Consumer Studies*, 36(4), 394–400.

Aprile, M. C., Caputo,V. & Nayga Jr, R. M. (2012). Consumers' valuation of food quality labels: the case of the European geographic indication and organic farming labels. *International Journal of Consumer Studies*, 36(2), 158–165.

Archer, D. W., Jaradat, A. A., Johnson, J. M-F., Weyers, S. L., Gesch, R. W., Forcella, F. & Kludze, H. K. (2007). Crop productivity and economics during the transition to alternative cropping systems. *Agronomy Journal*, 99(6), 1538–1547.

Barber, N., Kuo, P.-J., Bishop, M. & Goodman Jr., R. (2012). Measuring psychographics to assess purchase intention and willingness to pay. *Journal of Consumer Marketing*, 29(4), 280–292.

Bask, A., Halme, M., Kallio, M. & Kuula, M. (2013). Consumer preferences for sustainability and their impact on supply chain management: the case of mobile phones. *International Journal of Physical Distribution and Logistics Management*, 43(5/6), 380–406.

Bauer, H. H., Heinrich, D. & Schafer, D. B. (2013). The effects of organic labels on global, local, and private brands. More hype than substance? *Journal of Business Research*, 66(8), 1035–1043.

BBC (2019). 'Sexist' shopping tax targeted by Lib Dem MP's bill. https://www.bbc.com/news/uk-politics-47448623 (accessed 15 March 2024).

Bertini, M., & Koenigsberg, O. (2014). When customers help set prices. MIT Sloan Management Review. https://sloanreview.mit.edu/article/when-customers-help-set-prices (accessed 23 March 2024).

Bertini, M., & Koenigsberg, O. (2021). The pitfalls of pricing algorithms: be mindful of how they can hurt your brand *Harvard Business Review* 99(5), 74–83.

Bloomers, R., Magnani, F. & Peters, M. (2001). Paying a green premium. *McKinsey Quarterly*, 3, 15–17.

Brouwer, R., Brander, L., & Beukering, P. (2008). "A convenient truth": air travel passengers' willingness to pay to offset their CO_2 emissions. *Climatic Change*, 90(3), 299–313.

Cao, C., & Xu, Q. (2023). A new perspective on extra consumer costs for green parcel packaging—An exploration of signal theory and green values. *Journal of Cleaner Production*, 382, 135361.

Chen, C., Zhang, D., Zhu, L. and Zhang, F. (2024). Promoting green choices: how price premium displays influence consumer preference for green products. *Resources, Conservation and Recycling*, 207, 107682.

Cotte, J., Yvey, R. & Trudel, R. (2009). *Socially Conscious Consumerism: A Systematic Review of the Body of Knowledge*. Network for Business Sustainability Knowledge Project Series.

De Pelsmacker, P., Driesen, L. & Rayp, G. (2005). Do consumers care about ethics? Willingness to pay for fair-trade coffee. *Journal of Consumer Affairs*, 39(2), 363–385

Delate, K., Duffy, M., Chase, C., Holste, A., Friedrich, H. & Wantate, N. (2003). An economic comparison of organic and conventional grain crops in a long-term agroecological research (LTAR) site in Iowa. *American Journal of Alternative Agriculture*, 18(2), 59–69.

Didier, T. & Lucie, S. (2008). Measuring consumer's willingness to pay for organic and fair trade products. *International Journal of Consumer Studies*, 32(5), 479–490.

DiPerna, P. (2023). *Pricing the Priceless: The Financial Transformation to Value the Planet, Solve the Climate Crisis, and Protect our Most Precious Assets*. Hoboken, NJ: Wiley.

Essoussi, L. H. & Linton, J. D. (2010). New or recycled products: how much are consumers willing to pay? *Journal of Consumer Marketing*, 27(5), 458–468.

Gifford, K. & Bernard, J. C. (2011). The effect of information on consumers' willingness to pay for natural and organic chicken. *International Journal of Consumer Studies*, 35(3), 282–289.

Gleim, M. R., Smith, J. S., Andrews, D. & Cronin, J. J. (2013). Against the green: a multi-method examination of the barriers to green consumption. *Journal of Retailing*, 89(1), 44–61.

Grunert, K.G., Hieke, S. & Wills, J. (2014). Sustainability labels on food products: consumer motivation, understanding and use. *Food Policy*, 44(2), 177–189.

Guyader, H., Ottosson, M. and Witell, L. (2017). You can't buy what you can't see: retailer practices to increase the green premium. *Journal of Retailing and Consumer Services*, 34, 319–325.

Ha-Brookshire, J. E. & Norum, P. S. (2011). Willingness to pay for socially responsible products: case of cotton apparel. *Journal of Consumer Marketing*, 28(5), 344–353.

Henion, K. E. (1972). The effect of ecologically relevant information on detergent sales. *Journal of Marketing Research*, 9(February), 10–14.

Hinterhuber, A., & Liozu, S. M. (2018). Thoughts: premium pricing in B2C and B2B. *Journal of Revenue and Pricing Management*, 17, 301–305.

Holmes, M. R., Dodds, R., & Frochot, I. (2021). At home or abroad, does our behavior change? Examining how everyday behavior influences sustainable travel behavior and tourist clusters. *Journal of Travel Research*, 60(1), 102–116.

Hustvedt, G. & Bernard J. C. (2008). Consumer willingness to pay for sustainable apparel: the influence of labelling for fibre origin and production methods. *International Journal of Consumer Studies*, 32(5), 491–498.

Johnston, R. J., Wessells, C. R., Donath, H. & Asche, F. (2001). Measuring consumer preferences for ecolabeled seafood: an international comparison. *Journal of Agricultural and Resource Economics*, 26(1), 20–39.

Joly, C. (1990). The Green Premium and the Polluter Discount. *The Greening of Enterprise: Business Leaders Speak Out on Environmental Issues; Industry Forum of Environment for the UN Conference, "Action for a Common Future," Bergen, Norway (10–11 May 1990)*. Paris: ICC Publication 487E.

Killian, B., Jones, C., Pratt, L. & Villalobos, A. (2006). Is sustainable agriculture a viable strategy to improve farm income in Central America? A case study on coffee. *Journal of Business Research*, 59(3), 322–330

Koschate-Fischer, N., Diamantopoulos, A. & Oldenkotte, K. (2012). Are consumers really willing to pay more for a favorable country image? A study of country-of-origin effects on willingness to pay. *Journal of International Marketing*, 20(1), 19–41.

Kotler, P. (2011). Reinventing marketing to manage the environmental imperative. *Journal of Marketing*, 75(July), 132–135.

Kotler, P., Armstrong, A. & Balasubramanian, S. (2024), *Principles of Marketing*, nineteenth edition. Hoboken, NJ: Pearson.

Krav. (2011). Den hållbara maten 2021 https://wwwkravse.cdn.triggerfish.cloud/uploads/sites/2/2021/05/krav-den-hallbara-maten-2021.pdf (accessed 16 March 2024).

Kriwy, P. & Mecking, R.A. (2012). Health and environmental consciousness, costs of behavior and the purchase of organic food. *International Journal of Consumer Studies*, 36(1), 30–37.

Krystallis, A. Fotopoulos, C. & Zotos, Y. (2006). Organic consumers ' profile and their willingness to pay (WTP) for selected organic food products in Greece. *Journal of International Consumer Marketing*, 19(1), 81–106.

Laroche, M., Bergeron, J. & Barbaro-Forleo, G. (2001). Targeting consumers who are willing to pay more for environmentally friendly products. *Journal of Consumer Marketing*, 18(6), 503–520.

Li, F., Zhang, K., Yang, P., Jiao, J., Yin, Y., Zhang, Y. & Yin, C. (2022). Information exposure incentivizes consumers to pay a premium for emerging pro-environmental food: evidence from China. *Journal of Cleaner Production*, 363, 132412.

Liozu, S.M. & Cros, F. (2023). *Monetizing and Pricing Sustainability: Beyond Good Intentions.* Anthem, AZ: P4P Publishing.

Litvine, D. & Wüstenhagen, R. (2011). Helping 'light green' consumers walk the talk: results of a behavioral intervention survey in the Swiss electricity market. *Ecological Economics*, 70(3), 462–474.

Lohr, L. (1998). Implications of organic certification for market structure and trade. *American Journal of Agricultural Economics,* 80(5), 1125–1129.

Loureiro, M. L. & Lotade, J. (2005). Do fair trade and eco-labels in coffee wake up the consumer conscience? *Ecological Economics*, 53(11), 129–138.

Loureiro, M. L., McCluskey, J. J. & Mittelhammer, R. C. (2002). Will consumers pay a premium for eco-labeled apples? *Journal of Consumer Affairs*, 36(2), 203–219.

Lyngbæk, A. E., Muschler, R. G. & Sinclair F. L. (2001). Productivity and profitability of multi-strata organic versus conventional coffee farms in Costa Rica. *Agroforestry Systems*, 53, 205–213.

McDonald, S., Oates, C., Thyne, M., Alevizou, P. & McMorland, L. A. (2009). Comparing sustainable consumption patterns across product sectors. *International Journal of Consumer Studies*, 33(2), 137–145.

Meise, J.N., Rudolph, T., Kenning, P., & Phillips, D.M. (2014). Feed them facts: value perceptions and consumer use of sustainability-related product information. *Journal of Retailing and Consumer Services*, 21(4), 510–519.

Murphy, A. & Jenner-Leuthart, B. (2011). Fairly sold? Adding value with fair trade coffee in cafés. *Journal of Consumer Marketing*, 28(7), 508–515.

NYU. (2023). Sustainable Market Share Index. https://www.stern.nyu.edu/experience-stern/about/departments-centers-initiatives/centers-of-research/center-sustainable-business/research/csb-sustainable-market-share-index (accessed 16 March 2024).

Olesen, I., Alfnes, F., Røra, M. B. & Kolstad, K. (2010). Eliciting consumers' willingness to pay for organic and welfare-labelled salmon in a non-hypothetical choice experiment. *Livestock Science*, 127(2–3), 218–226.

Olson, E. L. (2013). It's not easy being green: the effects of attribute tradeoffs on green product preference and choice. *Journal of the Academy of Marketing Science*, 41(2), 171–184.

Pickett-Baker, J. & Ozaki, R. (2008). Pro-environmental products: marketing influence on consumer purchase decision. *Journal of Consumer Marketing*, 25(5), 281–293.

Pleters, L., Casone, J., Rogers, S., & Pankratz, D. (2023). Green products come of age. *Deloitte Insights.* https://www2.deloitte.com/xe/en/insights/industry/retail-distribution/consumer-behavior-trends-state-of-the-consumer-tracker/sustainable-products-customer-expectations.html (accessed 29 May 2024).

Porter, M.E. & van der Linde, C. (1995). Toward a new conception of the environment: competitiveness relationship. *Journal of Economic Perspectives*, 9, 97–118.

Rousu, M. C. & Corrigan, J. R. (2008). Consumer preferences for fair trade foods: implications for trade policy. *Choices: The Magazine of Food, Farm and Resource Issues*, 23(2), 53–55.

Simms, C. (1992). Green issues and strategic management in the grocery retail sector. *International Journal of Retail and Distribution Management*, 20(1). 32–42.

Stanton J. L., Wiley, J. B. & Wirth, F. F. (2012). Who are the locavores? *Journal of Consumer Marketing*, 29(4), 248–261.

Swedish Consumer Agency. (2021). Attityder till ekologiska livsmedel En konsumentstudie om hinder för att välja ekologiskt. *Konsumentverket*. https://www.konsumentverket.se/globalassets/publikationer/hallbarhet-och-miljo/attityder-till-ekologiska-livsmedel-konsumentverket.pdf (accessed 16 March 2024).

Taylor, J. & Boasson, V. (2014). Who buys fair trade and why (or why not)? A random survey of households. *Journal of Consumer Affairs*, 48(2), 418–430.

Ubilava, D., Foster, K. A., Lusk, J. L. & Nilsson, T. (2010). Effects of income and social awareness on consumer WTP for social product attributes. *Technological Forecasting and Social Change*, 77, 587–593.

Ureña, F., Bernabéu, R., & Olmeda, M. (2008). Women, men and organic food: differences in their attitudes and willingness to pay. A Spanish case study. *International Journal of Consumer Studies*, 32(1), 18–26.

Valkila, J. & Nygren, A. (2010). Impacts of fair trade certification on coffee farmers, cooperatives, and laborers in Nicaragua. *Agriculture and Human Values*, 27, 321–333.

Van Loo, E. J., Caputo, V., Nayga, R. M., Meullenet, J-F. & Ricke, S. C. (2011). Consumers' willingness to pay for organic chicken breast: evidence from choice experiment. *Food Quality and Preference*, 22(7), 603–613.

Wathieu, L. & Bertini, M. (2007). Price as a stimulus to think: the case for willful overpricing. *Marketing Science*, 26(1), 118–129.

White, K., Habib, R. & Hardisty, D.J. (2019). How to SHIFT consumer behaviors to be more sustainable: a literature review and guiding framework. *Journal of Marketing*, 83(3), 22–49.

Yang, C. C., Cheng, L. Y., Sung, D., & Withiam, G. (2009). Strategic-pricing policy based on analysis of service attributes. *Cornell Hospitality Quarterly*, 50(4), 498–509.

Yue, C., Alfnes, F. & Jensen, H. H. (2009). Discounting spotted apples: investigating consumers' willingness to accept cosmetic damage in an organic product. *Journal of Agricultural and Applied Economics*, 41(1), 29–46.

Zeithaml, V. A. (1988). Consumer perceptions of price, quality, and value: a means-end model and synthesis of evidence. *Journal of Marketing*, 52(3), 2–22.

Zhang, H., Gallardo, R. K., McCluskey, J. J. & Kupferman, E. M. (2010). Consumers' willingness to pay for treatment-induced quality attributes in Anjou pears. *Journal of Agricultural and Resource Economics*, 35(1), 105–117.

Author Acknowledgments

First, we would like to thank Dr. O. C. Ferrell who is the Director of the Center for Ethical Organizational Cultures at Auburn University for writing the foreword to this book.

Second, this book would not have been possible without the research conducted by many scholars and organizations around the world. We have given credit to all original research and company ideas presented in this book. It is our hope that our synthesis of combined work will inspire additional sustainability-oriented research, integration in higher education courses, and industry practices.

Third, we would like to acknowledge the work of graduate assistants Kazi Samina Afroz, Noelle Meeker, and Brett Porterfield at Appalachian State University for their assistance in adapting the chapter figures from their original design and content and for their assistance in creating some of the supplemental instructor materials available on Wiley's textbook companion website.

About the Authors

Pia A. Albinsson, PhD, is a professor of marketing at Appalachian State University. While native to Sweden, she has gained an international perspective by having lived and worked lived and worked in Greece, Malaysia, Portugal, France, New Zealand, and the United States. Prior to entering academe, she worked in tourism, banking, and retailing. She has conducted research and written three books on the sharing economy and collaborative consumption. She also conducts research on sustainability, consumer activism and well-being, and strategic value co-creation. In 2023, she was awarded the Triple E Award for her sustained research and teaching on sustainability-related topics in the Walker College of Business.

Hugo Guyader, PhD, is an associate professor of marketing at Linköping University, Sweden. As a visiting scholar, he travels to his native France, the United States, the United Kingdom, and Switzerland. His research is focused on sustainable consumer behaviors and business models that challenge traditional modes of consumption, particularly in the contemporary contexts of the sharing economy and the circular economy. Based on a mixed-method approach to data collection, he has published in marketing, sustainability, and service journals.

Mikael Ottosson, PhD, is a senior associate professor of marketing at Linköping University, Sweden. In his research, Mikael focuses on how firms can develop their market strategies and market offers in relation to sustainability. He has extensive experience in research, consultancy, and educational activities on the topic.

Currently, he is studying the shaping of sustainable markets, such as the biogas market and markets for sustainable fertilizers.

Anders Parment, PhD, is a research fellow at Stockholm Business School and a well-known public speaker and advisor across European countries, e.g. Norway, Germany, and Austria. In addition, he teaches at Linköping University, where he received his PhD, and University of Innsbruck, and he has written more than 50 books on various themes related to marketing, business, and sustainability, in addition to numerous journal articles on generational cohorts, marketing channels, segmentation, sustainability, and other core issues relating to society, business and marketing.

Index

M

N

O

P

T

U